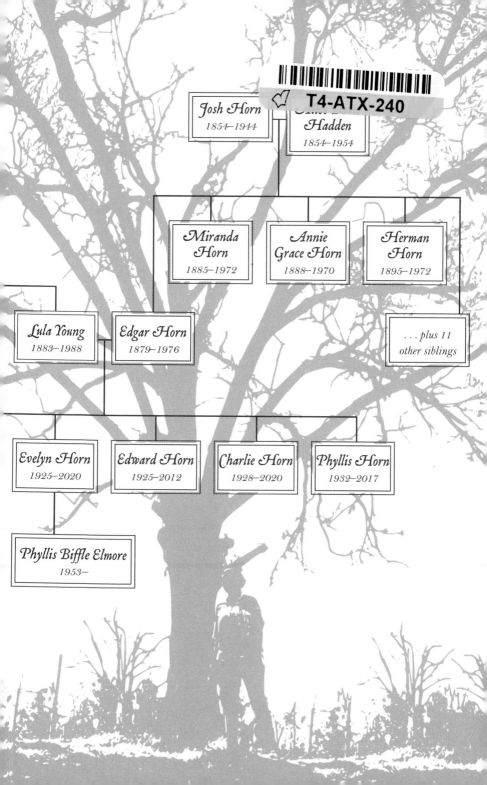

Josh Horn
1854–1944

Hadden
1854–1954

Miranda
Horn
1885–1972

Annie
Grace Horn
1888–1970

Herman
Horn
1895–1972

Lula Young
1883–1988

Edgar Horn
1879–1976

. . . plus 11
other siblings

Evelyn Horn
1925–2020

Edward Horn
1925–2012

Charlie Horn
1928–2020

Phyllis Horn
1932–2017

Phyllis Biffle Elmore
1953–

QUILT
OF SOULS

Lula Young Horn
c. 1905

QUILT
OF SOULS

A Memoir

Phyllis Biffle Elmore

imagine!

At the time of publication, all URLs printed in this book were accurate and active. Charlesbridge and the author are not responsible for the content or accessibility of any website.

An Imagine Book
Published by Charlesbridge
9 Galen Street
Watertown, MA 02472
(617) 926-0329
www.imaginebooks.net

Library of Congress Cataloging-in-Publication Data
Names: Elmore, Phyllis Biffle, author.
Title: Quilt of souls: a memoir / by Phyllis Biffle Elmore.
Description: [Watertown, Massachusetts]: Charlesbridge Publishing, [2022]
  | Summary: "A memoir of a Detroit child raised in Alabama by her grand-
  mother, whose storytelling and quilt-making open up a world of drama,
  passion, and African American identity."—Provided by publisher.
Identifiers: LCCN 2022002561 (print) | LCCN 2022002562 (ebook) |
  ISBN 9781623545161 (hardback) | ISBN 9781632892430 (ebook)
Subjects: LCSH: Elmore, Phyllis Biffle. | African American Women—
  Alabama—Biography. | Grandparent and child.
Classification: LCC E185.97.E47 A3 2022 (print) | LCC E185.97.E47 (ebook) |
  DDC 305.48/896073092 [B]—dc23/eng/20220222
LC record available at https://lccn.loc.gov/2022002561
LC ebook record available at https://lccn.loc.gov/2022002562

Display type set in Arboria by Adobe, Beloved Sans by Adobe, and MrsEaves
  by Zuzana Licko
Text type set in BellMT by Richard Austin
Printed by Bang Printing in Brainerd, Minnesota
Production supervision by Jennifer Most Delaney
Jacket design by Nicole Turner
Interior design by Mira Kennedy

Printed in the United States of America
(hc) 10 9 8 7 6 5 4 3 2 1

All photographs are printed courtesy of the author.

For my grandmother, Lula Young Horn,
and the unsung women of her era

In memory of Rufus Biffle Jr.
and McCullah Biffle

And to Joean Henry, with love

Introduction

THE DAY I WAS TAKEN from my home and driven sixteen hours down a road in a car filled with strangers, to a house in the middle of nowhere, to be delivered to grandparents I'd never met, I felt alone, abandoned, angry, and very scared. It was 1957. I was four years old. The stigma of being given away would follow me for years, like a lost puppy nipping at my heels. It took my grandmother Lula's love and a tattered, centuries-old quilt to bring about my healing.

Lula Young Horn was born in the small town of Sandersville, Mississippi, in 1883. She grew up on the Young plantation, in an environment that sat heavy under the shadow of slavery, and she was destined to quilt. In quilting and in life, she was the catalyst of my upbringing. As she worked, she told me stories of the women who wore or were connected to the strips of fabric she wove into the hand-sewn quilts I would later name "quilts of souls." It is a powerful title, for her quilts hold the consciousness of a long-ago generation. These women had no voice until my grandma gave them one.

During the nine years I lived in Alabama, many elderly women who resided nearby, born around the time of the Civil War and during the years of Reconstruction, became part of my extended family. They were an extension of my grandmother's life and represented all she believed in. She felt their stories were as relevant as hers, and I connected with these women too. Collectively, they were instrumental in preparing me to overcome so many obstacles. They tilled the soil of my resilience and, along with my grandmother, built within me a solid foundation as I prepared to face an uncertain future.

All these women are embodied inside of me.

African American quilting has long been an enigma for scholars and historians. It is a tradition older than the history of America itself, originating in Africa long before the first ships carrying slaves arrived in the Americas. Before and after the Civil War, African American women used scraps of clothing from white households to make bed coverings for both themselves and their slave-owners. Enslaved women also made quilts that were guides for escaping slaves. These quilts were hung on gates and clotheslines across the South. The patterns embedded in them showed slaves the way to freedom and included stars, railroad tracks, trees, and midnight-blue patches that represented river crossings, all coded symbols pointing the way north.

For many years, Grandma took the clothes of those who'd passed on and turned them into quilts, which were both a source of warmth on cold nights and family heirlooms to be preserved for future generations. Many of my grandmother's quilts also used railroad crossing designs, in a wide range of colors. In all likelihood, this pattern was passed down from my great-grandmother, Emma Young, who was born into slavery in Mississippi around 1840.

I'll always be grateful to my grandmother, who gave me the opportunity to listen to her first-person tales of quilting, stories that reached far back into my maternal lineage. Grandma's quilts laid the foundation for future quilters, too, who now use some of the same patterns and skills my grandmother displayed. Quilting has become one of the most popular international hobbies of our time. Modern quilters have established quilt making as an art form, and their work is showcased in museums, quilting shows, and quilting guilds across the country. These new-wave quilts are visual works of art calling for social change, a way to bring attention to racial injustice and to galvanize communities to action. They are not designed to be placed at the foot of a bed or snuggled under on wintry nights. Instead, they have evolved into magnificent pieces of fabric aptly referred to as fiber or textile art.

In many ways, these quilts carry the same messages embedded in those sewn before and during Reconstruction. Current quilters, however, have the freedom to use their quilts as a way of raising awareness of inequality. They can address injustice without fear of reprisal, unlike the women of my grandmother's time. Lula Horn's quilts of souls were also art, but she worked in a quieter tradition and a far different atmosphere from the present day's.

I may have forgotten the first time I rode a bike, received my first kiss, or got my driver's license, but I will never forget Grandma's quilts of souls stories or the elderly women I met growing up in the rural South. The vast amount of history conveyed to me by my grandma and these women, all of whom were born while the ink was still drying on the Emancipation Proclamation, fascinated and intrigued me. Barefoot, I'd run along the sandy roads, under the tall Alabama pines, and return to lie in the cool dirt under my grandparents' house and listen to the conversation of the folks gathered in our front yard. Through their colloquy I gained knowledge, strength, purpose, and the grit I'd rely on to sustain me in adulthood.

I'm honored to have spent most of my childhood in a community of powerful Black women. With Grandma at the helm, these women molded and transformed me. I longed to model my own character on the traits they exhibited during the course of their lives. They had an extraordinary ability to overcome horrendous indignities, even though the knee of the status quo was firmly placed on their backs because of the color of their skin. This memoir is my tribute to them, a recounting of their stories that I hope will give them their well-deserved recognition.

In their unsung lives, these women suffered sexism, racism, colorism, and other "isms" still to be identified. Many endured unfathomable abuses, yet they persevered and overcame. Butter churners, laundresses, teachers, farmers, healers, and storytellers, their fascinating lives have largely gone unnoticed because no one has told their stories.

Until now.

The stories of these women were given to me long ago. My grandmother's edict was to make them part of not only my oral history but the world's. To this day, I'll never know or understand why she chose me as the vessel to carry and one day pour out these beautiful stories. But as a little girl, she'd take me to an old slave cemetery not far from our five-room farmhouse, where she'd stand and silently pray over the makeshift graves. Before we left, she'd say: "Chile, these are the best stories you ain't never heard."

Once, as we were leaving the cemetery, I turned and glanced back at the scattered markers. As I did, Grandma stopped me in my tracks and said, "Don' you never look back at them, only forward, and forever think about what you seent here today."

Her words were true. Those poor souls helped empower me to fulfill a promise I made to myself long ago: never to allow my grandmother's stories to be forgotten or remain untold. Over the years, the tradition of passing down oral history has eroded. But knowing the stories behind my grandmother's quilts, I'm more convinced than ever that each one—or any other artifact passed down through the generations—has meaning for us all. Our experiences transcend race and color, because as humans we are all exposed to the same types of emotional pain and hurt. More often than not, we respond in the same manner too. As my grandma would say, "We all cry wet." Tears don't discriminate.

Gradually, our elderly population is passing away, particularly those who were born in the 1920s and '30s. This book is a call to action, to seize the moment and capture the great stories this generation has stored in their memory banks. Scores of people from my parents' era never had the opportunity to talk about their past. No one cared, asked, or had the time to listen. As a result, tremendous moments in history have gone unspoken. Once this generation ceases to exist, their stories will be buried along with them.

Even though my grandmother had no formal schooling, in her own way she was able to articulate how we all are more alike than different. The stories she told me as we sat under the old oak tree illustrate her many beliefs about humankind. She believed that some of us choose our life's path, while for others it's forced upon us through no fault of our own. She felt that this world would be a better place if we'd only learn to walk in the shoes of those who are hurting. And if she were alive, I'm certain that she could sew today's political cloud of division into a mesmerizing sunset, where there is hope for forgiveness and for unifying souls past and present.

I say this because not only was she a weaver of fabric, she was an agent of change. She made folks' lives better after she met them. Through her storytelling and quilt making, she sewed tales of bravery, heroism, perseverance, and courage into the hearts of her listeners and into the quilts of souls she made for family members. The depth of her wisdom is embedded in each chapter. Whoever has read or listened to the stories I've told about Lula Horn has been left with a longing to know and sit with her. This is the reason I chose to share her with the world.

Even though Grandma now sleeps with the angels, her spirit surrounds me during these ruminations. I can feel, smell, and touch her. I have been increasingly awed by her innate ability to fuse together people's intricate lives, as though the events she recalled happened yesterday. It has been well over fifty years since I first listened to her tales of the past, but I can still recall the stories that floated from her lips and landed in my ever-expanding heart. When all is quiet, the windows of reflection and introspection open wide. My room fills with the stories that shaped my life and speak through me now, as I weave my own quilt in the form of words upon these pages. My pen is their needle, my ink is their thread.

This is their history.

And yours.

City Girl Going Country

MEMORY CAN BE A STRANGE THING. Sometimes you'd much rather forget. I remember climbing into the backseat of a black automobile with two large men, one on each side of me. Three towering women were in the front seat; one of them had a mountain of gray hair that sat on top of her head like a giant bush. The driver had teeth protruding from her mouth even when her lips were closed. Looking back, they might not have been tall, but to a young, scared four-year-old, they were larger than life and piled in the vehicle like canned sardines.

I can't recall anyone getting out of the crowded automobile when it arrived at our large concrete driveway in Detroit. They just sat there, smiling. The lady in the front seat made small talk with my sister as I was ushered into the car. As we slowly backed out of the driveway, my sister stood, watching, a comb still in her hand. My brothers looked as baffled as I did.

Only moments before, I'd been sitting on an old milk crate while my eldest sister braided my hair. She'd popped me upside the head with the comb because I was fighting her as she wrestled with the tangles. The awful pink ribbons kept falling in my face as she attempted to tie them into neat little bows. I hated girlie ribbons. All I wanted to do was join my brothers, who were crouched on the sidewalk, playing a game of marbles called knuckles.

I'll never forget the deafening sound of the long black car, which drowned out the noise of my brothers cackling as they played. Old engine oil fumes rose up the steps and through the front screen door and settled in my throat. I wrenched myself away from my sister right before she tied the ribbon on the final braid. It hung there, dangling out of place. I was an innocent child, and in the blink of an eye I would be taken from Detroit to a place unknown to me. As I stared through the screen door, I didn't realize that this would be the last time I'd be anywhere near my sister for a very long time.

Many of the events of that day remain obscure, as though a dark storm welled up and thundered out the memories. I don't remember the exact moment when I began to miss my family or recognize that I was on my way to some unknown place far away from them. I didn't inquire, either, because I knew children weren't allowed to question grown-ups. Children were to be seen, not heard.

Before the car took me away, I don't remember spending much time with my mother. Both she and my father seemed to dart in and out of my life in microseconds. It was my eldest sister that I saw as the mother figure in my house. She tended to my sores when I was marked from ear to ear with chicken pox and cared for me at night when I had a bad dream or peed in the bed. I loved curling up in her lap and letting her rock me when I was upset.

My parents spent most of their waking hours working, especially Father, who was holding down two jobs. I suspect they had to work that much to support eight children. Maybe mother was tired or fast asleep when the big people came and whisked me from my home. Maybe she couldn't face that she had to send me away for a long time.

In the car, that lone pink ribbon swung back and forth across my forehead, irritating my eyelid every time I moved. I was afraid to speak or cry and too petrified to ask for a drink of water or to go to the bathroom. A constant shiver made my lips quiver uncontrollably. I could barely breathe, sitting between two men whose big behinds took up every inch of available space. If they'd moved a fraction in either direction, they'd have been sitting in my lap.

As the engine churned and hummed down the long highway, I sank into the black leather seat. I closed my eyes and tried to imagine something familiar, like the sounds of my brothers and sisters yapping around our crowded dinner table. Balled up in the small space I'd carved, I lulled myself into a sleep so deep I didn't realize we'd stopped by the side of the road until I heard the woman who was driving say:

"Ain't no cullud hotels near here, so we just gone have to pull over and make do."

My insides churned with fear. I longed for an explanation as to why I'd been torn away from my family. The silence from those who knew the answers pounded inside my head. I knew the strict rules of how a child "stays in a child's place." I was not about to cross those boundaries. Whenever adult friends or relatives knocked on the door of our house in Detroit, my siblings and I knew the routine: say "Good evening"; answer any questions with a "Yes, ma'am" or a "No, sir"; then head off to the basement, where we remained until we could no longer hear the chatter of my parents or their visitors' voices. This usually meant it was safe to go back upstairs. If we even showed signs that we wanted to question or talk back to adults, Mother or Father would flash an if-looks-could-kill glare.

So I didn't utter a word. I never asked where I was going or why. I didn't ask who these strangers were. All I knew was that they surrounded me on that sixteen-hour drive on one of the hottest days of my life. As we passed through the countryside, I saw all sorts of four-legged animals I'd seen only on our old black-and-white television. There were big cows and bigger horses; everything was bigger than me. I was a small, lost child swirling in a world of bigness.

The car wove along dirt roads, past tin-roofed homes. Trees of every shape and size lined the way. As I sat on my knees, peering out the back window at the trail of white dust that rose behind us, I knew I was entering new territory. I watched the highway disappear, replaced with blood-red dirt, and the finality struck me like a lightning bolt. My stomach tightened, tears ready to bust through like a storm.

Suddenly, the car stopped in front of a house. With its tin roof, it looked like all the others we had passed. A chill shook my body, and my hands and feet turned ice-cold. Even though the blazing Alabama sun scorched the side of my face, I shivered like I was standing dead center in a snowstorm. I tumbled my three-foot frame out of the big car, my feet searching for the ground, and sank into warm, feathery-white sand that went up to my ankles. I was so caught up in the warmth of the sand as it settled around my feet that I barely heard one of the men look at me and say, "This is your Grandpa Edgar and Ma Lula's house."

The only thing that separated the car from the house was a dirt road and wire fence, attached to four wooden posts that stretched the length of the front yard. A wooden gate kept the barbed wire from falling to the ground. An elderly man rose from his seat and made his way to where we stood. He looked old and worn-out. His khaki pants were held high above his waist with suspenders. I'd never in my life seen anyone move that slow.

The lady driver commented, "Y'all know Uncle Edgar is hard of hearin'."

It seemed like it took him forever to remove the wire hook before the gate swung open. Once inside, the men shook hands with Grandpa Edgar while the ladies waited their turn to give him a quick hug. He looked at me and didn't utter a word. He just shook his head and smiled.

Being deathly afraid made everything stand still and cold. Even though people were moving around, laughing and talking, everything warped into slow motion. My eyes darted back and forth from the big people who had been with me on the long ride to the old man they called Uncle Edgar.

Then a smiling lady emerged from the backyard, wiping her hands on a flowery apron draped around her like a dress.

"Madea Lula, how you doin'?"

"Kickin', but not too high, Brother Needham," she said as she looked down at me for the first time. "Now, who this lil skinny chile? I'm your Grandma Lula, baby. You gone stay here with Grandma and Grandpa for a spell and we gone be jus' fine."

The first thing I noted about Grandma was this: she was breathtaking. Her skin was like Hershey chocolate, my favorite candy in the whole world. Her steel-gray hair was pulled up into a tight ball that sat on the back of her head, and her piercing grayish-blue eyes were mesmerizing. Even though this was the first time I'd laid eyes on her, I felt safe in her presence. The fear of the unknown that had taken every ounce of my strength dissipated as I stood there, enraptured by how she glowed. Her silver hair matched the color of her eyes, and her chocolate skin looked like it'd been carefully poured into a cast, molded, and smoothed into a mahogany sculpture.

With one swoop, Grandma Lula lifted me off the ground, hugging and wet-kissing me on both jaws. Her embrace was so warm and inviting, I never wanted her to put me down. I felt like her arms were exactly where I belonged. This beautiful, creamy cocoa-skinned woman took my hand, filling my senses with a distinct aroma that alternated between chocolate and mothballs.

My fascination with Grandma was disrupted by the sounds of farm animals running around. I'd never seen the likes of those creatures in my life. They were feathery things in all different colors and sizes, scurrying about the yard. Some had black-and-white

11

polka dots with globs of red skin hanging from their beaks. Later, I found out they were chickens and roosters, and the polka-dotted ones were guinea fowl. But that day, I clutched Grandma's hand tight, afraid. But it seemed they were just as scared of me, because each time I moved, they scurried away in a frenzy. Grandma shooed them, flapping her apron, and they scattered in fifty different directions, leaving little balls of droppings as they ran away.

Grandma ushered all the big people to the front yard, offering them a seat and demanding that they rest themselves in various chairs under the largest tree I'd ever seen. Grandma told me to take a seat on the concrete stoop nearby and said that she'd be back with a treat for me "direc'ly."

Sure enough, she wasn't gone but a couple of minutes before reappearing with a square chunk of something I'd never seen before.

"Lookit what yo' Grandma gots for you right yere. I knows you gone like this. It gone make your heart and liver sang."

I bit into the glob of gooey peanut and caramel. I didn't know what my heart and liver were doing, but in that moment Detroit, the road, the big people, even the scary feather creatures were a distant memory. Grandma winked at me and smiled, and I watched as she dashed back and forth from the house to the front yard, delivering ice-cold tea to her guests. One of the big men from the car picked up his Mason jar and gulped it down in one swoop. He let out a big *ahhhhhhh* like he'd just quenched his thirst after crossing the desert.

As the big people talked and laughed, Grandma said, "Y'all look mighty hungry, so I'm gone fry up that pool of bass Edgar jus' catch this mo'nin'."

Grandma cooked up a feast in no time. When she called out, "Come on in, y'all," I thought I'd be trampled by everyone rushing up the two concrete block steps and through the front door. I followed them down a long hallway in the middle of the house and into the kitchen, where the table was steaming with fresh bass from Grandpa Edgar's pond. There was fried chicken, sweet potatoes, peas, and tons of other dishes I'd never seen before, enough to feed a multitude. The house filled with aromas. My mouth watered.

Grandpa Edgar sat at the head of the table. I climbed into a chair, my feet dangling way above the linoleum floor.

"Thank ye Lawd for this here food we 'bout to 'ceive fo' yo' blessin'. Bless the folks gather here and bless the cook, 'cause Lawd knows she a good cook and a sho nuff good wife. I jus' wants to thank you 'gin, Lawd, for this here bounty and all the folks here at yo' table to eat of this here food. Amen."

Everyone looked overjoyed when the "Amen" came. Hands reached across the table from all directions, pulling fried chicken and fish from the serving platter, filling glasses with iced tea. Gravy overflowed onto the white tablecloth. No one said a word until all the plates were loaded and everyone's mouth was half full. Then the woman with the big teeth asked Grandpa, "So, Edgar, what's that nosy sister of yours up to?"

"You must be talkin' 'bout that meddlin' Bessie. She still mean as a snake and walkin' roun' gettin' in everybody's bizness. If y'all waitin' for Bessie to change her stripes, y'all be waitin' a long time."

They laughed and began talking loudly about other relatives, the weather, and how good the food looked. People on both sides of me loaded up my plate. My stomach growled, but somehow the message from my belly didn't reach my brain; I felt too overwhelmed to eat. Grandma Lula hovered around the table, refilling glasses and urging everybody to take second helpings. She was making sure everyone was well taken care of. I longed for her to sit down and be still, so I could study her chocolate face and steel-gray hair, but she never did.

The big people looked even larger after digesting Grandma's food. Afterward, they sat around the table burping, giggling, small-talking, and chewing on toothpicks. One of

13

the men who'd been in the backseat with me proclaimed how much he "hate to eat an' run," but he didn't want to be caught down there in the backwoods after dark, so he "gone ease on up the road."

They filed out of the kitchen and into the front yard as if it was the end of church service, each one pausing to give Grandma, Grandpa, and me a hug before they jumped in the car and drove off down the long dirt road, past the oak and pine trees.

In their absence, a gaping hole opened inside me. There I sat, all alone, in a strange place, full of sand and trees and God knew what else. I hunkered down on the concrete steps with my legs bent and my head buried between them, trying to smother my heartbreak. All I wanted was to remain in darkness while I waited for Grandma to reappear.

At that moment, someone broke into that small space I'd created for myself.

"Whatcha name, gal?" Grandpa's question knocked me out of my thoughts and sent tears erupting out of me, like hot lava flowing from a volcano.

My mouth filled with salt as I feebly said, "Phyllistene."

Grandpa just stared. Maybe he'd never seen tears come out of anyone like that. Grandma shook her head, came over, and gathered me up in her all-consuming arms.

The day didn't improve after that. There was no running water, no inside toilet or bathtub. No toilet paper, electricity, telephone, and no radio or television. All food stuff was grown or made. Our sugar, syrup, and flour were from the ground, otherwise known as not store-bought. The meat that we ate came from chickens, cows, hogs, or anything else raised right there on my grandparents' farm.

Grandma took me to the homemade well in the backyard, which accounted for all our drinking, cooking, and bath water.

When it rained, water flowed into the gutters, which traveled along the lip of the roof and down into the well. Screens covered the top to keep out leaves and bird droppings. She showed me the outhouse, an oven-like, four-by-four wooden shack where bugs, wasps, and every other flying insect on the planet appeared to have taken up permanent residence.

Newspaper was piled high inside, almost reaching the ceiling. I thought it was for reading until Grandma took a page from the stack and demonstrated how to rub it between my hands to soften it up. She wanted to make sure I did it correctly.

"If you don' get them papers sof', you gone get yo'self a big case of the piles. You gots to be real careful with that newspaper, chile."

That was the moment when I realized the newspaper was for cleaning my backside after I finished doing my business.

I held onto Grandma's hand so tightly she must've felt it all the way to her toes. Each time she explained the layout of the farm, my lips trembled. Since my two front teeth were missing, I kept my tongue firmly planted in the hole. That seemed to stop my teeth from chattering.

In Detroit, I was used to everything being compact; I could walk out the front door and the rest of the world was right there in front of me. Neighbors were a stone's throw away and farm animals were nonexistent. Mother hated anything with four legs, maybe because it reminded her of the unpleasantness of growing up in the country. Once, my brother brought home a stray cat, and Mother was livid. She beat my brother and the cat. My brother sat for hours on the front porch, white tear tracks drying on his face.

In Alabama, everything in my new environment frightened me. The animals had their own personal habitat, so not only did I have to adapt to my new surroundings, I had to adjust to theirs. I cried constantly and clung to Grandma for dear life. I was her shadow; when she moved, I moved.

That day, she led me through the backyard, beyond the smell and noise of the chickens to a huge pasture surrounded by barbed-wire fence. Inside this meadow was a herd of brown, polka dot, and black cows. They came sauntering toward us, chewing their cud. In her southern drawl, Grandma assured me, "Chile, them cows more scared of you than you of them."

We went from the cow pasture to the barn. I held on to her apron strings, dodging cow pies. She grabbed a large silver pail that hung on the side of the barn, pulled up a stool, and plunked it down next to one of the cows. I timidly stood behind her, but she told me to come closer so I could see. I edged in. The smell from the cow made me want to puke; each time her tail swished from left to right, the odor shot straight up my nose and down my throat. It stunk twice as bad as the outhouse. I felt like I'd eaten a cow pie.

As Grandma watched me gag, she shook her head and promised, "The smell gone grow on you, chile."

She wrapped her hands around the udders and began pulling. Her hands were like a machine. I could tell she'd been doing this for a long time. The eye contact between her and the cow astounded me. The cow was chewing on the mess in her mouth while Grandma sucked on a mouth full of snuff. They were different species, but they were in harmony with each other.

"See that? Now you try it."

It took every bit of my courage, but I sat myself down on the stool, stuck my hands under there, and tried to wrap them around the cow's teats. My fingers couldn't reach all the way. I managed to get some sort of grip in order to get my yanking somewhat coordinated. Brownie the cow wasn't enjoying herself as much as when Grandma was at the helm. Her chewing stopped and her eyes evaded mine. She let out a long, pained *moo*, which made me drop her teat right out of my hand.

Grandma kept telling me, "Go on, gal, ol' Brownie jus' full of milk." If she had as much milk in her as I had tears flowing into that bucket, there'd be enough milk to feed the entire town of Livingston.

"Gone now, squeeze and pull, squeeze and pull, ol' Brownie waitin' on you, you hear me?"

When I saw milk come squirting out, I couldn't believe it. Grandma laughed. "Why, I do declare! You a country gal now!" I didn't know whether to take my newfound status as a compliment or an insult. Grandma seemed a whole lot happier than I was about the results. She was so proud of my milking ability that she went and found Grandpa Edgar to tell him.

Since there was no electricity, my grandparents prepared for darkness well before the first stars appeared. Otherwise, we'd stumble over each other in the dark. The preparation included gathering and filling kerosene lanterns. Never in my life had I felt so cold. I stood in the half-lit room, shaking like a leaf.

I guess Grandpa felt sorry for me. "Don' stand thar watchin' me, gal," he said. "Git in dat bed while I start dis yere fire."

My large bed, made of duck and goose feathers, was next to Grandma and Grandpa's. It sat so high off the floor I had a difficult time launching myself up. No matter how many blankets were heaped on me, I couldn't get warm. I lay, shivering despite the heat from the roaring fire. My body shook uncontrollably as I listened to something inside the walls scratching and clawing. It sounded like it was marching, getting ready to fight to the death. This went on for hours.

Grandma and Grandpa were clearly accustomed to the racket. They lay in their bed, unmoving, oblivious to the sounds. Then, out of nowhere, an angry storm blew in. Wind and lashes of rain battered the house. A deep groaning sound rose and fell. The rain pounded the metal roof like it was punching holes through the tin. I wanted to crawl under the bed, but I was afraid of what might be under there.

That was the worst night of my life.

Those first few nights, I cried myself to sleep. My crying became as predictable as a face on a clock. The cold was unbearable, and my body would convulse like I was having a seizure. I tried to remember Detroit and the family I'd been stripped away from, but I could conjure only shadowy silhouettes. I had no way to articulate how deeply this scared me.

I continued to wrestle with the cold until, finally, Grandma got up from her bed in the middle of a shaking episode and placed a partially completed quilt on top of the blankets already covering me. Warmth swept over me. For the first time in days, I relaxed. It felt as though I was being swaddled like a newborn in a receiving blanket. Snug, immovable, and warm. The quilt's colors enthralled me, the reds and blues reflecting the bright firelight. I noticed it had missing pieces, that parts of it were barely hanging on to their backing. Other parts consisted of large open spaces with only a cloth foundation to hold it together. Still, it was dazzling—a beautiful mix of soft prints, gaudy corduroys, stripes, plaids, and every other type of cloth you could imagine.

Along with the quilt, Grandma provided additional comfort that night. I felt the warmth of her breath as she lay next to me, soothing me with a gentle song. Her hand glided back and forth over the small of my back, on beat with her rhythmic singing:

This little light of mine,
I's gonna let it shine;
Let it shine, let it shine, let it shine.

"Grandma gone tuck this here ol' quilt 'rounds you and it gone keep them shakes away. This quilt gone be your quilt of souls, and you gone keep it with you all your born days, you hear me, chile? It's your quilt now. Your Grandma gone make it all full, one piece atta time, then it gone look brand spankin' new. I'm gone put some ol' clothes that's sittin' out back in the smokehouse that gone fill in all them missin' pieces. It's gone be new spirits and old spirits in your quilt, and all of them gone watch over you, chile, fo'ever. Jus' trust what Grandma say. Your ol' Grandma layin' here gone see it through by and by. You jus' watch, you gone be alright when the mo'nin' come.

"Gone now, get some sleep. Grandma gone mosey on back over here in the bed with your Grandpa. Sun gone be up direc'ly, so we needs to get some shut-eye."

As I drifted off, wrapped in the smelly but strangely beautiful quilt, I tried to make sense of Grandma's words about how it would be with me forever. I didn't understand, but still, I couldn't help pulling it over my head as I fell, warm and content, into a deep sleep.

Grandma sitting on our screened-in front
porch, her usual perch. Here she'd rest a
spell while others enjoyed her food.

2

The Country

I WOKE THE MORNING after Grandma gave me my quilt of souls still thinking about its warmth, how in its presence the chills that had dominated my body disappeared like darkness in the morning. I didn't want to move from its cocoon. But after hearing Grandpa's faint voice calling, I reluctantly hopped out of bed. Before rinsing the sleep from my eyes, I walked outside and stood in the front yard. Everywhere there was palpable silence. Everything was woods, woods, and more woods, the pine and sycamore trees as tall as the sky.

My grandparents' yard was huge, and flowering plants abounded—honeysuckle; black-eyed Susans; and beds of yellow, pink, red, and white roses. Then there were the ones that became my favorite: the four-o'clock flowers, magnificent crimson blooms that only opened their buds at four in the afternoon. The grandeur of Grandma's flower garden relieved some of my sadness.

As I sat on the concrete stoop, taking it in, Grandpa's voice interrupted my thoughts. It rang in my ear so loud you'd have thought he was talking through a megaphone.

"Whatcha doin' over thar, gal?" He was sitting in his rocker under the old oak tree, chewing on a twig. "You hongry'? Lula gone fix somethin' t'eat direc'ly."

I nodded my head. My stomach was growling louder than a tiger in the San Diego Zoo.

"Gal, you ain't said two words since you got here. What wrong wit' ya? Dat cat got yo' tongue?"

"No, sir," I answered, even though I hadn't a clue what a cat's tongue had to do with me not talking. Grandpa just shrugged his shoulders and shook his head as he walked up the two steps past me.

Out of the corner of my eye, I saw Grandma making her way down the dogtrot—the long, open hallway down the middle of the house that separated our bedroom from the front room. She was belting out one of her old Negro spirituals, which sent shivers down my spine.

"Grandma jus' checkin' on you and yo' grandpa 'fore I get on in here and cook y'all some vittles."

And what a breakfast! Oversized homemade biscuits, apple preserves, and grits. Grandma said she thought I had a tapeworm by the way the food flew off my plate and into my mouth.

"Chile, you ain't knee high to a duck's behind. Jus' don' know where you puttin' all that food."

Grandpa howled with laughter, spraying a mouthful of biscuits and grits clear across the table. Watching him sent me into a giggling fit. For the first time since landing on their doorstep, I smiled.

My grandparents' house cast a spell on me. Above the fireplace in the bedroom, a photograph collection was neatly displayed on the mantelpiece. The dogtrot was set up like a living room, though in actuality it was a long, wide hallway that ran from the screened-in front porch to the back of the house, connecting with the large dining room. The kitchen area was small, with a wood-and-coal-burning stove. Pots and pans hung from the walls below the pinewood cabinets. A section of the wall in the dogtrot was stuffed with old newspapers to seal the cracks from wind and rain.

On the other side of the hallway, on the flower-papered wall, a picture commanded the space. It was of a tall, remarkable-looking woman in a long white dress and matching hat. Of all the photographs, that one intrigued me most. Grandma told me it was her sister, Ella. Her stare was piercing, and I longed to know more about her. To me she seemed larger than life.

The most magical room of all was my grandparents' front room. Grandma made it clear that it was off-limits unless I was with her or Grandpa or they gave me permission to enter. Inside was a pinkish sofa covered in hard plastic. A gigantic old chifforobe sat in the corner, and Grandma kept the long metal key that unlocked it in her apron pocket.

My eyes got wide as saucers when she opened the cabinet door and pulled out a glass plate filled with homemade tea cakes. Grandma shook her head as she watched me devour two of them at once. I almost got a crick in my neck trying to look over her shoulder to see what other treasures she had stored in there. But Grandma was too quick. She put the key back in the lock and shut the door.

Just like our bedroom, the front room had two beds with large head and foot posts. It had a fireplace, too, the mantel adorned with pictures in rustic frames. I was struck by one of an older couple. The woman looked just like Grandpa, with her high cheekbones, fair skin, and sharp nose. The man standing behind her was a distinguished-looking gentleman with dark, silky skin. He wore a starched, collared shirt under a gray suit. Grandma told me it was a picture of my grandpa's mama, Alice, and his papa, Josh Horn. She said that they were "with the Lawd now."

One day, my curiosity got the better of me. When Grandma returned to the field to finish up her plowing for the day, I decided to make my move. I was desperate to find out what other goodies were inside the glass and wood chifforobe. The thought of doing something that I shouldn't was tempting and only made my curiosity grow.

I waited as Grandma made her way down the dogtrot to the kitchen, way in the back of the house. When I heard the screen door on the back porch shut, I was off on my adventure, into the front room, where I stood, soaking up the thrill of being in an off-limits paradise. I looked over at the sofa, and it beckoned me to sit. Since it was covered in hard plastic and my bare legs were sweating profusely from the Alabama humidity, each time I lifted my legs, they stuck to the plastic before coming free with a crackling sound. I giggled and enjoyed a few minutes of lifting my legs up and down, just to hear that sound.

Then I got up, went over to the chifforobe, and pulled on the door. To my surprise, it swung wide on its own. It was unlocked! I climbed up on the wooden sleeve so that I could scan the contents. My eyes lit up as I homed in on two round red and blue decorative metal tins. I pulled them down from the shelf one at a time and laid them on the pale wooden floor. Inside the blue one were pressed flowered handkerchiefs and a handful of silver coins.

As I struggled to remove the lid from the red one, it popped open and all its contents flew out. Black-and-white photographs covered the floor. I saw a picture of what looked like a younger Grandma smiling and holding hands with a heavyset lady. Just as I was about to start picking up the pictures, Grandma walked into the room. There I sat, open tin in my hot little hands, photographs scattered all around me. She looked as shocked to see me as I was to see her. I regretted not grabbing another tea cake before getting caught.

She didn't scold me. Instead she pointed to my great-grand-parents' picture on the mantel and said, "Papa Josh and Mama Alice's spirit live in this here room. You can mess 'roun in here and break somethin' if you want. They are haints in here and them spirits'll chase you out if you come in here again. Now, gone. I'll clean up this here mess you done made, Lawd Jesus."

I couldn't fully grasp the concept of ghosts and haints, yet from Grandma's voice I knew they were something very unpleasant. It reminded me of how back in Detroit my brothers would chase me, sheets draped over their heads, making all types of ghastly noises. I'd run and jump in my sister's lap and she'd scold them, threaten to beat their behinds. The thought of my great-grandparents' spirits chasing me made me shake in my shoes. Being busted cold by Grandma, I probably looked more like a ghost than Papa Josh and Mama Alice ever could.

What saddened me more than anything was disappointing Grandma. I retreated to the screened-in front porch. It was my favorite part of the house, because of the long wooden swing, which had become my perch. It hung from two half-rusted chains that clanked and clattered as it swayed. I'd stretch out with my legs cocked up over the back for hours. That day I sat, wondering at what point those haints would attack my little behind. My encounter with Grandma had thrown me back into my sitting-on-the-pity-pot mode, and I babbled uncontrollably as tears rolled down my cheeks.

Grandpa was in the front yard, whittling branches into his favorite chewing and gnawing toothpicks. The chickens were there, too, clawing for worms and bugs, flapping and flipping their wings. Grandma had returned to the field out back; I could faintly hear the plow and chain banging against each other. A woodpecker hammered away on a piece of wood that Grandma had put up as a brace to keep her yellow rose branches from falling over onto her bed of orchids.

Talk-crying was an art form I'd learned since arriving in the country. It's when you ramble through a babble of muffled tears. The blessing of being surrounded by all that wild and boisterous nature was not having to worry about anyone hearing me sobbing. Least of all Grandpa. As Grandma would often say, "Grandpa so deaf, he ain't able to hear the dinner bell even if it was rangin' direc'ly in his ear."

Then, in the middle of all my slobbering and sobbing, I heard Grandpa making his way up the two steps toward the raggedy screen door. So many flies and other bugs had smashed onto the screen that it was permanently marked with blobs of residue. I could hear him sucking wind as he began banging and shaking the door. I'd put the latch on before I lay down in the swing. It was a habit drilled into me and my siblings in Detroit: always put the latch on the door, no matter what.

"Chile, hurry up and went. You hear what I say, chile? Hurry up and went rat now."

I ran to the door. Grandpa was standing there, out of breath, repeating the same thing over and over. "What wrong wit' you, chile; you hear me talkin' atcha?"

Just as I unlocked the screen door, I heard Grandma making her way down the dogtrot. Grandpa stepped inside, trying desperately to catch his breath. "I d'clare, dis yere chile sumptin else, Miss Lula. She done messed 'round an puts dis hook on dis yere do'. That gal rat yere knows I needs hep to git in de house. Um 'bout to keel over tryin' to make it to git my med'cine."

The tears returned, gushing down my face.

"Pay no mind to yo ol' grandpa, baby; he jus' tryin' to get in the house to get his med'cine. You gots to remember that yo' ol' grandpa gots real bad consumption. He jus' wants you to make haste 'fore he keel over."

I cried even louder because I didn't know what "make haste" or "keel over" meant. Boo-hooing, I stood there, trying to figure out whether I was more disappointed in myself for not hearing Grandpa calling, for putting the latch on the screen door, or because I couldn't make out what Grandma and Grandpa were saying. The only thing left for me to do was bury my face in Grandma's apron, which smelled of dirt and sweat. Tasted like it too.

Whenever I allow the struggles of my first few months in the country to fill my memory, they give me pause. I was a small child, just four years old, living in a world completely contrary to the one I'd been torn away from. But I can describe with pinpoint accuracy when I began to discover a small level of comfort and peace in my new life.

It was during my first few weeks in the country, when folks started to drop off bags of clothing. The clothes had belonged to their loved ones who'd passed on. Grandma would use these clothes to make quilts for their family members. Even though I was too young to fully grasp the concept of the lives these folks had led prior to their passing, her sewing while humming, barely pursing her lips, was hypnotic. Watching her pull thread in and out of fabric as she told stories consoled me. She made me feel safe, like I was in a cocoon where nothing could touch me, and the physical aura she cast seemed larger than the front yard. Sometimes she'd comment, "You such a pretty lil gal, Grandma loves yo' heart and yo' liver too." Other times she'd set the quilt aside and motion me to her lap, where she'd lay a wet kiss on my forehead while rocking me like a newborn baby. Her lap was enormous.

I never spoke a word while she held me. Absolute quiet reigned, except for the sounds of insects, birds, and Grandma's lullabies. It was during those moments that the sadness that filled me began to recede. Each hug provided the strength, courage, and stability I needed to survive the trauma of being dropped off in unfamiliar surroundings. Layers of insecurity began to peel away from me like the dead skin of a garden snake.

And with each strip of fabric Grandma placed in her quilts, I became more intrigued by the stories they told. Quilting became synonymous with storytelling. As she worked, Grandma would tell me, "You gone grow into these stories, chile."

Over the years, I noticed Grandma had a certain pattern and timing to her storytelling. Each story and each piece of cloth seemed to fit like a puzzle. Every one had a beginning, middle, and end. More and more, I was aware of—and amazed by—the way she was able to weave people's lives into her quilts, telling me how they lived and how they died. Sometimes I'd have to wait until she gave me one special piece of information before I could grasp the magnitude of their stories. Then, as if a lightbulb had been turned on in my head, the other pieces would come together. Only in that moment would I be able to understand the fullness and completeness of it, just like a finished quilt.

With each story, the agony of missing Detroit and my inability to grasp the language and culture of my new environment began to subside. I never wanted to be far from Grandma. I didn't think I could endure the hurt of being removed ever again.

Over time, I came to consider myself a pretty good translator of euphemisms and the colloquial language of my new home. Sometimes I communicated with my grandparents by mimicking their words. It was like picking up a foreign language. For instance, there was no such thing as aunt or cousin, it was "ant" and "cuttin." Steadily, I began replacing my small vocabulary with the local vernacular. I'd laugh at myself over the way I was able to jumble or mispronounce words and leave off letters, just like the old folks.

Grandpa got a kick out of me talking like him, and would say, "You thank ya grown now, don't ya?" Sometimes, when I'd be on my way to the outhouse and he'd ask "Whar ya goin'?" I'd say, "I'm goin' to see a man 'bout a horse, Grandpapa"—the very words he used when Grandma asked him the same question. A little wry smile would fill his face, like he was pleased with my answer.

I also began to understand country etiquette, culture, and traditions. Men and women were always referred to as "Mister" or "Miss"; it didn't matter whether the woman was married or not, it was still pronounced "Miss." For addressing every adult directly, it was either "Ma'am" or "Sir."

As the months passed, the vastness of everything around me no longer bothered me. Nor did the feeling that I was lost in a never-ending forest. Yes, I'd arrived. Gradually, I became a part of the rural countryside and basked in its beauty, and I found peace in the silky white sand and honeysuckle. On the banks of a cool water basin, I'd daydream about Grandma's stories. Sometimes I'd create the characters in my mind until I could feel, touch, and smell them. With the sensation of cool earth on my back, I closed my eyes and felt the warmth of the sun beating against my eyelids. Even with my eyes shut tight, I saw ribbons of orange and crimson. It felt as though I'd been born there, nestled in the arms of the tall Alabama pines.

As a result of this newfound love of the country, time seemed to pass rapidly. I'd turned five and finally felt free of the sadness that had consumed me almost four months ago. It was already hot and hazy, though it was still morning. I could barely see the tin roof of our house. The spring that sat about two hundred or so feet from our front yard cascaded with fresh blue water. This was my hideaway in the woods, my aqua-filled playhouse. Greenery and blooming flowers were everywhere; tall blades of grass and dogwood and green maple trees cast shadows in the noonday sun. Daisies and other wildflowers grew along the water's edge.

At the spring, I found a solitude I'd never known before. It was an escape far enough from the farm that it seemed as though I'd traveled somewhere. I wasn't so far, though, that I couldn't hear Grandma's booming voice calling out for me. My ears were attuned to her. I made sure that whenever she called, I was ready to burst uphill to help with her quilting or any other task. When she called, I knew I only had a few minutes to make my way through the brush and flowers and along the tree-lined path that crossed over the white sand road. On the other side was our small, sparsely furnished five-room house.

Until Grandma called, all I wanted to do was lie there, nestled next to the blue waters of the spring. Grandpa and his brothers had dug it back in the mid-1890s, when they were boys. It was knee deep, with water so clear you could see your feet. I loved standing in it, wiggling each toe, curling them into the squishy mud that formed at the bottom. I'd watch how quickly the cloud of dirty water would disappear and turn clear blue again. I spent so much time frolicking through the spring waters, the tadpoles that congregated there became a part of my family. They'd swim near my feet, like they wanted a nibble, then take off in a flurry downstream. Watching them swim back and forth without a care in the world was mesmerizing. I'd lie there, my mind drifting into daydreams, until I heard the familiar sound of Grandma calling my name—singing it, carefully emphasizing each syllable.

"Phyl-liss-tene…"

I knew I'd better get up the hill to the front yard with lightning speed. Grandma's favorite words were, "You bet' not let me call you more 'n once." She always said that, even though sometimes she'd call me two or three times. I wasn't about to push my luck or test her patience though. Grandma would have none of that.

By the time I got to the front yard, Grandma had taken her seat under the old oak tree. She sat with her legs slightly sprawled, wiping the sweat from her forehead with her apron.

"Chile, been callin' you pert'near an hour. We needs to get started on your old quilt. Gone in the house and grab it off your bed, we got jus' 'nough time to make some headway 'fore I got to get supper on. Gone try to get a good piece of it sewed 'fore nightfall."

"Yes'm, Grandma."

"Get your Grandma's snuff from the mantel; bring it on with you. Make sure you don' wake your old grandpa. He down with his rheumatiz, an' he sleep mighty poorly las' night."

"Yes'm."

I tiptoed inside and slowly pulled my unfinished quilt off my bed. Sure enough, Grandpa was snoring loud enough to raise the dead, as Grandma liked to say. My quilt needed a lot of work. The batting, or the insides of the quilt, which consisted of cotton picked from somebody's field long, long ago, was seeping through the holes in the cloth. Grandma had told me she was going to make my quilt larger and fill it with more clothing from her loved ones. She'd spent the last few months trying to pry it away from me, but I'd been reluctant to surrender it. I had to feel it next to my body to fall asleep.

Grandma said, "High time we get started. Them kind spirits in your quilt took a hol' of you ever since I gives it to you that night. Don' you worry, chile, Grandma gone make sure when she done workin' on the quilt for the day, she gone put it right back on yo' bed."

I was so glad to hear that she wasn't going to throw it in a croker sack and put it in the smokehouse, like she did with other quilts and bags of tattered clothing she was still working on. Each time she began quilting, she'd send me to get the bag of clothes she'd be working on that day. I'd drag the sack to the front yard and sit it right next to her rocker. Then I'd watch as she dug around inside it.

That day, she pulled out a piece of faded off-white cloth, smiling like she'd found a long-lost treasure. Slowly, she held it up and began rocking in her chair. She said it was from Ella's wedding dress. Ella was the woman whose portrait graced the hallway, the woman I longed to know more about. When Grandma began pulling pieces of her dress from the bag, I thought I'd choke on my own spit. I couldn't believe that Ella's clothing would be part of my quilt.

"This yere the firs' cloth we puttin' in yo' quilt."

My grandma had many memories of times past. She'd refer to those days as "after slavery times," or "during slavery times." It was her way of measuring the span of her life. As she worked, she would stop intermittently to bark out, "You payin' 'tention, chile?" This was her way of letting me know how important these stories were, and how they were intimately attached to her past. In her quilts, she could stitch the broken pieces of her heart back together, somehow mending it.

I picked up a soiled piece of cloth—another piece of Ella's wedding dress. The stains were so set in that even soap and water couldn't remove them. I imagined that some of Ella's clothes bore invisible tears from loss and abandonment. These were emotions I understood.

Grandma was meticulous in her placement of the clothing in her quilts. She'd gently cut the fabric to ensure a perfect fit, using only her hand to measure each piece. She began to sew, and it wasn't long before she'd enter into what folks down South call a "stitchin' rhythm." Looking as though she were in a trance, her body stoic and focused, she began to tell me the story of her sister Ella.

3

Courageous Ella

"MY MAMA TELLS ME THE STORY 'bout me and Ella so many times. She say, 'I wants you to know how you and your big sista Ella came to be and don' wants you to never forget.' And I tells you what, I's so glad she did, 'cause I wouldn't be sittin' here in this front yard tellin' you all 'bout my family right now if it wasn't so. You hear me, chile? That's why I don' wants you to never tire of yo' ol' grandma talkin' 'bout my Ella. I'm gone tell you 'bout Ella more times than you can count, 'cause you needs to know. You a lil gal, but you gots somethin' inside you that's older then Methuselah. This here ol' quilt gots folks clothes in it. Grandma don' even know who they is, but whats I do know is that they prob'ly done passed on. My mama starts to make yo' quilt soons she finds out that she gone have Ella. But Ella comes early, and she never finish it. We gone finish it now. I tells you somethin' else, I wo'n't be surprise if Mama knew all 'long that she wa'n't gone finish it. She may know your lil self was gone come to your grandma direc'ly and you's the one that s'pose' to have it all along. Now, how you like that?"

A wide smile crossed Grandma's face as she looked at me.

Her sister Ella, she said, was born around 1876, somewhere near Sandersville, Jones County, Mississippi. She and Grandma were the daughters of two emancipated slaves named Emma and Joe Young. Emma and Joe had been owned by a Mr. Young, one of the evilest slave-owners you could imagine. Emma would tell Ella and Grandma how he worked his slaves coming and going, morning until night, every day except Sunday. Any time he'd get into one of his hateful moods, all the slaves would watch as he'd come barreling out of his house, which sat at the top of Devil's Hill. They could hear him coming before seeing him. He'd be breathing so hard, you'd think he'd just plowed forty acres nonstop. It seemed as though he lived for ways to punish his slaves, like whipping the skins off their backs for no good reason. He'd make some of them go to work in the fields with large wooden blocks chained to their feet.

Before the war was over, when slaves were still slaves, Emma birthed three children. The evil Mr. Young sold all three while they were still nursing. The pain of him taking her children, only days removed from her belly, was so extreme that Emma thought she'd never bear another child as a result. The pain and heartache were just too much. Emma told Ella and Grandma about her missing children many times over the years. It was as though she was trying to will them back into her life each time she told the story. Through the telling and retelling of what happened to Grandma's sister and brothers, my great-grandmother was able to remember all the details as though it had happened only yesterday.

Mr. Young passed on right after the South's surrender, making way for his only son, the young Mr. Young, to take over. The young Mr. Young was the spitting image of his father, potbelly and all. But he didn't appear to be quite as mean-spirited. As a result, many of the ex-slaves stayed on to work the fields, including Grandma Emma and Papa Joe.

The young Mr. Young married soon after he took over the plantation. His wife was said to be the kindest white woman you'd ever want to meet. She gave Blacks liberties never seen before, like allowing them to read and be taught right there on the plantation. She also prevented her husband from making his workers do any fieldwork on Saturdays or Sundays. She was not at all like old Mr. Young's wife, who was almost as bad as he was in her treatment of slaves. Old Mr. Young's wife had ended up moving to Savannah with her married daughter after old Mr. Young passed.

Now, just when Emma thought she wasn't able to bear any more children, along came Ella. Ella was born nine or ten summers after slavery. Joe and Emma were as happy as they were surprised to be having another child. And Ella was born into freedom. She was also special because she was born with what country folks call a veil over her face. Word of the veil spread through the country pipeline, and it didn't take long before folks from miles around knew about her. According to folklore, a veil is a thin film that very rarely forms over an infant's face during childbirth. Legend states that any child born in this way has magical powers. These children were said to have the ability to change people's luck; just a touch from their hand was rumored to have curative powers. Some said they could even see into the future.

Folks from near and far lined up to see baby Ella, to lay their hands on her, to hold and squeeze her tight. A child entering the world with a veil was rarer than a three-legged calf. Emma was grateful for Ella's gift, yet at the same time couldn't decide whether it was a blessing or a curse. A veiled child is given so much attention. Even young Mr. Young almost broke his neck making his way down to the Black settlement to view the beautiful Ella.

This was the first time he'd ever been down to the old slave quarters. Like his father, he'd inherited a breathing problem that folks down South called the consumption. His was supposedly even worse than his father's. As a matter of fact, he came close to leaving this world many a time. He knew that he'd better make things right in order to keep Ella near to hand, where he could benefit from her healing abilities.

Mr. Young called Papa Joe up to the big house and offered him a piece of land he could farm. He also gave him the house that used to belong to the overseer. He told Papa Joe that he could pay for the land from his crop in installments. Papa Joe was so glad to get his own land and move to a larger place that he agreed to the deal right away.

So it came to be that Ella grew up working in the Young household like no Black person ever had before. She had the run of the entire big house. Little did Joe know that the evil plan young Mr. Young had cooked up with that land would one day tear Grandma's family every which way but loose.

Before that day, though, more good news came for Emma and Joe, with Grandma bursting into the world in 1883, seven years after Ella was born. She was a late-life child, or what Emma called her miracle baby—she was in her forties at the time of Grandma's birth. Together, Ella and Grandma grew up on the little piece of land that young Mr. Young had sold to Papa Joe.

Ella was a young girl when she began laying hands on Mr. Young. After using homemade salves, plasters, and potions that she and Emma had made, Mr. Young didn't have any more consumption spells. Ella would use those remedies on him every day, rain or shine, spell or not, and Mr. Young was happier than a pig in slop. He began to smile more than ever, in addition to treating his workers more like real people instead of machines.

Ella also spent a lot of time in the big house learning to speak well and read fluently. She was taught to read and write by the young Mrs. Young. Around that time, Mr. Young's business started booming. He became one of the largest producers of cotton and timber in all of southern Mississippi. He couldn't believe his good fortune. Even though he didn't go around announcing it, he credited Ella. Having her on the plantation, he thought, was the best thing that had ever happened to him.

Ella became the recipient of all the old clothes Miss Young no longer wanted. She'd make clothes for everybody who lived on the Young place. Young Mr. Young never refused her anything. He knew that she was the person that kept him healthy, wealthy, and endowed with good fortune. Ella knew it, too, and used every bit of his goodwill to her advantage.

In addition to her mastery of potions and healing ointments, she sewed like she was born with a needle and thread in her little hands. She was only six or seven when she picked up quilting like it was second nature. Her mother, Emma, taught both Ella and Grandma how to make quilts for folks who'd passed on, and while they quilted Emma would preach about how it was a sin to mix new cloth with the clothes of folks who "done gone on to glory." Their soul would never find rest if they were mixed, she told her daughters.

Many times, Grandma, Emma, and Ella would stay up half the night, sewing quilts. Those quilts were special and unlike anyone else's. They zigged and zagged, crissed and crossed, and burst with an assortment of colors. The Youngs loved showing them off to their visitors.

One day, Miss Young gave Ella some books she didn't want any more. Ella was almost fifteen by then and could probably read better than Mr. Young. Even Miss Young was surprised at how quickly Ella had picked up reading and writing. Her speaking skills and command of the English language were near impeccable, all thanks to Miss Young. Mr. Young had no idea just how well Ella had grasped learning, nor did he care. Ella overheard him tell his wife that there was no way she could learn to read much, and all she'd ever be able to do was to look at the pictures. His words set a fire under her. As sure as night follows day, she had almost everyone in the Black settlement reading and writing their names. She taught Grandma to read and write too. My great-grandparents, Ella, and Grandma would sit around the fire on Sunday nights while Ella read Bible passages. It wasn't long before Grandma had many verses from the Bible memorized.

Ella was Grandma's sun and moon. Everywhere Ella went, Grandma Lula was right on her heels, walking in her footsteps when she wasn't helping in the fields. She'd sit quietly watching Ella make tinctures and teas for Mr. Young. Ella never got involved in the fieldwork; her only job was to ensure that she had a constant supply of Mr. Young's healing herbs and special plasters. Much of her time was spent in the big house.

Ella had such a way with Mr. Young that her mother thought she was getting "too uppity for a cullud gal." Ella had reached the point where she'd tell Mr. Young exactly what was on her mind without hesitation. She knew that she had him where she wanted him and could control each situation just as she wanted. But around 1895, Ella's life changed. She messed around and fell in love with Jeremiah Thomas, a boy from the adjoining plantation. Ella was what Joe and Emma called courting age when she fell head over heels for Jeremiah. She walked around in a daze day and night and could barely talk about anything else.

Mr. Young noticed that Ella had lost some of her zeal for being on time with his teas and plasters. Late one night, he knocked on Joe and Emma's door. Mr. Young rarely came anywhere near the Black settlement, but Ella had missed his daily dose, and he was looking for her. Emma gave Ella the who and what for when she came home later that night, and Ella apologized before darting up the hill to give Mr. Young his treatment, even though it was almost midnight.

As the months passed, Ella's attention focused more and more on Jeremiah. Every minute of free time they had, they'd spend in each other's company. She'd talk about Jeremiah from sunup to sundown. He could do no wrong in her eyes. They were attached, as Grandma would say, at the hip. On Sundays, they'd spend time in the grove eating apples and dreaming about their future. They were like two bookends. To remove one would cause everything to fall.

Then Jeremiah's father announced that his family would be moving to New York to provide better opportunities for everyone, including Jeremiah and his younger siblings. Ella was broken up. Jeremiah begged and pleaded with her to marry him, but she couldn't imagine leaving Joe, Emma, and Grandma. Jeremiah told her that he would come back after he found a job, that one way or another, they'd marry and he'd convince her to go back with him. They swore their hearts to each other. To the day he left, Jeremiah continued to plead with Emma and Joe to leave the Young plantation. But they would not budge.

In the months that followed, Jeremiah wrote constantly, and Emma and Joe were proud of him, because he had found himself a good job as a porter up North. Each time a letter came, Grandma could see it in Ella's eyes: she wanted Jeremiah to come back for her. It was a long year, but Jeremiah did return and asked Joe for Ella's hand in marriage. Ella was so happy to see him, she nearly floated off the ground. She said yes to his marriage proposal, and their mama began making her a wedding dress that exuded charm and sophistication. With its high neckline and fitted waist, it was exquisite.

Once again, Jeremiah offered to bring Emma, Joe, and Grandma up North with him, but Grandma knew there was no way her mama and papa would leave Mississippi. As Papa Joe would say, "Young Mr. Young ain't got good sense, but he treats us halfway decent for us being cullud folks. Ella gone jus' have to go all by herself."

There was another reason Emma and Joe didn't want to leave, a sadder one. They always believed that somehow their children, the four little babies that had been sold so long ago, would find their way back to the Young plantation. Unrealistic as it may sound, they held out hope that, through some miracle, they'd be reunited with their lost children. But Ella was determined to go north. Before the night was over, she'd have to go up to the big house and tell Mr. Young she was leaving.

Ever since Jeremiah put the idea of moving to New York into Ella's head, Emma had known there'd be trouble. It was a premonition, one she felt very deeply. Ella was Mr. Young's lifeline. He'd resist her leaving, and it didn't matter whether slavery had ended or not; he'd always thought of Ella as his property, there to serve him first and foremost. Her happiness was secondary. Her number-one responsibility was to take care of him. Emma claimed that the only way he'd let Ella go would be over his dead body.

What was Ella to do? She had to go with her Jeremiah, and she needed her monthly earnings Mr. Young owed her for the services she'd provided. Ten dollars was a lot of money. But Ella was fearless, never acknowledging what her mother was afraid of. Though she had never witnessed the wrath that would come from Mr. Young that night.

It was late in the evening when Ella decided to go up to the big house with her news. She'd just seen Mr. Young that morning to give him his tea and make a plaster for his chest. She had decided against telling him then, but chose to wait until she and Jeremiah had made their final arrangements to meet the Reverend Eddie. He'd marry them and then they'd be on their way north.

Ella walked up the steps and into the front room. Mr. Young was sitting in his favorite old leather chair, a glass of whiskey in his hand. She stood across from him. So many times, she'd seen him sit in that chair and drink the many elixirs and teas she'd made for him over the years. He looked at her through bloodshot eyes. Ella met his gaze directly and told him she was getting married and moving to New York the first thing in the morning.

Grandma found out what happened next when she went back to visit Miss Young years after the young Mr. Young had passed on. Miss Young had been standing in the doorway the entire time, listening to Ella go on about marrying Jeremiah and how she'd no longer be able to take care of Mr. Young. Miss Young witnessed the entire nightmare of what her husband did to Ella.

She saw it all.

Miss Young wanted Grandma to know that she'd tried her best to help Ella that night. She tried several times to stop her husband from hitting Ella, but the liquor had him fired up. Ella acted as though she didn't feel him slapping her again and again, even as her nose and mouth bled profusely. He wouldn't stop. Ella would stand up, compose herself, and eye him like he was an attack dog. Then he'd strike her back down to the floor.

Miss Young watched helplessly as blood trickled from Ella's nose and mouth. Each time she spoke, Ella sounded like she was choking on her own blood. But she refused to give up, to stop making her case. She was leaving, she repeated, and never coming back. She wanted the money that he owed her. She wasn't backing down, which only made Mr. Young angrier.

Miss Young pleaded for him to stop. She even tried to stand in his way so he couldn't strike Ella, only to be slammed up against the wall by his force. Mr. Young couldn't believe Ella was this defiant and determined, not only to get the wages due her but to walk out of his house with her head held high. I guess he figured that he wasn't going to allow an insolent Black girl to get the best of him. That's when he saw a hot poker lying in the fireplace, and, with precision, lifted it and swung.

The scorching heat from the blow badly burned the side of her face and a section of her lips. It was as though Mr. Young were trying to brand her like cattle. Ella's knees buckled, and she slowly fell to the floor. Unable to stand, she crawled out of the house to the front porch, moaning and groaning, in excruciating pain. I have no idea how she made it back to her family's house that night. Mr. Young watched and wouldn't allow his wife to help Ella in any way.

When she finally made her way home, and Joe, Emma, and Grandma saw her face, her horrible wounds, they went into a state of shock. No one, they felt, not even Satan himself, should be allowed to suffer like that. The look in Grandma's eyes as she told the story of what had transpired that night was heartbreaking. The entire house was in an uproar, she told me. Papa Joe grabbed his shotgun and began fumbling through the chifforobe to get his shells. Everyone was crying at the top of their lungs, including Ella herself.

Emma grabbed Joe, pleading and screaming for him not to go after Mr. Young. You could see the anger in Joe's eyes, Grandma told me; you could almost feel the heat from his blood as it boiled with rage. Feeling helpless and powerless, Joe slammed his gun to the floor, ran out the door, and disappeared into the woods. He never returned. No one ever saw him again. It was as though my great-grandpa had never existed.

When Jeremiah saw Ella's face, he turned pale as a billy goat. Grandma felt that after that, Jeremiah might as well have died too. He was just that broken. Every day he'd come to the house, but Ella wouldn't allow him anywhere near her. She pleaded with Grandma never to allow Jeremiah to see her like that again. Her face was too scarred, the pain unfathomable.

Emma and Grandma treated Ella with all the healing herbs they could, but nothing seemed to heal her face, her mouth, or her spirit. Jeremiah refused to go back to New York; instead, he ended up moving back to the small plot of land that he'd lived on before he and his family went north. I suppose he just wanted to be near his Ella. He was heartbroken over her, and as a result he lost his mind as well as any reason to live.

And poor Emma. The emotional pain of seeing her daughter in that condition took a physical toll on her that was so deep, a week later she went to sleep and never woke up. Grandma was only thirteen years old. She now had the task of burying her mama, taking care of Ella as best she could, and watching Jeremiah waste away.

But she had to bear it. She was the only one left.

Things got much worse. Two weeks after Mr. Young's horrific abuse, he showed up unexpectedly at their door and ordered Grandma and what was left of Ella to get on their way. He was taking back his land. Grandma felt helpless, but luckily Emma's church family helped to bury her and took both Grandma and Ella into their home. They lived with Miss Della, who had a small shanty with a pretty green pasture out back. In Ella's last days upon this earth, she loved lying in the grass, even though she was in horrific pain. She thought Miss Della's place was what heaven looked like. Grandma made a promise to Ella that she'd bring her back to this place when she got ready to meet the Lord.

A month later, Ella's mouth just wouldn't heal. She was at the point where she couldn't open it at all, making it impossible for her to eat or drink. As a result, she wasted away. She was only nineteen, and just beginning to blossom and grow into adulthood when she was stricken by white anger, greed, and selfishness. When the good Lord took her that night, she faced it straight on. Her eyes stared right through Grandma. She fought hard not to leave her, because she knew Grandma would be all alone and would have to fend for herself. All the family members they knew of were now gone.

Grandma held Ella so tight she felt her sister's spirit rise up and plant itself right in the base of her spine. She then gave Ella permission to cross over, as she put it, because Grandma knew she would be all right. But not before she told Ella that she loved her heart and her liver too.

All this happened in 1896, when Grandma was only thirteen. But that night, she used all her strength to pick up her sister's limp body from the cold, wet grass and carry her to the nearby Black undertaker's house. She never bent or bowed beneath the weight of Ella. Her back remained straight as an arrow. That was the way my grandma Lula was. She never complained, ever. Even during those days when she was obviously in pain, hurt, or abused.

After Ella passed, Grandma went to see Jeremiah over at the Thomas place. She had a difficult time mustering up the courage to tell him that Ella was gone but knew it had to be done. When she told him, he just dropped his head a bit lower. She couldn't see his eyes, only the tears that landed in his lap. He wouldn't lift his head, no matter how hard Grandma tried to make eye contact. He never was the same boy with the hundred-dollar smile, and he hardly made enough money from the little farm to keep the place up. Grandma used to sit with him for a while right after Ella passed on, but he just looked at the floor or the ground, and when he talked, she could barely make out what he was saying.

One day when Grandma went to see him, she couldn't find him anywhere. As she made her way back down the road past Ma Cherry's house, she saw Ma Cherry outside, sweeping off her front porch. When she saw Grandma, she called out.

"Come over here, gal. If you come by here to see that Thomas boy, he done gone on to glory. They finds him hangin' from a tree down yonder. Ain't got a stitch a clothes on."

After Jeremiah's death, Grandma didn't know why she went back to his shanty, but she was glad she did, because that's how she ended up with Jeremiah's blue shirt. I suspect she was trying to find a way to keep him and Ella together, because in their life, the two fit like hand in glove. I watched as she meticulously stitched pieces of them into my quilt, Ella and Jeremiah now bound together in the same squares.

Grandma then took more pieces of Ella's wedding dress, the dress Ella never got to wear, and sewed it along the four sides of the quilt, where the fabric was missing. It blended in beautifully with the red-checkered and black-and-white-flowered fabric next to it. After she'd finished, she told me that whenever I got too tired and weary or felt like giving up, I should remember Ella and what she went through.

"You see, chile," she said, "trouble don' las' always."

I was always amazed at how Grandma could tell the story of Ella without flinching. I'd search her eyes, but the tears never came. After a while, I began to understand why. Ella was such a pinnacle of strength, and Grandma wanted to exhibit the same strength she herself had used to lift and carry her sister through the darkness on that long night so many years ago. Over sixty years had passed, but she could still feel Ella's spirit within her. That's why she was able to stand proud and strong.

I was almost six when Grandma first told me the story of Ella. I hadn't yet grasped the concept of death and adult fear. I knew Ella as the woman in the beautiful long white dress, the one whose image I'd stare at first thing in the morning and catch a glimpse of before I went to sleep. She was a captivating figure in a way I couldn't explain, and I couldn't imagine her being hurt or exposed to danger. As Grandma described what had happened to her, I struggled to comprehend the pain she'd suffered.

Ella was the first person who gave life to my quilt of souls. Even though Grandma Lula sewed other folks' clothing into my old quilt, Ella's heartbeat permeated it most. Her fabric became the anchor to which the other pieces of clothing—and other stories—were attached. She was the last of Grandma's lost, sold, and deceased family members, a stark reminder for me of a vanished generation.

After she finished sewing Ella's and Jeremiah's pieces into my quilt, the stillness between me and my grandma was haunting, yet beautiful. From the bag, she pulled out a section of a yellow dress with small gray polka dots and an orange dress that was missing its sleeves.

"Now this here is parts a Miss Cooter's dresses." She pointed to the yellow-polka-dotted-and-orange fabric. "I'm gone put some of Miss Cooter's yellow dress pieces right here in the middle next to Ella, 'cause she like a sista to me."

At that moment, Grandpa poked his head out the front door and spoke in a voice just above a whisper, "Miss Lula, I need some of dat lin'ment and sulfur."

Grandma put down her sewing and rushed into the house. I knew this meant that Grandpa was having one of his spells. The sun was going down and Grandma would be tied up tending to him for Lord knew how long. I wouldn't be hearing any more about this Miss Cooter that day. Who was she, I wondered, and how did she fit into Grandma's life?

4

Cooter

THE NEXT DAY WAS SATURDAY, and Grandma wasn't planning on doing any plowing. This meant extra time spent quilting. Even though it was the weekend, we still got up around
six in the morning. As Grandma said, "If flowers bloom, the
rooster crow, and birds sang every single day at the same time,
we ain't no diff'rent."

After placing our chairs away from the sun's rays, I was
happy as a fat rat in a cheese factory. Grandma had told me that
she'd tell me about Miss Cooter today. Then, right before she
started her quilting, she did something she'd never done before:
she let me pick cloth from her bag to use. I almost fell out of
my seat.

"I wants you to look in there and gets me some more of
them yalla pieces of Cooter's dress. Jus' like the one I pulled out
yestiddy. Now, it's some more orange pieces somewhere in that
bag, too. Grab them, chile, that's pieces of Cooter's fav'rite dress."

Grandma seemed happier than me after I found the torn
clothing and laid the scraps across my knee. I found a large

orange piece that was half torn but still had buttons on it. Other pieces of the yellow polka-dotted fabric looked like the sleeve of a dress, oddly shaped and needing to be cut. Grandma showed me how to gently remove the buttons and cut the fabric into neat strips and squares. She did the same with the yellow until we had ten perfectly straight pieces. She placed five of the yellow ones and five of the orange ones next to Ella's wedding dress, then used straight pins to hold them in place until she could sew them together.

As usual, she didn't start her story until she was sewing. It seemed like she had to be in the right state of mind. With a little wry smile filling her face, she began to talk about the days when she'd worked for Doc Murphy in Laurel, Mississippi.

After Ella passed, Grandma told me, she started working for the Williams family as a housekeeper. Mr. Williams passed away during her second year working for them, and his wife and children moved to Memphis. But Mrs. Williams was blood kin to a man named Doc Murphy, so before leaving for Tennessee, she put in a good word for Grandma, and that's how Grandma came to work for the Murphy family around 1900, when she was sixteen.

Grandma ended up working for the Murphy family for over forty years. She tended to all Doc Murphy's children and even some of the Murphy grandchildren. At one time Mrs. Murphy had four young children, all within a year of each other, and Grandma not only cooked, cleaned, washed, and sewed for a family of six five days a week, she was the nursemaid and caregiver for the children.

When Mrs. Murphy saw how busy Grandma was, she hired a washwoman to pick up the laundry on Wednesdays to take some of the load off. The washwoman's name was Cooter Mae Berry, and this was the beginning of a special friendship between her and Grandma. As their relationship grew, if Miss Cooter had extra time on Wednesday, she'd sit in the Murphy kitchen, talking, laughing, and singing spirituals with Grandma. Cooter always made sure Doc Murphy was her last stop on Wednesdays. If time allowed, she'd stop in on Fridays too, after delivering laundry to her other customers.

Now, Cooter had four sisters, and they all worked together getting out laundry. Cooter was the oldest and the only sister who had married. Her husband's name was Jake Greenfield and he started out all right, but when one of his hands got caught in a cotton gin, it messed him up so bad he couldn't get work anywhere. This misfortune was said to contribute to him turning into an alcoholic and an abuser. He did nothing all day but drink, then he'd come home and start whaling away on Cooter. He'd beat her black and blue.

Cooter put up with his abuse because of their four children, twin girls named Jan and June, and twin boys named Thursday and Friday. She stayed with Jake so the children could have a father, even if he wasn't home half the time, and when he was home he was cruel or abusive to Cooter. She figured she could hang in there for her children's sake. And no matter how much she had to work, she told Grandma, she'd make sure that her children got a good education. She often talked about wanting to go to her grave knowing they were going to be all right. She always asked the Lord to make things better.

Grandma would always tell me a washwoman's work was the most backbreaking and soul-robbing you'd ever want to see. Most folks thought that picking cotton or sharecropping was brutal, but the job of a washwoman was incredibly grueling. These women were also known as laundresses, and they picked up laundry from their customers on Mondays and Wednesdays. Monday's laundry was due back on Wednesdays and Wednesday's laundry on Fridays. There wasn't room to breathe in between. The next week, it started all over again.

The washing assembly line that Cooter and her sisters had going on was nothing short of amazing. The sisters had houses next to each other in the Black settlement. A bunch of clothes-lines hung from the first sister's house to the last sister's. Huge black steel pots were used for "cooking" the clothes. Cooter and her sisters would boil the water in those pots over a blazing fire until it was scalding hot. They had to be careful transferring the clothes from the black pot to the rinsing tub, because the water was so hot it could cause severe burns. They also had to move opposite the direction of the wind to prevent the piping-hot steam from burning their faces. Once, the feet of one of the sisters were badly burned when scalding water spilled on her and she had no choice but to keep on washing and singing. They were singing about the goodness of the Lord, which Grandma believed eased many folks' pain.

For each load of laundry, Cooter and her sisters would separate all the clothes by color. When they finished washing the colored clothes in warm water, they'd toss them down into big aluminum tubs full of cool water. The white clothes, and the extra dirty ones, they sent through boiling water two times with a bar of devil lye soap to loosen up the dirt and make them white as snow. After the clothes sat in the steamy water for about thirty minutes, they'd pull them out with oak poles before tossing them in cool water.

"Then," Grandma Lula told me, "they'd scrub them clothes on that scrub board like you wouldn't believe."

Cooter and her sisters would be lined up, side by side, each sister with her equipment: two silver washtubs, a big black iron pot for boiling clothes, and a wooden scrub board. After the clothes were wrung out, they'd go up on the line to dry in the hot sun.

The sisters made their own soap from devil lye. This was a dangerous chemical, which I knew because Grandma made her soap with it, too. It came in a white can with a red skull and crossbones on it. The crystals would burn a hole in you if they ever came in contact with your skin. When Grandma would ask me to bring it to her, I'd be scared it would spill on me. How could you scare the mess out of a little girl with that talk and in the next breath ask her to go fetch it? I'd wrap an old rag around the can when I delivered it to her.

The washwomen, or laundresses, also made their own starch from flour, water, and Lord knows what else. Cooter and her sisters could heavy-starch a shirt so much it'd stand up on its own. Grandma would get a kick out of describing how Cooter and her sisters scrubbed their clothes on their individual scrub boards in perfect rhythm. The sound of scrubbing mixed in with their songs. You could hear their voices bouncing off the trees in the distance. Singing and scrubbing, scrubbing and singing.

Steal away, steal away, steal away to Jesus;
I ain't got long to stay here.
Lord I'm a-tired and weary;
Jus' wants to be with the Lord.

They sang their hearts out. I imagine that most of the songs were about pain and misery. Old Black hands going up and down on those scrub boards, swoosh, swoosh, swoosh.

"Sunup till sundown, weekdays, all year long they're out there," Grandma told me.

A slew of other poor women who lived in the Black settlement took in wash too. Their songs would mix with Cooter's and her sisters'. I guess all those women had to make a living some kind of way.

The scene of washwomen was familiar to me. Whenever Grandpa and I went to Livingston, we'd pass the settlement where these local women lived and worked. Sitting in the back of Cuttin Jeff's truck on the way into town, I'd see them lined up with washtubs and scrub boards, grinding away and singing. I imagined this was the same setup that Grandma was talking about. Even though Cooter Mae and her sisters had lived in Laurel, Mississippi, during Grandma's era and were long gone, a new set of women right here in Livingston had taken their place. I'd hunker down in the back of Cuttin Jeff's truck so only my eyes were peeking over the side to catch a glimpse of the present-day laundresses.

There they were, in torrid conditions, sawing away on their scrub boards, washing and tussling with the clothes as we slowed down at the railroad track. It awed me to think how tired they must be. Sometimes I'd see one of the women sitting under a shade tree, fanning herself with an old cardboard church fan, the one with a picture of the white baby Jesus with a halo around his head. Her dress would be pulled up above her knees like she was trying to catch a breath before she'd have to go back to work, arms deep in the silver washtub.

When it rained, Grandma told me, Cooter and her sisters had to make up for lost time, seeing how some of their customers showed no mercy just because of the weather. Every now and then, a winter snow'd hit Mississippi. On those days, the sisters had to work through the night in order to get the clothes to their customers on time. Some days they'd have to drape clothes all over their houses. They'd build a roaring fire in the fireplace to dry them faster.

The washwomen's work never ceased. It didn't matter if it was 0 or over 100 degrees. They were outside in the heat or the cold, with nothing but the roaring fire and steam to keep them warm. Twice weekly, Cooter and her sisters would deliver baskets of clean clothes to their customers in wooden wagons attached to two mules. They'd carry the heavy baskets around to the back door, because no washwoman was ever allowed to come to the front. It would sometimes take them half the day to pick up and drop off laundry to their Wednesday and Friday customers. If the two old mules felt cantankerous, it only slowed the process down more.

Through all the hard work, Cooter never fussed or had a harsh word for anybody. She was only a few years younger than Grandma, but already she was bent over like a woman twice her age. Cooter was very soft-spoken, and Grandma worried about her constantly. Between her laundry, raising her children, and an abusive husband, she already had one leg in the grave. It got to the point where Cooter began talking to Grandma about dying.

"One day," Grandma told me, "Cooter came by Doc Murphy's place to see me. I remembers it was on a Friday. She look like she gone fall down right there on the kitchen floor. That poor woman plops down so hard she miss the chair and lands right on her bottom on that hard floor. I gots to get down and pull her up. That woman cryin' like it ain't no tomorry. She gots the weight a the worl' on her, chile. I guess she been holdin' them tears for years. Her face all swole and she cryin' like nobody's bizness. I jus' grabs her and tell her it gone be alright. She tells me that nothin' she do is right. She say her body feel like she been fightin' the devil all night and she ain't eat in two days 'cause Jake done knocked out three a her teeth. That poor woman puts her head in her hand and cry like a baby. She says, 'Miss Lula, I thank the Lord is callin' me home, and I wants to go when he get ready 'cause I'm jus' so tired, Miss Lula. I'm jus' plain ol' tired.'

"I grabs her hand and talks with her a spell. I tells her that trouble ain't gone las' always, the good Lord gone see to it. I sat in that kitchen for hours, combed and braided her hair, put some potion on her face to take some of the swell down. Mama always tol' me, 'Scratch the scalp, soothe the soul.' That's why I combs Cooter's hair that day. 'Fore I put the last plait in her head, she says, 'Miss Lula, I don' never wants my chil'ren to feels like I feel mos' days. If they do, they might as well be dead. My chil'ren the only thang that give me some kinda peace. I'm a gone take every ounce to bring them on into the finish line. I don' never wants them to see through my eyes, though. They ain't never see me cry, not one drop a water. You the only one, Miss Lula, that see me cry, not even my sistas. I gots to stay strong for my chil'ren and my sistas 'cause I'm my mama's ol'es' chile and when Mama passed on, I promise her I look over my sistas till the day I go on to glory. I tells her 'fore she pass that a herd a mules ain't gone stop me, long as the Lord keeps me standin'. But I gots to admit to you and the Lord that I sho nuff gets tired sometimes. The good Lord, you, and them trees over yonder only ones see me like this.'"

Grandma's sorrowful expression told me that she'd reached back in time and was recalling Cooter's pain that day. Her lips quivered, and she reached out and grabbed my hands as she continued, speaking as though Miss Cooter was right there in our front yard.

"I jus' grabs her hand and I prays over that woman like she gettin' ready to leave this worl'. I jus' wants Cooter to be alright, but she gots such a hard row to hoe. Miss Cooter put me in mind of my Ella when I had to hold up for her when Mama and Papa left, jus' like Miss Cooter gots to hol' up for her sistas."

Cooter's sisters worried about her as well, especially with Jake beating on her every chance he got, driving her farther and farther down a path from which they feared she might not return. They were getting fed up with their brother-in-law's antics. If it wasn't for Cooter telling her sisters to let him be, that he'd get better, Jake would've disappeared a long time ago. But regardless of Cooter's pleading, his luck was getting ready to run out.

And, sure enough, the very week after Cooter had sat in Doc Murphy's kitchen with Grandma all busted and bruised from Jake's abuse, he did what he'd done many times before: came home around ten o'clock drunk as a skunk. He banged around, cursing, screaming, and calling for Cooter loud enough, it woke up everybody in the house. The kids were screaming and clinging to their mama. Cooter was calling out for Jesus.

Jake was so drunk he couldn't hear nothing but that rotgut liquor, which made him even more brazen and bold. He kicked over furniture and, through bloodshot eyes, noticed Cooter's clean laundry: beautifully starched shirts hanging from the rafters, the rest folded up in neat wooden baskets in front of the fireplace. He snarled and grabbed both baskets, hurling them across the room, then smiled to himself like he'd just won the war. Clean clothes littered the room like a tornado had struck, leaving a mile of debris in its wake. Then Jake busted through the bedroom and lit into Cooter like he usually did whenever he got sloppy drunk.

Little did he know that he'd crossed a line. He'd messed up a large portion of Cooter's clean laundry. Luckily, he only messed up the white ones. Still, Cooter's sisters were up until six o'clock that morning, redoing those soiled clothes. It took a lot of doing to get them to dry. The next day, Jake was sitting around the juke joint, talking big with his other sorry, good-for-nothing menfolk when up popped Cooter's four sisters. These sisters were strong, big-boned women. All them years spent lifting heavy baskets of clothes, Grandma told me, had given them the strength of Job.

The look on Jake's face when he saw all four sisters hovering over him was priceless. They were like hawks cornering a jackrabbit. They drug him out of that juke joint and walloped him and let him know they'd do it again if he ever lifted one finger against Cooter.

He definitely got the message, Grandma told me, because no one had heard anything from him since. If only Cooter could've seen it! But he'd beaten her so badly that night, she couldn't get out of bed for a week.

After the beating her sisters put on Jake, Cooter's spirits revived. The spring in her step returned. She even started singing in the wash assembly line again. All the sisters were glad to see her heaving clothes around, just like she used to. She saved enough money to send her children up North to college. After moving to Chicago and Detroit, all four ended up as doctors and lawyers. They bought her a big house in Livingston, where she lived until she went to be with the Lord. But not before she'd raised three of her grandchildren, who were sent back South to live with her after her working days came to a close. Just like me and my grandma Lula.

As I got older, I realized how Cooter's life was a microcosm of the lives led by many Black women from my grandma's era. They fought the hard fight. I witnessed with my own eyes how they took the most arduous, low-paying, thankless jobs to support their families, all while working to raise and educate their children. On top of all that, they'd often end up raising their children's children, otherwise known as "Grandma's other babies."

Miss Cooter was one of those women. She went to her grave before her time with calloused hands, a hard-fought spirit, and a bruised soul. Her two sets of twins, who'd grown up hearing the story of how my grandma made quilts from the clothes of those who'd passed on, brought Grandma the clothing that had belonged to Cooter, her mother, and two of her sisters so Grandma could turn them into quilts of souls.

The pieces of cloth we put in my quilt were left over from those quilts. Grandma arranged the polka-dotted yellow dress and orange prints, made of combed cotton, throughout the top portion of the quilt, next to pieces of Ella's wedding dress. Cooter's sisters' dingy blue-and-white dresses were aligned beside Cooter's fabric, forming a zigzag pattern inside two large squares. In my quilt, Cooter and her sisters, along with Ella, formed a quartet of strength.

Grandma placing Cooter's clothing next to Ella's felt right. These two women displayed toughness and an incredible ability to withstand brutality. I couldn't help but cringe at the pain and misery Cooter must've endured from her husband and her white customers. Laundresses and washwomen lived long ago—there's no mention of them in any books I've read, yet they were involved in strenuous, backbreaking work. They, like Miss Cooter and Ant Ella, were survivors.

Over the years, I saw Grandma place leftover fabric from Cooter's and her sisters' clothing in many of the quilts of souls she made for others. Eventually, the bag was exhausted. I remember the day she placed the last piece of Cooter's yellow polka-dotted dress. A broad smile and a look of contentment crossed her face. I recall her saying that it was done in a way that held such reverence. She told me that whoever received pieces of Cooter's and Ella's fabric in their quilts was truly blessed.

That day, in her yard in Alabama, Grandma left me with a song. It was one of Cooter's favorites, a song she and her sisters often sang on their wash days. A song Grandma would also sing when she'd come home from toiling in the fields:

Bringing in the sheaves,
Bringing in the sheaves.
Here we come rejoicing,
Bringing in the sheaves.

Annie Grace Horn Downson (Ant Tudney), my
grandfather Edgar Horn's sister. Her songs, field calls,
and story are in the Library of Congress and National
Archives. I spent many days listening to her tales.

5

Livingston

GOING INTO TOWN WITH GRANDPA became a monthly ritual. Grandma no longer had to preach about the chores I'd have to complete beforehand; they were as automatic as ticks on a hound. The words *town* and *Livingston* barely left her lips before I was up and moving about the farm like I was plugged into an electrical socket.

My grandparents' house sat about ten miles from downtown Livingston proper. I'd often hear old folks talk about the town as though it was a booming metropolis. Maybe because it was the county seat for Sumter County, or because it had a courthouse larger than probably the whole town. I'm sure many people who lived there had never been too far outside the area. As a result, they had no other city to compare it to, except for the tiny towns with only a hundred people or so spread throughout Sumter County.

In the dead center of Livingston, a small building the size of my grandparents' front room housed the single grocery store. It sold sundry produce items and my favorite sour balls and candy canes, which came in every color of the rainbow.

Since my grandparents' little farming community was considered far enough from the outskirts of Livingston, the powers that be gave it its own name—Brewersville. It consisted of only a couple dozen families, and almost everyone there was said to be related. Most didn't know how, nor did they care. Brewersville was as rural as it was confined, and when relatives or friends visited us from out of state, they always made sure they were gone before sundown. I couldn't rightly blame them, because when the sun no longer showed its face, you couldn't see a foot in front of you. There were no streetlights, zero paved roads, not one traffic signal of any kind.

I'm just as certain that some got out before sundown because they were afraid of being in the shadowy backwoods after dark. They'd likely heard from their family and friends the ghastly stories of the area, from headless horses to tormented and tortured Black women, men, and children, their spirits still lurking about, trying to get their just rewards. These horrific stories originated from actual accounts of African Americans who were murdered, many by lynching, in the murky boondocks of Livingston and its outlying areas.

Grandma told me that some Black folks around there could recall every story ever told or heard about the brutality that went on in those woods. I'd hear some of the folks who sat in our front yard spin these stories like a top, turning them into the most mystical, edge-of-your-seat truths you'd ever hear. I was the eager auditor of many such tales. I'd listen to other old folks, too, people who were five and six years old during slavery, speak about these atrocities. By then it was 1958, and I was about to turn five. I still remember how folks would tell my grandparents about recent incidents of Black folks being lynched, maimed, or outright murdered in the stillness and coldness of those woodlands.

Route 28 was the main thoroughfare in Livingston, a two-lane highway that ran east to west for about ninety-seventy miles. After crossing over the Conkabayou Bridge off 28 West, an inconspicuous cutoff led to a single-lane dirt road, lined on both sides by towering trees. The rarely used road had to be shared by both incoming and outgoing automobiles, tractors, and horse-pulled wagons. This was the path that wound its way next to my school, Bethel Hill, before eventually running past my grandparents' front yard.

Within sparsely populated Brewersville, there was no such thing as next-door neighbors—or neighborhoods, for that matter. From our little farmhouse, Cuttin Jeff and his wife lived a mile up the road in one direction; Grandpa's two sisters, Ant Money and Ant Tudney, and his brother, Uncle Herman, were three long cornfields and a cotton field to the south of us, in the opposite direction of Cuttin Jeff. Grandpa's mean sister, Ant Bessie, resided to the east in a one-bedroom shack that could be reached by going out our backdoor, through the cow pasture, and over to the other side of our pond.

Grandpa was the second eldest of fifteen siblings. His three sisters and one brother were the only ones still in rural Alabama. The others lit out of the country long, long ago for greener pastures. They'd do a return visit every now and then, and believe me, they were short visits.

Downtown Livingston, small as it was, was the only thing that brought back at least a smidgen of my life in Detroit, vague recollections of things like concrete roads and large brick houses with landscaped yards. Cuttin Jeff would pick up Grandpa and me in his old blue truck, and off we'd go into town, a thirty-minute ride. For me, it may as well have been an around-the-world excursion. Going-to-town day always added pep to my step, even though I had to get up extra early in the morning. Feeding the chickens, gathering their eggs, and drawing water to fill the gallon tubs for Monday wash day took a few hours. Sometimes Grandma added additional duties, like "pickin' up chips" for Grandpa's fire.

My last chore before going to town was my Achilles heel. It began early on in my farm-orientation days and became one of my greatest challenges, a grueling job but one I considered pure competition between myself and Grandma's mangy chickens: a clandestine operation where I'd have to crawl under the house to gather their eggs. Most times, the hens weren't on their nests, so it was a search, grab, and go mission.

This same area had become the habitat I'd sometimes have to share with all Grandma's chickens, ducks, and guinea hens. At first, I was a stranger dropped in from Detroit who invaded their space. But now that I'd been there more than a year and a half, as far as I was concerned, under the house was as much mine as theirs. It was where 90 percent of Grandma's chickens laid their eggs, but it gradually also turned into my listening post, an area where I could eavesdrop on grown folks as they talked about the goings-on around Livingston and beyond. I could hide and view the entire front yard with ease, and no one ever discovered I was there. That's why I had to make sure that those chickens and I were of the same accord. They had to get used to me, just as I had to get used to them.

Over time it all worked out. It no longer was like my early days, when I was afraid of the birds' shadows. Grandma would send me out to grab their eggs, and I'd jump every time they made a move. It took time to build up my courage. But Grandma would tell me that I could go to town with Grandpa after this chore was done, so slowly but surely my fear diminished.

The chickens had their own special space under the house where they made their nests. But a few of them, I guess to piss me off and make my life miserable, chose not to spit out their wares under the part that was easily accessible. Instead, they laid their eggs in the deepest, darkest crevices. This meant I had to crawl about, searching around corners of wooden beams and concrete blocks, digging in globs of stinking chicken mess. Not to mention my run-in with a snake or two. Those chickens seemed to love playing hide-and-seek with their eggs.

Gathering eggs from six or seven hens was more than enough to fill my basket. But it was the fat devil hen that laid nothing but light brown eggs that I considered Public Enemy Number One. I couldn't take a basketful of eggs to Grandma with no brown eggs in it. She'd say, "Don' see no brown eggs in yo' pail; now gone back out and find that dev'l hen—you know Grandma gotta have her brown eggs."

Reluctantly, I'd crawl back under the house, starting in the front and making my way midway to the back. The devil hen would have moved her nest from the last time, so I'd scratch and claw through the darkness until I found her in the corner, where the foundation of the fireplace sat. As I reached in my pocket like Grandma had taught me and pulled out a handful of corn, I could've sworn she was laughing at me. Before I could throw it, she was off her nest. All I could see was her skinny legs running after the corn. I gently grabbed the golden eggs, placed them in my basket, and left her pecking and staring at me with one eye cocked to the side.

I absolutely hated this chicken—she had a vendetta against me, because in her chicken sense, she knew I needed her eggs. I thought to myself, Grandma should wring her neck and cook her up for dinner. I didn't even want to think of that hen making me miss time with Miss Jubilee, an eccentric, sharp-minded old neighbor woman I adored, or a trip to town. The mere thought made my blood boil.

I could usually hear Cuttin Jeff blowing his truck horn about two or three minutes before he pulled up to our front door. The echo would linger in the air until I'd see the outline of his blue truck. Today, after we dropped in to check on Miss Jubilee, we'd be making a trip to downtown Livingston to take Miss Caroline her quilt of souls.

Grandpa hated spending time with Miss Jubilee. He said she talked more than a runaway freight train and she was old as Methuselah. Even though I didn't know exactly who Methuselah was, Grandpa might have been onto something. The first time I met Miss Jubilee, I thought she was the scariest-looking person I'd ever seen. Not only did she look ancient, she had a towering presence. I would stare at her the entire time Grandpa and I sat in her front room. It took seeing her a few times for the novelty to wear off. Then it wasn't long before Grandpa would leave me with her while he and Cuttin Jeff went into town. He'd return an hour or so later to retrieve me.

During that time, Miss Jubilee would talk about her hunting dogs or tell me scary stories about men and women who'd passed on and returned as haints. I remember the time she told me about how her dogs had chased a ghost through the woods out back, or the night one dog was killed by an animal that looked half giraffe but had a head like a tiger. Her descriptions scared the holy crap out of me. Like Grandma, she knew how to weave verbal works of art. The only difference was the contents of Miss Jubilee's stories were mostly scary and spine-tingling, and after hearing them it was almost guaranteed I'd have nightmares. Grandma would get up and set me right in the middle of her and Grandpa, and I'd drift into sweet dreams to the deep sounds of Grandpa's snoring.

Today, Grandpa was already telling Grandma he was not looking forward to visiting Miss Jubilee. "Lawd, every time I see that uman, she say she gone die tomorry and she ain't gots long to stay yere. Lawd, that uman a worry de horns off a billy goat and she been tryin' to see the Lawd fo' the las' forty years."

Grandma wasn't hearing it.

"Edgar, you jus' stop that foolishness, now. Miss Jubilee born 'fore the surrender with no mama or papa. Lord knows, all she wants is to be with them in glory. Gone now, Edgar Horn, 'cause I ain't stuttin' you. I got to get these tea cakes out the oven 'fore they get black as tar. I needs to make sure I send a sack of them to Miss Jubilee. She jus' loves the way I puts a pecan right in the middle of them. Take her them two jars of fig preserves sittin' back there on the back porch table too."

Grandpa motioned me to pick up the homemade preserves, which Grandma had made yesterday. "Me and the gal gone see her for jus' a spell 'cause we gots to drop off Miss Caroline's quilt too," he told Grandma. "We wants to get back here 'fore too late."

It was now my turn to receive Grandma's going-to-town speech. But not before she pulled a piping-hot tea cake cookie from the pan and set it aside for me to eat on the way. Grandma's tea cakes were large, round pieces of delight. Folks from miles around would brag about how she made the best tea cakes in the world.

"Come here, chile. Now, Grandma don' wants you to get over to Miss Jubilee's cryin' po-mouf, 'cause you ain't one bit hungry. Grandma wants you to mind your manners, and it's always 'No, ma'am' or 'Yes'm.' If she offers you some to eat, you makes sure you thank her kin'ly and tell her 'No, ma'am.' You let Miss Jubilee know I be prayin' for her."

No matter how many times I went with Grandpa to visit Miss Jubilee or anyone else, Grandma always gave me the same speech. She was a proud woman who took offense to the idea of accepting food from old folks. She felt that "crying po-mouf" meant that folks would get the impression your family wasn't feeding you.

Cuttin Jeff's truck was extra loud as it pulled up in front of the house that day, the black smoke from the tailpipe thicker than the fog that settled over our pond on an overcast summer morning. Looking at it, Grandpa said, "Come on, chile, clumb on up here an' sit 'twixt me an' Jeff; don' wantcha gettin' the consumption sittin' on dat back."

I'd been looking forward to riding in the truck bed, my usual spot. In the cab I looked so small, sitting between Cuttin Jeff and Grandpa. My feet barely touched the floorboards.

As we drove, I began thinking that I might as well be sniffing the fumes from the exhaust, because Cuttin Jeff smelled like he'd just finished raking cow and horse dung, and Grandpa wasn't far from it himself. Old men that I encountered growing up in the country had a musty smell that was a cross between week-old sweat and farm animals.

Miss Jubilee's house was about three miles from downtown Livingston and about six or so from our farmhouse, right off Route 28, down a dirt road and about three miles before the Conkabayou Bridge. She lived in a three-room, tin-roof place, surrounded by bushes and shrubs that demanded space right at the edge of the road. A short grassy path led to her two front steps.

As we pulled up, I barely had one leg out of the truck when I heard Miss Jubilee approaching the screen door. Around her neck she wore a mess of rattlesnake carcasses, rabbit tails, and a pair of chicken feet, and it all clicked and clacked with every step. Hearing that sound, I brimmed with excitement. The way Miss Jubilee's eyes danced when she saw Grandma's tea cakes was wonderful, and I ran off to meet her, leaving Grandpa to bring up the rear. He walked super slow, and I could've had an entire conversation with Miss Jubilee before he made it to her front porch.

"Hey Edgar. Hey Jeff. How y'all doing?" Miss Jubilee called. Catlike whiskers poked out from her jaws, and the smell that emanated from her was like the sulfur Grandma burned during the summer to keep flies and mosquitoes away. "You come on in too, Jeff. You ain't got to sit out in that truck."

"No, ma'am, um gone sit here 'cause my rheumatiz actin' up this mo'nin'. Much oblige anyhow."

"Come here, gal, and hug Miss Jubilee's neck. I swear, every times I sees you, you gettin' bigger an' bigger. What yo' Grandma feedin' you?"

Before I had a chance to answer, Miss Jubilee's eyes zeroed in on the sack of tea cakes. Some parts of the brown bag were saturated with butter, which had seeped from the cookies and made large grease circles on the paper. But they were still warm, and they smelled scrumptious. Miss Jubilee reached for the bag and popped an entire cookie in her mouth. She closed her eyes and looked as though she was caught up in rapture.

"Well, Miss Jubilee," Grandpa said, "we ain't gone stay long 'cause we gots to drop off Miss Caroline's quilt 'fore it gets too far 'long past three. Go on, chile, helps Miss Jubilee on back inside."

Even though Miss Jubilee could walk almost better than me, this was Grandpa's way of hurrying her along before Miss Jubilee talked his ears off, as he liked to say. But I did as he said, grabbing her hand and leading her to the middle of her dogtrot.

"C'mon Miss Jubilee, I'm gonna walk with you for a spell."

"Thank you, gal. Now, you be sure to come by and visit ol' Miss Jubilee nex' time you on yo' way to town, you hear me?"

"Yes'm."

I skipped and hopped back to the truck and begged Grandpa to let me get in the bed. He acquiesced, especially since the smoke flowing from the tailpipe had dissipated. With the wind blowing up my nose and down my throat, I felt free as a bird. I stood up like I was an airplane ready to take off and soar through the air. My mind was somewhere far away—until Grandpa beat on the back window for me to sit down.

I loved bouncing around in the truck. My little body wasn't heavy enough to stay balanced, and every dip in the road sent me flying into fits of laughter. As the truck wove up and down hills and valleys, I felt like I was on a roller coaster. My stomach did somersaults. I didn't care if we went to town or not, I just wanted more of that belly-bouncing laughter.

I was having so much fun, I didn't even notice that we were nearly in front of Miss Caroline's house. I didn't know much about her, only what I'd heard the old folks say about her being a very well-off white woman. She lived near the intersection of the courthouse and town square, in a large white house with a picket fence wrapped around it. Three huge white columns reached from the bottom of her front porch to the rooftop.

Grandma's reputation for making quilts of souls stretched from Alabama to Mississippi. Her quilts were legendary and crossed racial lines: she'd make them for both Blacks and white folks. So I was never surprised where they ended up. Grandma always told me that the only colors she really saw and concerned herself with were the ones laid out in her quilts, and that I needed to think along those lines. Sometimes she'd talk about how her mother made quilts for the Youngs, who would sell them to the highest bidder. The Youngs would in turn give Emma only a piddling of what they sold for.

The day before, Grandma had finished putting the last few pieces in Miss Caroline's quilt. It was alight with bright colors. From the blue-and-white border the inside alternated between red and green, with a burst of yellow radiating out from its middle. It looked like the sun had dropped out of the sky and landed on top of it. I loved watching Grandma add the finishing touches, all those colors coexisting together without clashing one bit.

As Cuttin Jeff's truck pulled up in Miss Caroline's expansive driveway, I jumped out of the back and Grandpa handed me the cotton sack with her quilt. It was clear that he and Cuttin Jeff were not getting out of the truck. Miss Caroline was sitting on the front porch, sipping what looked like iced tea in a tall, frosted plastic cup. She smiled when she saw me walking toward her. Miss Caroline was white as a sheep, with a big, squishy stomach. I had to restrain myself from poking her belly with my finger. As she stood up, waving to Grandpa and Cuttin Jeff, her belly shook back and forth with the same intensity as her hand motion.

"You must be Miss Lula's lil grandbaby."

"Yes ma'am, Miss Caroline."

She had a sweet smell, like Grandma's rosebushes in the early morning dew. I was as captivated by the fragrance as by her deep southern twang, which was on full display, but different from that of my grandparents and Cuttin Jeff.

"Come on inside, chile, so I can see what you got for Miss Caroline in that sack."

She took the bag and *ooh*'ed and *ahh*'ed as she unfurled the quilt and stretched it out along the length of her sofa. As I watched, her pasty face turned blood red and she began to sob uncontrollably. I stood there like a knot on a log, as Grandma would say, while Miss Caroline pointed to various pieces of clothing in the quilt.

"This is my mama's favorite dress. It used to have pearl-colored buttons, and this gray piece was the dress she told me she was baptized in. And this is a piece of my papa's brown work shirt. This was the last shirt he wore before the accident."

As she wept, I felt tears well up in my own eyes. The next thing I knew, Miss Caroline was hugging me and rubbing my back. Then, out of nowhere, she kissed me on my forehead. I'd never had this much close contact with a white person, period. I was shocked by her behavior, though I can't explain why. I was still a little girl; I wasn't supposed to have this type of awareness about race relations. Grandma was mostly color-blind and often shielded me from the prejudices of the world, although I was adept at identifying the differences between the races. My feelings concerning the treatment of Black people were based on what I read in school and heard in Grandma's quilts of souls stories, but mostly on what I saw through my own eyes.

During this period of my life, I'd begun to learn that anything to do with white people or the word "white" itself was considered good, pure, and wholesome, and anything related to being Black was inferior or bad. In all my years attending school down South, we had only hand-me-down books from the white schools and Sears and Roebuck catalogs, which we'd page through before placing them in the outhouse to be used as toilet paper. Every model in the entire book was white. Then there were the toilets and water fountains in downtown Livingston, which were labeled "White" and "Colored." The ones for whites were pristine and in good repair; those marked "Colored" were old and dilapidated.

It was Grandma and the other strong Black women I'd spend time with over my years in Alabama who would teach me my skin was not a sin and that being Black was an honor, not a curse. So, in that brief moment with Miss Caroline, I considered myself fortunate to be hugging a woman who just happened to be white. It stayed in my mind, too, that Miss Caroline might have found the same joy I did—not because I was Black, but because I'd delivered her a gift that made her smile. It was Grandma's quilt of souls that had bridged that racial divide.

I suppose Grandpa got restless sitting in the truck, waiting for me. I could see him through the screen door, slowly making his way up the four steps to Miss Caroline's porch. Inside, Miss Caroline was telling me how Grandma had brought to life the parents she'd tragically lost long ago, when she was a child. Now their clothes were transformed into sunshine.

By this time Grandpa was knocking on the screen door. "Chile, ya done got los' in there or somethin'?"

I told Miss Caroline I had to go. Before leaving, she motioned me to grab a brown paper bag that sat on a table next to a colorful lamp. I thanked her as I walked away, while peeking inside. I couldn't believe my eyes. Candy canes! At first I was hesitant to take them, because I knew how Grandma felt about taking food from folks. But after mulling it over in my head for all of ten seconds, I realized that candy wasn't food. What a stroke of luck!

My mouth watered as I thanked Miss Caroline. She in turn thanked me and Grandpa for bringing the quilt. She was effusive in her praise for Grandma and her quilt making and said that she'd treasure her quilt forever. As we drove away, I saw her standing in the doorway of her white frame house, clutching her quilt of souls as if her parents had come back to life and were standing there with her. Watching her embrace her quilt, I no longer focused in on the color of her skin. I saw the same longing and sense of peace in her eyes as I'd seen in other folks when they received their quilts of souls from Grandma. Before I left, Miss Caroline had told me she would keep her quilt folded at the foot of her bed. I knew what that meant. She'd cover herself in her parents' love every night before falling asleep. And I knew exactly how she felt. The moment when I'd held my quilt or wrapped myself up in it at night.... Well, I was always reluctant to be away from it for long.

But my quilt was still unfinished. I was waiting for Grandma to continue filling it up with the fabric and the stories that would make it whole.

Grandpa Edgar Horn standing next
to one of my uncle's automobiles

6

Bethel Hill

IN THE FALL OF 1959, as I was turning six years old, two life-changing events occurred simultaneously. I started my first year of school in September, and two weeks before the beginning of the school year a surprise visitor showed up in my grandparents' front yard, arriving in a familiar black automobile.

I was shocked. I wracked my brain trying to remember that face, but I couldn't.

"Gone, child," Grandma Lula said. "Give yo' mama a big hug."

Seeing Mother made my heart pound. She was a stranger to me. In that moment, I became the same little girl who'd arrived in Alabama almost two years ago, scared, distraught, and filled with overwhelming sadness. I clung to Grandma like a piece of lint. No matter how much she nudged me, I was determined not to go anywhere near this woman.

Before I knew it, I'd run back into the house and hidden under the bed, my quilt wrapped tight around me. When Grandma finally coaxed me out, tears streamed down my face. My mother smiled at me, which made me cry even more.

Grandma looked confused; shaking her head, she gave me a bear hug, then went off with Mother to sit in the rocking chairs inside the screened front porch, where they talked until well after dark.

The cold returned that night. Mother and I slept in the same bed on the first night of her visit. I was determined not to touch any part of her body while lying there, though I can't explain why. I scrunched my small frame up into a tight ball and stuck my fist in my mouth to stop my teeth from chattering. Even my quilt provided little comfort.

I guess Grandma must've recognized what I was going through, because she got up in the middle of the night, lifted me up like I was a six-month-old, and laid me in the bed between her and Grandpa. The warmth emanating from those two old folks was indescribable. I felt safe again, and there I slept until Mother's visit was over.

The entire time she was visiting, I almost broke my neck trying to avoid her. I can't believe how frightened I was of her. She might as well have been the bogeyman. Looking back, I was probably terrified that she was going to take me away from Grandma Lula—I dreaded being taken away again. I thought if I disappeared, I'd be out of sight, out of mind. At least that's what the old folks down in the country would say. Or my angst could've been a gut reaction; it might have been the only way I knew to express my frustration at what I saw as being unwanted and unloved by my mother.

I had to be polite; Grandma wouldn't have it any other way. But other than that, I wouldn't say a word. And in the end, I didn't have to worry much about being courteous, because Mother never attempted to engage me in conversation, except for her usual "Good morning" and "Good night." This suited me just fine.

Then, like an east wind on a summer day, she was gone. And I was still there—with Grandma, watching her quilt and listening to her storytelling.

Mother would visit periodically over my years in the country. She would stay a few days or a weekend, then ride off in the black car with the folks I came to know as her brothers and sisters. During my first three or four years in Alabama, I'd periodically remember small things that had occurred in Detroit. I had only glimpses of my parents' faces, but the welfare cheese and extra-large bag of generic Cheerios stood out. Before long, though, all the trepidations and misgivings I'd had about being sent to stay with my grandparents disappeared. Grandma and the country became my entire universe. Her hugs, kisses, and being constantly around her gave me a sense of security and comfort I'd never experienced in Detroit.

Sometimes, I'd have a sickening feeling that one day I would be herded into a car and taken away from my grandmother. It was a fear that haunted me. I'd drown out these feelings by listening to Grandma's soothing humming and stories of those who'd suffered much more than my feelings of speculative loss.

In those days, there was no kindergarten. You went right into first grade as soon as you turned six. Since I was born the first week of September, I transitioned into school at the start of the school year. I didn't think too much about it; the end of summer was still a few weeks away, and there was nothing that indicated the school year was right around the corner.

Absolutely zero children lived near my grandparents. In fact, I rarely saw other kids until I started school. Elderly friends of my grandparents, my great-aunts and great-uncle who lived a mile down the road, and Cuttin Jeff were the only other folks I had a chance to interact with.

Looking back, I could faintly recall my sisters. The three of us slept together in the same bed. You couldn't get much closer than that. I remembered them coming home with bags of clothes from the local secondhand store. I'd watch as they tried on every garment, spinning around in the mirror, admiring themselves in their new used duds. I hated when they went off to school. I felt abandoned, and I struggled to remember what transpired on the days they left me. The only memory I had was watching them run out the front door, the screen door slamming behind them. I couldn't recall anything from the time they left for school until the time they came home, but I imagine my brothers and I were left with Mother. She was probably tired from working nights, especially after having eight children, four of whom were "stair-step," and two of whom were twins. It must've been taxing—barely thirty-five with a crop of children. Her body must've been broken and her mind weary.

Down in the country, I didn't do any school shopping. Grandma insisted we "jus' make do with what we got." My school, Bethel Hill, drew largely from the Moore Place, a small community of ten or twelve families who lived nearby. The current residents of the Moore Place and their ancestors dated back to slavery, and many of them were distantly related to my family.

It was over a two-and-a-half-mile walk from my grandparents' home to school along a white and gritty dirt road. There was no such thing as bus transportation for children who went to Bethel Hill. It was a long way, but Grandma was going to walk with me and teach me everything I needed to know about the path. She accompanied me for the first couple of months before I lit out on my own.

On the first day, Grandma and I woke up before the chickens. We had to leave the farm by 6:30 a.m. in order to make it to the fork in the road, which was over a mile away. There, Miss Clay, my teacher, would pick me up. As we passed through the small wooden gate, Grandma told me not to be afraid. "God done cast you, chile, so you ain't got nothin' to fear."

I wasn't sure exactly what that meant, but if Grandma said it, I knew it was true. Later, I'd figure out that this was her way of saying that the Lord had chosen me as one of his own, a special child, so to speak, and that was why I'd have his favor forever. When I told her how scared I was of leaving her, all she said was, "Nobody want you but the devil and yo' ol' grandma, chile."

Up ahead of us was a massive pine tree. It would become a fixture for me, a mark of where home was. Each day, I'd glance back at it as I left and greet it with relief on the way back.

My stomach felt like two cats were fighting inside as Grandma and I walked along. Woodlands rose up on each side of us. The deep brush and weeds grew wild, lining the sides of the road. The sand was as white and grainy as table salt. It was barely daylight, but it was eerily quiet, with only birds chirping. We saw deer, snakes, and glimpses of other wildlife along the way. Grandma showed me how the dirt road had no turns and would lead me straight to where I could look down into a small valley and see Cuttin Jeff's house—an indication that I was almost at my destination, where I would wait for my ride.

"Don' you worry yo'self, chile," she told me. "I be goin' with you for a bit."

After what seemed like forever, we got to the fork in the road, and Grandma eased herself down onto a huge boulder. As always, despite the early hour and long walk, she never complained. Minutes later, an old pale-green Buick with peeling paint on the driver's side stopped right in front of us. A rotund woman sat in the driver's seat. She had a jolly face and cat-eye glasses resting on her nose. It was Miss Clay, the woman who'd be my teacher for the next six years. She was the daughter-in-law of Cuttin Jeff, and she and her husband, Robert, lived with him.

As she stopped her car in front of us, she leaned out the window and said, "Mo'nin,' Miss Lula. Hi you?"

"I'm a kickin' but not high, Miss Clay. Get on in, chile."

I crawled in the car, trying not to look at my grandma. I was afraid if I did, I'd burst into an endless round of tears.

Miss Clay took off with a jerk. I turned around in my seat and caught a glimpse of Grandma with her walking stick, heading back toward home. That familiar sinking feeling of being left behind caught in the back of my throat. The tires rattled as we passed over cattle crossings with their metal bars embedded in the ground to prevent runaway cows. Miss Clay drove so fast I thought the engine was going to conk out. Then, suddenly, we screeched to a stop in front of Bethel Hill Elementary School.

I tumbled out of the car as barefooted as I'd come into the world six years ago. I didn't have much experience with other children, but I knew right away I'd be forever branded the teacher's pet, and worse, because I'd come to school in the car with my teacher. Other children stood around, dressed in their first-day-of-school clothes. I could smell the newness of the girls' dresses and plastic barrettes, of the boys' crisp short-sleeve dress shirts. All eyes were on me. They snickered and whispered to each other like only little kids can. I must've looked a hot mess with my ashy legs and no ribbons in my hair. Instead, I had small plaits all over my head, which felt like they were sticking out in all directions from the breeze of my wild ride.

Miss Clay waddled up to the schoolhouse door. There I stood, right where she'd dropped me off, alone with thirty-five or so children I'd never seen before. Illogically, I searched for my grandmother's face in the crowd. One of the boys began ringing a big bell that swung from a rope attached to a mulberry tree. Everyone took off running toward the school, laughing and shoving each other as they jostled to get inside the door at the same time. I reluctantly trailed behind.

Bethel Hill was an old white building plastered with peeling paint. Each classroom held about twenty-five students. The cloakroom separated the two classrooms. I was in the group taught by Miss Clay, whose enormous presence commanded the room. She must've weighed over three hundred pounds. Her poor feet looked as though they were squished into shoes two sizes too small; they couldn't have been comfortable. She had a robust laugh with one gold tooth that shone brightly when she smiled, which she did a lot.

The morning went by in a jumble of new impressions. At recess I sat, alone and miserable, as the other children ran around screaming and playing. All the girls had pressed hair that was either neatly braided in three plaits or fixed in the three-pony-tail look, one on the top and one on each side. Grandma had tried to press my hair the night before with the hot comb, but I'd run away, afraid of the scorching, smoking thing. I had no one but myself to blame for going to school with crappy-looking hair.

When I came home that afternoon, I asked Grandma to press my hair super straight. Peer pressure gave me the courage to face the hot comb. Grandma didn't say a word, but her eyes twinkled as she heated it up. The comb slid through my hair, making crackly sounds, like when my brothers would put a match to firecrackers. I loved every minute of it because now my hair would look like the other girls' did.

When mine was straight as an arrow, Grandma said, "Nigh go get them pink ribbons that you came here with." I lied and told her that I'd made a mistake and dropped them down the outhouse while sitting there taking care of my business. She shook her head and said "Chile, what I'm gonna do with you? You somethin' else."

I couldn't say that I hated those ribbons because they reminded me of the day I'd left Detroit. That was why I'd ditched them in the outhouse.

The next day, I went to school with pressed hair and three beautiful braids. I was still an eyesore, though. Most of my classmates dressed better than me and had what I considered tastier bag lunches. They'd bring Vienna sausages or potted meat packed in a new brown paper bag. My lunches consisted of cold biscuits with mystery meat in a stained old paper bag. Grandma made sure I brought that same bag home every day, no matter how many grease stains it had. I was constantly ridiculed for my greasy lunch bags. And some of my classmates teased me just because I was the new kid on the block.

As if the teasing wasn't enough, I was also classified as a left-handed misfit. For reasons unknown, back in the 1950s and 1960s, writing with the left hand was considered wrong. I was what you'd call a true lefty—until Miss Clay declared that I *had* to use my right hand for writing. She didn't care what other tasks were done with my left hand, but writing couldn't be one of them. To ensure I heeded her edict, she'd pop me on my knuckles if my pencil got anywhere near my left hand.

Miss Clay had a paddle called the "board of education." It had small circular holes in the fat part of it, and when it hit your skin, those holes became suction cups and sucked your skin up. It hurt like hell. I feared that board of education more than Grandma's switch. Miss Clay would keep it in the corner of the classroom. No matter where you sat, it was always in plain sight. This board became a huge deterrent to misbehavior during my years at Bethel Hill.

During my first year at school, I thought I was the only child there, maybe the only one in all of Livingston, not living with his or her parents. As the months passed and I began to make friends, I was pleased to find that over half my classmates were being raised by their grandparents too. Most of them resided in the Moore Place community. Brenda was one of those "Grandma's other babies," sent down from somewhere up North to live with her grandma Ada a year before I came south. She became my best friend. Every Friday, her grandma would put homemade pecan candy in her lunch. Grandma Ada made enough for me too. More than enough.

During my second week of school, Brenda and I would sit together on an old tree stump, watching two of our classmates play patty-cake. I was determined to learn the game and make up my own rhymes. Then, I thought, everybody's eyes would be on me. And that's what happened.

My momma and your momma went down to the lake.
My momma picked up a toad and your momma a snake.
The snake jumped and landed in your momma's lap.

The toad then jumped inside your momma's cap.
What color was the snake?
(double clap)
What color was the toad?
(double clap)

Before long, Brenda and I were spending the entire recess clapping our hands together. You could hear the smack of skin echoing through the trees. By the time we returned to the classroom, the insides of our palms would be beet red. Other kids would try to join in or beg me to teach them my rhymes. Both Miss Clay and my classmates admired my ability to make up jump rope songs, patty-cake rhymes, and riddles.

During my second year at Bethel Hill I discovered I loved telling stories. Grandma's influence had rubbed off on me. I could retain and recite any information that was read to me the first time, and I thirsted for the written and spoken word. Miss Clay called me a born orator and marveled at my inquisitiveness and recall. A couple of times, I overheard her talking to Grandma about how I possessed a special gift.

Miss Clay gave us an unusual education because Bethel Hill had terrible, worn-out textbooks, as was typical of most Black schools. The *Fun with Dick and Jane* books were old and outdated. As an inquiring, studious child, I often asked why no one in those books looked like me and my classmates. If I could have, I would've thrown Dick, Jane, and their parents into the brown gooey mess of the outhouse. Spot the Dog was the only member of that family I would've kept. After Grandma's stories, the Dick and Jane family was just not getting it for me.

The weekly readers were even worse. Miss Clay never bit her tongue when talking about how the books sent to us by the Sumter County Board of Education absolutely stunk. As a result, she began bringing in the *World Book* and *Britannica* encyclopedias and teaching us from them. She'd simplify the material for our grade level. The math books we had were also old and dilapidated, so Miss Clay wrote out her own math problems and used an old mimeograph machine donated by the Black high school to reproduce them. As sure as clockwork, the first Monday of every month, she'd hand out math problems and we'd sit in class working them out.

My days at Bethel Hill gave me the opportunity to hone my storytelling craft. I could barely sleep on Thursday nights, knowing that every Friday, we'd stand before the class and either bring an item for show-and-tell or pick a story we wanted to talk about from our readings or our real-life experiences. Miss Clay was adamant about us memorizing our topic. She never allowed us to read from our paper. I can still recall the way she rolled her words so precisely, placing emphasis on each syllable.

"Negro children," she would say, "must be able to *recollect* their work most *expeditiously* and *eloquently.*"

My classmates would constantly complain about Miss Clay's use of big, fancy words. But she'd always say, "There is no such thing as big words; they're called challenging words." From that point on, I was primed to learn as many challenging words as I possibly could.

Most kids did their best on Fridays, repeating standard fairy tales that they'd memorized. My presentations were different. I'd tell parts of Ella's story or bring my quilt to show off, even though it wasn't finished. I loved watching my classmates' reactions; how they'd gasp when I'd tell them stories I'd heard about the folks whose lives were part of my grandmother's quilts. I'd always start my story with:

"Once upon a time there was a woman named Ella. She was my antee, and she wasn't scared of nothing." I'd tell them about her being born with a veil, and about her magical powers. "Then one day Mr. Young got mad at her and he beat her 'til all her magical powers left. See this spot here?" I'd say, holding up my quilt. "This is Ant Ella's wedding dress that she didn't even wear yet because Mr. Young almost killed her. She didn't live but a little while after he beat her like that.

My grandma washed the blood off her face with this dress. Grandma said she washed it and washed it but most of the stains just won't go 'way."

When I spoke, there was total silence. The other students just sat there, enraptured. No one raised their hand for questions except booger-picking, trouble-making Earl Lee. With his longest finger up one of his nostrils and the other raised in the air, he said, "Miss Clay, I got something I wanna ask. Was Phyllistene's antee a booty-scratching African?"

My eyes darted between Miss Clay and the class, trying to gauge their reactions to Earl Lee's stupid question. Most of my classmates sat glued to their chairs, trying to stifle their laughter. I think they were afraid of the wrath of Miss Clay.

As they should have been. With one hand, she grabbed Earl Lee by the ear and nearly slung him into the far corner of the room. That boy was a nuisance in every sense of the word. Not a day would go by that he wasn't getting into some sort of trouble. He'd take the bologna off his sandwich and throw it up at the ceiling, just so it could land on someone's notebook or head. And he was forever making stupid sounds with his mouth. Miss Clay had an all-but-permanent space for him in the corner of the classroom.

After finishing my talk about Ella and the quilt, Miss Clay said that my story was the best she'd heard. I felt even more like the teacher's pet when she added, "I want all you children to be like Phyllistene. She's so smart and she always follows directions. That's why she's going to go forth and do great and wonderful things."

From the corner of my eye, I could see Brenda beaming. After that I didn't care whether my classmates considered me Miss Clay's favorite or not, because Brenda was my best friend and she'd liked my story. When class ended for the day, Brenda and I locked arms. Together, we walked down the three concrete steps. Then she went north and I went south, both of us heading down the long dirt road toward our farms in the woods. Over my nine years living in the country, Brenda and her grandma Ada visited us only twice. Brenda wasn't allowed to travel the road between Bethel Hill and my grandparents' farm alone, and whenever I'd ask her if she could come over, she'd say, "Big Mama scared of them haints up near your house. That's why she don' like me nowhere near that road unless she with me."

As I walked home that day, I spotted Earl Lee squatting on one knee on top of the grassy mound in front of the school, tying his shoe. I ran as fast as I could and tipped him right over into the ant bed in front of him. He squealed like a stuck pig, then took off like he'd been shot out of a cannon, his signature finger still up his nose.

Miss Daisy

A PINK HOUSE with a rusted orange tin roof sat in the backyard of Bethel Hill Elementary School, right next to the playground. It was an eyesore—the boards were rotted, the paint peeling. That was Miss Daisy's place, a juke joint for folks looking for a good time. It was a source of regular gossip for Grandma's visitors, who always complained about "all that sinnin' goin' on right next to the schoolhouse door."

It was true: we'd see drunks stumbling out of Miss Daisy's in the morning, as we arrived at school. When we went outside for recess, the smell of old liquor from the night before hung in the air like wet clothes.

Miss Daisy was young, but living that sort of life had aged her. Her face showed signs of deep trouble and her long red hair was streaked with gray. You could tell at one time she'd been a beauty. I might've been young, but my senses told me Miss Daisy wasn't quite right.

Still, she provided a lot of entertainment during recess. Me and my classmates would sit under the tree and watch the goings-on over at her establishment. Grandpa's cousin Bennie was one of Miss Daisy's regular patrons. He didn't drink a little; he drank until he couldn't stand up. We'd see Miss Daisy holding him up so he wouldn't fall flat on his face. Most times, they'd both fall down right in the middle of the road, just from the weight of him. We'd watch in amazement as they'd fumble their way up, faces covered in white Alabama sand, and we'd laugh so hard our sides split.

Sometimes, while the other kids were playing games, I'd hide behind the mulberry tree and watch Miss Daisy. She'd sit on the stoop in front of the old pink shanty, sucking on a Pall Mall cigarette. I knew they were Pall Malls because when me and my classmates snuck over to her yard and picked up the butts, we'd see empty red Pall Mall boxes scattered all over. We'd walk around with those lipstick-stained butts hanging off our lips, pretending we were smoking.

Poor Miss Daisy. She'd sit at the opening of her front door, looking forlorn, strands of hair hanging over one of her eyes like they were hiding her shame and guilt. I think she longed to be engaged in our silly games. She never shooed us away or said a word. She just sat there with the saddest look you'd ever see as my classmates said mean things about her and cackled wildly with laughter. I felt sorry for her, but I still cracked up when they called her a slut, even though I had no idea what it meant.

One day, I figured I ought to know the term, since I was laughing my tail off about it. Brenda and I asked Little Lee and Clarence what a slut was. Clarence responded, "I dunno, I just hear Grandpapa callin' her that all the time. Don' ask me nothing 'bout what that is, and I ain't gone ask Grandpapa either. He ain't gone beat my behind like no polecat, and I ain't gone get in no trouble for some dumb girl like y'all either."

He had the audacity to stick out his tongue at us before taking off like a jackrabbit; otherwise Brenda would've trounced him. Since no one could give me a definition, my curiosity grew.

During recess, I talked Brenda into coming with me to peek inside the window of Miss Daisy's house.

"Come on, Brenda," I entreated, "stop being such a scaredy cat. Ain't nobody gone see you. If we get caught, I'll tell Miss Clay it was all my fault. Come on, girl…"

It was a hard sell because Brenda's grandma's house was only a stone's throw across the road from the old pink house.

"My Big Mama gone see me and I'm gone get in a whole heap of trouble," she told me. "You gone make me get a whupping. Let's just sit under the tree and watch her when she come out. I like watching her. We can wait till she throw out one them cigarettes, then we can play grown-up." She paused and added, "I wonder, do she got another slut in there too?"

I rolled my eyes at her. I wanted to see what was going on *inside*. Still, Brenda resisted. She said she didn't want any part of Miss Clay if our teacher got wind of what we were planning.

Now, Brenda was a thumb-sucker, especially when she got nervous, so that's what she did: placed her thumb so far back in her mouth I thought I heard her gag. With her feet dug in the dirt, her body became almost immovable. In response, I began tugging on her with all the force I could muster. I ended up pulling her by the arm of her long-sleeved green sweater, almost tumbling her down the small incline to Miss Daisy's house. Her thumb never moved from her mouth the entire time.

"Stop it, I ain't going down there. I told you I ain't going!" I often wondered how she could speak so clearly with a thumb planted underneath her two top teeth. She was definitely a pro at thumb-talking, I guess in the same way I was a cry-talker. "You gone get me in trouble!" she shouted. "Turn me loose. Stop—I'm gone tell Miss Clay!"

Even though I'd pulled her almost all the way to Miss Daisy's, her whining got so loud she attracted our classmates, who were playing tag and swinging from makeshift swings between two birch trees. That's how we ended up with a trail of kids following along. In the end we had to turn back, and when we did, we saw Miss Clay standing on the front steps, watching us. From that day forward, I gave up the whole idea of spying. I had to put my curiosity to rest or risk getting myself in big trouble.

Then came the biggest surprise of my young life. Miss Daisy appeared in our front yard, clutching an old quilt. And to my even greater surprise, Grandma embraced her with warmth and affection, giving her that big chocolatey hug I thought was exclusively mine. For reasons unbeknownst to me, I felt a twinge of jealousy, a feeling I'd never had before.

Miss Daisy looked disheveled. Her hair was jutting out all over her head and tears streaked her face with dirt. Grandma motioned for her to sit on the ground between her legs. She reached in her apron pocket and pulled out a raggedy black comb and a clean white handkerchief, which she gave to Miss Daisy to wipe her face. Grandma began combing Miss Daisy's hair and humming the song that always soothed my spirit. I could tell it soothed Miss Daisy's too. Grandma ran the comb gently through Miss Daisy's tangled strands, lulling her into a deep calm.

Grandma was probably the only person in Livingston who'd entertain Miss Daisy in her home, let alone treat her with such tenderness. It was just her way. I'd heard folks sitting in my grandparents' front yard talking with disgust about Miss Daisy and saying she should be ashamed of herself. Grandma would always shush them right in midsentence.

I watched Miss Daisy hand Grandma her quilt, which looked like it'd been badly burnt. I couldn't figure out a way to get close enough to hear their conversation. Miss Daisy's visit was such a surprise, I forgot all about escaping to my secret place under the house. Instead, I sat plastered to the front step, trying to act like I was disinterested, even though I was dying to find out what they were talking about.

Grandma spent well over two hours talking with Miss Daisy. When she left, I couldn't wait to tell Grandma what I'd heard the kids at school saying about her. Having heard the term used so often in descriptions of Miss Daisy, I didn't think twice about it when I blurted out, "Grandma, what did that slut want?"

I learned right away that was a word that should never come out of a little girl's mouth. That was the first time I'd seen Grandma's ire, and she gave me the double whammy: a scolding and a spanking. When Grandma used the switch, that meant I'd messed up miserably. She picked a branch from a tree, the kind that bent but didn't break. It made a swish-swish noise as I was getting it—and you wouldn't believe how bad I was getting it. Bad-mouthing people was a serious offense in Grandma's eyes, something that would never be tolerated, even in jest. That lesson was imprinted on my brain for the rest of my life.

Part of the lesson was a story from Grandma.

"Poor Daisy," Grandma told me, shaking her head. "It took that chile the longes' time to say one word to me. For years she los' her will to say nothin'. It was beat outta her, I 'spose. Daisy was the gal everybody talk 'bout, but mos' folks don' know 'xactly what that chile done been through. Folks can be mean as they come, 'cause they ain't able to step in somebody else's shoes. If you can't do that, how in the worl' you gone be able to hol' somebody else's pain and know when they heart breakin'? Lord knows I'm glad that chile finds your grandma. Don' knows who sends her to me. Probably won't nobody buts the Lord. But I'm sure glad she show up here with that quilt so your grandma can fix it.

"All the time I'm workin' on it she still ain't open up her mouth for the longes' time. You jus' don' know what that chile went through, but she makes it to this here front yard, and I'm so glad of it."

I saw the sadness in Grandma's eyes and heard it in her voice as she began to tell me the story.

Miss Daisy was born right here in Livingston to Miss Rachel Demps. She was Miss Rachel's only child, as far as anyone knew. Before Miss Rachel had Daisy, people in the country considered her a spinster, because she was over thirty-five and had never married. Her parents were from somewhere up North, and no one had any idea how she'd ended up in tiny Livingston. She was very articulate, elegant, and refined, and she possessed a physical beauty that was difficult to ignore. Grandma raved about her cocoa-colored skin and waist-length hair.

Grandma met Miss Rachel at a Sunday church service. The entire time she lived in Livingston, Miss Rachel only attended church twice. With the exception of Grandma and Miss Jubilee, the other church members avoided her like she had leprosy. She felt rejected by the community, which might be the reason she never came back.

Miss Rachel had traveled extensively before coming to Livingston, and she never lived in the so-called Black part of town. Her house sat in the northwest corner and was pretty much isolated. She was the only Black person who lived in that close proximity to the white citizens. As far as anyone knew she never worked, but she had the best fineries anyone could buy. She was elusive and very private in her dealings. My grandma's friend, Miss Sugar, was the only person that communicated with Miss Rachel more than once or twice, and who at least had some key pieces of her life. Miss Sugar was also the only person that had ever stepped foot inside Miss Rachel's home. For the rest, she was a recluse that folks knew very little about.

One summer, Miss Rachel disappeared from view altogether. No one, not even Miss Sugar, saw her. But like Grandma would say, "Every shut eye ain't 'sleep." Rumors swirled that the local white newspaperman was tipping and catting around with Miss Rachel.

She and her man friend carried on for years, until one day up popped Daisy. Lo and behold, she was the spitting image of the newspaper man: fire-engine-red hair, pale skin, and a dime-sized black mole over one eye. Her papa, the white man, had the same red hair and pale skin, and a black mole in the exact same spot as Daisy's.

I suspect Rachel saw immediately that there wasn't any way to hide the truth. I guess she was too ashamed, or she feared for her safety. Maybe she wanted to protect the identity of Daisy's father. Whatever the reason, she did what no mother should ever do to her newborn. She got up during the wee hours of the night, wrapped the baby in a beautiful quilt, ran miles through the woods until she reached the Black settlement, and laid the baby on the porch of the first house she came to. Then she waltzed off down the road to Lord knows where. What went through her mind and heart as she ran away from a part of her?

It was a cold February morning, and I imagine that poor little girl almost froze to death. I thought about the quilt she was wrapped in, how it might have been the only thing that saved Daisy's life. An old woman found Daisy on her doorstep. When she pulled the quilt back, the first thing she probably saw was that child's red hair and black mole. Most Blacks and whites in Livingston had seen the newspaperman, and obviously saw the resemblance. With that black mole on his face, he was difficult to miss.

The story unraveled from there. Most considered Miss Daisy marked by the sins of her mama and papa. Word spread, and the next thing you knew, the newspaperman fled town too. Miss Daisy ended up being raised by a community of Black people. Black children teased her for being white; whites talked about her in whispers for being the child of a whore and a white man who couldn't keep his fly buttoned. She was ridiculed beyond belief and called a bastard so many times she thought that was her last name. Some of the women tried to protect her, but their efforts were doomed from the start. At the age of twelve, my grandma Lula told me, she ended up with a young family who lived in the Black settlement. The husband did some bad things to her. His wife never knew. Three years later, it got to the point where Daisy couldn't take it anymore, so she ran.

Not long after that, Miss Sugar tried coaxing Miss Daisy into living with her. But by this time, distrust toward others was so deeply ingrained in Daisy's spirit that her stay with Miss Sugar was brief. She ended up scraping and scrounging for food. Many times, she slept in the woods. A few times she practically starved to death. That's how she ended up at the juke joint next to Bethel Hill, a place owned by old man Hank Chesterton, who was three times Daisy's age. In her quest for food and shelter, Daisy turned to alcohol and old man Chesterton, who sometimes beat her ragged. But she stayed. I guess that old pink house was the closest thing she'd ever had to a real home.

As the years and months went by, she became more and more worn down and used up. The saddest thing is that she lost a couple of children along the way, both born dead. Grandma Lula told me she'd heard folks say that Miss Daisy killed her babies. But that wasn't true at all. I think Miss Daisy just wanted a child, something of her own to love.

Miss Daisy's story struck me to my core. I felt horrible for all the mean things I'd said and thought about her. As I watched her and Grandma Lula, I felt guilty as sin, and I couldn't control the tears that welled at the corner of my eyes. Grandma took the bottom of her apron and tried washing them away, but they kept coming wildly, like a dam that had broken.

Grandma knew what was going on inside my head without me saying a word. She pulled me next to her and placed a corner of Daisy's quilt in my hands. She took the other end and started repairing some of the torn sections, placing white stitching along the inner and outer border. All the while, never missing a stitch, she looked me directly in the eye. Her stare was hypnotic. A feeling of absolute calm came over me, deeper than anything I'd experienced before. I couldn't let go of Daisy's quilt or Grandma's gaze. It was magical.

We worked on Miss Daisy's quilt all that day and into the next. We took a lot of material from Grandma's bags of rags to replace sections that were tattered or charred. Grandma said the quilt needed balance, just like Daisy's life. The fabric of those old spirits would watch over Daisy and help her get through the trials she was facing. Afterward, we washed the quilt with one of Grandma's special solutions to get rid of the burnt smell. As we worked, I regretted again the times I'd poked fun and listened to my classmates ridicule Miss Daisy. Grandma had taught me better. I could've defended her, but instead I let them pull me into their mess.

When I went to school the day after Miss Daisy's visit, I no longer possessed any desire to peek inside the raggedy pink house. And I was thrilled to see that Miss Daisy no longer sat perched on the step she'd occupied for years. She was gone. Hopefully forever. It was Friday, the day Miss Clay set aside for oral presentations. In the past, I'd used this time for quilt of souls stories.

Not today.

Instead, I stood before my classmates, closed my eyes, and told the abbreviated story of Miss Daisy. Hearing about her life might not have had the same impact on my classmates as it did on me, but it was still reassuring to know I'd set the record straight.

"My grandma say that Miss Daisy had a tough life. More than you, you—" As I spoke, I pointed to my classmates. "And even Miss Clay. Too tough for a young girl like her, but she made it through. She gots the scars to show for it, too, but she came through the storm. Grandma said that there is leaves that hang on the tree that don't fall, even when the rain and wind come. Miss Daisy was the leaf that ain't never fell. Grandma says it ain't nice to talk 'bout folks who can't help they self, 'cause they too young and ain't learnt nothing 'bout life yet. So just think about that the next time you want to talk about somebody. Just like you don' want nobody laughing and talking mean 'bout you, when you can't help yourself, think about how Miss Daisy must a felt."

I walked back to my seat in absolute silence. I can't explain what I felt, but I do recall the bear hug Miss Clay laid on me. It was the first time I could remember seeing her tear up.

When school ended, Miss Clay drove me all the way to my grandparents' house. I was concerned; it had been almost two years since the last time she'd taken me home. Did she want to talk to Grandma about my progress in school? In those days, so many elderly folks were raising their grandchildren that in-school parent-teacher conferences were almost nonexistent. At rural schools like mine, the teachers made house calls.

I jumped out of the car and had just enough time to sling my notebook on my bed and crawl under the house. From my pool of dirt, I could see Miss Clay and Grandma talking in the front yard. Miss Clay said that she'd never in her life met a child like me in over twenty years of teaching. Grandma just listened, not uttering a word, although she did nod in agreement. During Miss Clay's entire visit, she never sat down. I could see the gleaming rays of sun glisten off the metal of her cat-eye glasses as she described the story I'd told about Miss Daisy. She wanted to know whether my presentation was true.

I'll never forget the perplexed look on Grandma's face. She wiped her hands on her apron and took Miss Clay's hand in hers. "Miss Clay, that chile jus' born to talk, she learnt to soak up everything I tells her and she smart as a whip. Once I tells her, she sure ain't gone forget, 'cause that child gots a memory like a hawk. So I can stand here right now and lets you know that gal ain't wrong 'bout nothin' she say 'bout Miss Daisy, 'cause I tells it to her the best way I knows how. So now she know better how to treat folks, 'specially when they in a bad way."

Miss Clay just smiled and shook her head as she walked back toward her car.

After that initial visit, Miss Daisy started coming by to visit Grandma almost every week. She'd sit silently, listening to Grandma hum as she sewed. Each time, I'd watch her from under the house. I knew the feeling well, how just being around Grandma seemed to heal all the things that hurt.

When Grandma finished Miss Daisy's quilt, it looked almost brand-new. She'd skillfully woven in the vibrant blue, orange, and yellow clothing of her loved ones. Miss Cooter and Ella's dress pieces were placed in each corner and throughout the middle, in a dozen or so large squares. Grandma also added fabric I hadn't seen before, leftovers from some of the bags that had been sitting in the smokehouse before I arrived. I loved the richness of the plaid and red stripes, which reminded me of candy canes.

The completed quilt had so many smaller blocks, made with diagonal and horizontal designs, that I lost count. But just like in my quilt, Ella and Cooter were the anchor that kept the other pieces intact. Now Daisy would be symbolically connected to them too. They would lift her up and give her strength. The quilt was truly a sight for sore eyes.

When Grandma handed Miss Daisy the completed quilt and she unfolded it, her eyes got as wide and wet as a cornfield on a rainy day. Grandma took Miss Daisy in her ever-loving arms and rocked her like a baby while she whispered, "Thank you, Miss Lula," over and over again. She held that quilt like it was the newborn child she never got to have.

Before Miss Daisy left, Grandma told her snippets of the history of the pieces that made up her quilt, particularly the stories of Ella and Cooter. As she'd said to me on that night back in 1957, she told Daisy that if she wrapped herself in her quilt of souls, it would uplift her whenever she got too low, too tired, or felt like giving up. Before Miss Daisy left, even though she was a woman of very few words, I overheard her tell Grandma that she didn't know how she'd have survived without her. And then she repeated the words I'd heard Grandma utter many times: "Miss Lula, I jus' loves your heart and your liver too."

Miss Daisy also said that she no longer lived in the pink house and that she would never return. She was leaving Alabama to go up North with a woman who'd befriended her.

Even though I felt happy for Miss Daisy, in a strange sort of way, I knew I'd sorely miss seeing her.

Grandma never shared with me the story of how Miss Daisy ended up finding that woman. All she would say was that sometimes a miracle will find you, even when you're not looking for one. It wasn't until Miss Daisy left that I remembered wishing I'd reached out and embraced her.

8

G.C.

IT WAS EARLY MORNING and Grandma was off feeding the chickens and slopping the hogs. Grandpa stood in front of the unlit fireplace, his head drawn back as he dropped a glob of snuff behind his bottom lip. Since Grandma was working out back, I fixed him a biscuit and fried salt pork sandwich. Fried salt pork was a strip of fatty meat. In Detroit, we called it bacon. Before I put a biscuit anywhere near my lips, I laid the plate at Grandpa's spot at the head of the table, sat, and waited for him to shuffle down the dogtrot to the kitchen so he could say grace. Grandma would have a cow if she knew I'd put a morsel of food in my mouth before she or Grandpa had a chance to bless the meal.

By the time I'd eaten and done my chores, Grandma had set out a bag of clothes that Cuttin Jeff had dropped off yesterday. This meant she was getting ready to make a new quilt for someone who'd crossed over.

"C'mon, chile, we needs to get this quilt made for Mama Nall's lil grandboy 'fore his body lowered in the groun'."

Her words hit me like a thunderbolt. Grandma couldn't possibly be talking about G. C.! He was the same age as me. My eight-year-old body froze in place. I thought of the many times I'd seen folks visiting Grandma after they'd lost a loved one, their endless tears. Grandma would comfort them, wiping their faces with the bottom of her apron. I'd been to so many funerals with Grandpa that I'd lost count. But those were elderly folks who'd lived a full life. G. C. was only a child. Now he was gone.

It pained me to see folks mourning the loss of someone who'd passed on. What was most heartbreaking was knowing they'd never be able to see their loved ones on this side of life, as Grandma would say. Now I began to feel a sharp twisting and churning in the pit of my stomach, wondering what it would feel like not to see G. C. ever again. Tears began to stream down my face and into my mouth, mixing with my salty sweat. Cry-talking, I blurted out, "I miss G. C. so much, Grandma. He just a lil boy, just like I'm a lil girl, and now he gone and I can't play with him no more."

Grandma swooped me up in her lap and pulled me close. I could smell the odor of yesterday's dinner in her apron. "It's gone be alright, chile, you jus' wait an' see. Trouble don' las' always. That lil boy in a better place now. He ain't in no kinda pain."

My grandparents talked as though death was a place where someone would go on an extended visit—a place called "glory." The person who had passed would come back every now and then to visit, not as themselves, but as haints, or kind spirits. Grandma and Grandpa believed that spirits would sometimes return to the place they'd loved most. Or, if they were angry when they passed on, sometimes their spirit would roam or haunt the place.

In all my years living with my grandparents, I never heard them use the words *death, dying,* or *died.* It was always *gone, ceased, passed on, gone home, done left for glory, with the Lord, came to the end of their row, crossed over,* or *came to grace.* It was almost as though there was too much finality in the words *death* or *dying*. Over the years, I learned that this was a testament to my grandparents' deep faith and enduring strength. I was forbidden even to mumble the words *death* or *dying* in their presence. Sometimes, when I went to school, I'd hear classmates whisper about someone in their family who'd died, but always in hushed tones.

Ella's story was the first time I heard of someone being gone. Grandma talked about how her sister had gone home to a beautiful place beyond the skies. She often spoke about folks who'd gone on to be with the Lord and resided in a place called heaven. In this place, she said, "there be no more sufferin', 'cause they in the arms of the Almighty."

The first time I saw someone up close who'd passed on was a day I went into town with Grandpa. Sitting there with Grandma as she talked about G. C., my mind went back to that day, to old man Wilburn laid out in the dogtrot. I thought about G. C. lying in a cold wooden box like him and became more disheartened because I couldn't play with him anymore—forever.

G. C. had lived in a little house in the back of Bethel Hill School, about a football field away from Miss Daisy's place. From Bethel Hill, you could almost spit into his backyard. My classmates and I would see him feeding the chickens almost every school day. As I sat in Grandma's lap, I thought about the times I'd seen G. C. walking down the dirt road next to Bethel Hill. He'd always walk with his eyes lowered and his hands plunged inside his cruddy overall pockets. He'd stop right in front of me as I'd ask him a thousand questions.

"Where ya going? What you doing? Why they call you G. C.? Why don't you go to our school? What's your mama's name? Where you come from? You got sisters? Why you don't answer me, can't you talk? Do that cat got your tongue?"

I barely gave him enough time to answer one question before another would come barreling out of my mouth. For every single one, he'd just shrug his shoulders up and down.

I was excited because he was cute. Looking back, I had a mad crush on him. He was different, in an indescribable sort of way. He didn't talk much, but when he smiled, he had the widest grin I'd ever seen, exposing a chipped front tooth that was perfectly broken in half. He had a light almond complexion with coal-black hair so wavy, it made me dizzy. I'd stare intensely at his head every time I had a chance. He was what Grandpa called high yalla. Grandpa considered any Black person high yalla if they were light-complexioned. I'd crack up when he'd attach those characteristics to fair-skinned Black people. I often wondered if Grandpa considered himself high yalla, because his skin was lighter than G. C.'s.

I was so enamored with G. C.'s wavy hair, he could've been the color of cooking flour and I wouldn't have cared. Talking to Grandma, I couldn't wrap my mind around him passing on. I didn't know anything about his mother or father. Again, many of my classmates lived with their grandparents or grand-mothers; for us, living with a "grand" was as normal as the nose on your face, as Grandma put it. But it was strange how G. C. had just appeared one day, like he'd been living there all along.

G. C. lived with his great-grandma, whose name was Mama Nall. Everyone called her that except G. C., who called her Great. She was a scary-looking woman who carried herself strong and proud, even though she was almost one hundred. The first time I saw her, I was terrified, because she had one eye that stared at the ground or crept up into the corner of her eyelid when she talked. When she'd speak directly to me, I thought she was talking to someone else, because that eye would be looking in a completely different direction. Her other eye was almost shut. I wondered how she could steer a wagon and two mules with all that one-eye motion going on.

But Grandma told me not to worry about Mama Nall seeing, because she could hunt better than any man. Grandpa said she was cockeyed and that's why her eye went every which a-way. Once, she'd killed the fattest deer that folks had ever seen. Menfolk had been hunting this same deer for years, but Mama Nall shot and killed it with her double-barreled shotgun early one morning. Whenever I'd see her, she'd have that shotgun slung over her shoulder and a small pistol stuck in her argyle sock, the kind you'd see men wear. I just wanted to make sure I wasn't around when she started shooting at stuff.

Caught up in my thoughts of G. C. and Mama Nall, before I knew it I'd opened my mouth and asked, "Grandmama, how G. C. die?"

Right after those words came flying out, I knew I'd messed up. Grandma stopped rocking, and I jumped from her lap. She then scooted her rocking chair as close as she could to my four-foot frame, and with one hand gently grabbed my chin. She looked me in the eyes before spitting a big glob of snuff close enough that I could see the dirt separate as it hit the ground.

"Chile, that boy jus' sleeping. When he woke, he be with the Lord. You hear me, chile? Ain't nothin' die 'rounds here. Now we needs to git this mou'nin' quilt ready for his grandma direc'ly. Don' wants you worryin' one bit, 'cause trouble don' las' always."

Grandma started pulling G. C.'s overalls and plaid shirts from the sack. I knew those overalls well, but viewing them up close was scary. Once again, tears began to gather at the corners of my eyes. Was I really supposed to understand this thing called gone, ceased, or whatever name my grandmother chose in that moment? What I did know was that the person would never be seen by me, or anyone else, ever again. Unless, of course, they returned to the place they loved most as a haint and scared the living mess out of somebody.

The last time I saw G. C., he and his grandma had come by to do some fishing in my grandparents' pond out back of the house, past the hay barn. Folks from all around Livingston loved to fish in that pond, which was loaded with black bass and perch. Sometimes people left with so many fish, they'd have to tote them away in a large silver wash tub.

No matter how many times Mama Nall fished in my grandparents' pond, she'd ask permission before proceeding. Oftentimes she'd sit in the front yard and make small talk with Grandma and Grandpa beforehand. Like always, Grandpa would tell her, "Mama Nall, I done tol' you right smartly now 'bout umpteen times. You ain't gots to ask me first 'bout fishin' in dat ol' pond. It be heaps of fish down thar; you ain't gone catch all of 'em."

While Mama Nall and my grandparents sat in the front yard talking, I had time to play with G. C. You could tell by his accent that he hadn't lived in the country long. I didn't know much about his previous whereabouts, but to me he talked like a city boy. I knew all too well what that sounded like. It was funny how I'd pick up on G. C.'s frustration with understanding Mama Nall. He'd ask her over and over again, "Ma'am, what'd you say, Great?" or, "Ma'am, say that again, Great," and I'd chuckle inside, remembering how that used to be me.

On this trip, I took G. C. down the hill so he could see the spring. We soaked our feet in the blue waters, and when he saw the school of tadpoles, his eyes got as big as Grandma's homemade biscuits. Before I knew it, he took off running up the hill so fast I didn't have time to ask where he was going. Like a burst of lightning, there he went. I thought he would trip and fall face-first, he was running so fast.

When he returned, he had a Mason jar. He slid off the lid and dipped it into the water. This big-headed boy was trying to fill up his jar with *my* tadpoles! I couldn't believe my eyes. Every time he tried to put the jar in the water, I'd kick, beat, and stomp on his lanky body. You'd have thought that World War III was going on down at the bottom of the hill. G. C.'s lip was bruised and bloody when he ran off to blab to Mama Nall and Grandma.

"She thinks them tadpoles belong to her!" he blurted out.

"They my tadpoles and ya bet' not mess with them no more!" I shouted back in a high-pitched, almost crying voice.

Grandma and Mama Nall just stood there, ignoring the both of us. Finally, Mama Nall bid Grandma good-bye and said she and G. C. were "gonna go on down to the pond and get some fishin' in 'fore they stop jumpin'."

That was the very last time I saw him: G. C. and Mama Nall, leaving the pond, heading up the dirt road past the tall pine tree at the edge of my grandparents' property. All I could see was the back of the red-and-white plaid shirt he was wearing that day.

Now Grandma had that same shirt laid out, the first piece that would go in the quilt. I was so caught up in G. C.'s passing, I'd forgotten how I'd mistreated him that day at the spring. Guilt flooded me. I thought about the blood on his shirt and me hitting him in the head with a tree branch, all this coupled with not being able to tell him I was sorry. All he'd wanted was a few tadpoles. Now I wouldn't be able to give them to him—or anything else.

Grandma took the clothes, sat them on top of the bag, and patted her lap, encouraging me to take a seat. Once again, her lap became my refuge. She soothed my anguish, rocking me like an infant, assuring me that I had nothing to do with G. C.'s passing. She told me that the good Lord wanted G. C. to be with him in paradise. I sat, crying a river, until I entered a period of quiet reflection. I could feel Grandma's heartbeat. The rocking chair swayed along with her harmonious musical notes as she sang:

When I'm gone the last mile of the way,
I shall rest at the closing of the day.
For I know they be joy waitin'
When I go the las' mile o' the way.
Yes, Jesus... Yes, Lawd.

Grandma's singing was so soothing, I could've lain there and gone to sleep somewhere between 'the last mile' and 'the way.' I wanted her to take the fear of death from me—to make it go away. I thought about Ella, and of the feeling I'd had the first time I saw a person who'd passed on up close. It took a long time for me to get that picture out of my head.

This was the incident some four months ago, with old man Wilburn. Cuttin Jeff had fetched me and Grandpa early one morning and taken us to downtown Livingston, where Grandpa did his shopping at Millen's store. Across the street from Millen's, in the town square, was the old courthouse. It was so massive it seemed to swallow up the other buildings. Succulent flowers of every color surrounded it, making a fence of blossoms.

Two water fountains sat right below the steps. The hand-written word above one read "Colored"; the taller, prettier one said "Whites." No matter how many times I'd go to town with Grandpa, he gave me the same speech: "Don' let me catch you nowheres 'round that cotehouse, ya heah me, gal? If ya wants water, you drank till you bust from dis jar rat yere." He would always bring two large Mason jars filled to the brim with water and ice.

I didn't understand why something so beautiful caused so much ire from Grandpa. But I'd soon find out.

On our way home from town, we stopped on the outskirts of Livingston at an old farmhouse. It resembled my grandparents' place, except it had a room above the front porch with a window facing the yard. What was strange about this house was that a mattress was hanging out the window, slung over the sill. Sheets and quilts draped the fence.

As I hopped down from Cuttin Jeff's truck bed, Grandpa motioned for me to stay out in the front yard with two other children, who looked about my age. They were dressed in their Sunday going-to-church clothes. The boy sat in a chair, his feet barely touching the ground. He kicked sand and pebbles in the air with his shiny black church shoes. The girl laughed every time dirt and rocks flew up in the air. I joined in on the laughter not because it was funny, but because I wanted to be part of the hoopla. But I had one eye on the children and one on the mysterious dwelling. My curiosity was piqued further by the colorful quilts draped over the fence. There had to be more inside.

As I darted out of the front yard, I heard the boy yell, "I'm gonna tell," but I ignored him. I peered through the front door and down the long dogtrot. It felt like the first time I'd snuck into my grandparents' front room. I knew Grandpa would be angry at me for disobeying him, but this house was too intriguing to pass up. I'd deal with the consequences later.

As I stepped into the hall, I came face-to-face with a man lying on a long board with his eyes closed. He wore a white shirt and a little black bow tie. I hoped he wasn't mad at me for coming into his house without knocking. As with Grandma's hallway, a vast array of pictures graced the walls. I was distracted by the fresh flowers and plants on the shelves. It felt like I was in a flower garden.

Just as I was ready to go back and get more face time with the sleeping man, Grandpa and an older lady emerged from one of the rooms.

"Get over heah, gal!" That was the loudest I'd ever heard Grandpa raise his voice. I ran over to where he stood. He took his hand and slapped me on my backside. I ran away, crying like nobody's business, and jumped in the back of Cuttin Jeff's truck. Cuttin Jeff was still sitting in the driver's seat. Through the rearview mirror, he must've seen me crying my eyes out. I kept babbling over and over again, "Grandpa whupped me for looking at that old man sleeping in the hallway with all them pretty flowers."

Cuttin Jeff, who was aloof most of the time, busted out laughing. "Chile, 'twaint no man sleepin' in nair. Dat was a dead man on de coolin' board waitin' fo' de sun to go down so his spirit be carried away. Lord, chile, you a mess." He bellowed out another round of laughter.

I felt the cold steel from the truck as I lay balled up in a fetal position, my little ass shaking like I'd been dropped in an ice bucket. I must've dozed off, because when I woke, Grandpa was standing at the back of the truck calling out for me. "Hey gal, get on down heah, chile, and get dis ice cream."

Grandpa was all smiles, so he must've forgiven me.

We sat around in the front yard—me, Grandpa, the folks from the house, and the kids dressed in their Sunday clothes—and ate homemade vanilla ice cream until the entire batch was gone. Then the lady I'd seen in the hallway handed Grandpa a brown feed-sack filled with old clothes. I heard her tell him that she'd appreciate it if Grandma could make her a double-wide, double-ring quilt of souls. Grandpa nodded, still chewing on his wooden toothpick as he walked to the truck.

I couldn't wait to dive into the back of the truck and begin the journey home. The sun was setting, and it had started to rain, a warm, light drizzle. I was content to sit soaking up the smell of the fresh country air as we drove along the dirt road, past the cotton and cornfields. The mist from the rain and the taste of the homemade ice cream washed away any negative thoughts.

As we pulled up in front of the house, Grandma was standing at the front gate with her big apron and wide open arms, ready to hear about my day. Even though it'd only been a few hours, I felt like I hadn't seen her in weeks. Grandpa told her about my run-in with the corpse, and Grandma explained that the man had been laid out on the cooling board because he'd passed on a few days ago. She said that when a person passes inside of a house, you must hang the mattress, sheets, and quilts that were on the bed outside until the sun goes down. This allows the sun's shadow to pass over the bedding where the dead person had lain. If this wasn't done, their spirit would forever roam, and they'd be unable to rest in peace.

That night, when my grandparents thought I was fast asleep, I heard them discussing the fate of ol' man Wilburn. Since Grandpa was hard of hearing, he couldn't help but talk loudly. Grandma would end up repeating herself in response, loud enough for me to hear the entire agonizing story.

Poor Mr. Wilburn had been caught filling his jar with water from the "White" fountain in front of the courthouse for the second time. In my Grandpa's deep southern drawl, he kept saying how they'd chased that man up and down them backwoods. Mr. Wilburn hid out among the trees and brush for hours, trying to hide from the white night riders. But they caught him and they beat him half to death. When the Black folks found him, he was barely hanging on to life. He looked like he'd been doused in blood. They brought him back to his house and sent for Miss Jubilee. She brought all her herbs and healing tonics, but she couldn't save him. His wife said it wasn't any use going for the white doctor in Livingston, because he'd be too scared to come anywhere near their house.

It was the first time I'd witnessed fear in my grandpa. I couldn't see his facial expression in the pitch black of night, but I sure did feel it. Grandma told me later that Mr. Wilburn was one of Grandpa's best friends.

After laying out all the material for G. C.'s quilt, Grandma began cutting pieces of his shirts and trousers into strips. As she sewed, she told me the story of how three of Mama Nall's four great-grandbabies, all boys, had passed on.

Pearlie, G. C.'s mama, was Mama Nall's only grandchild. Pearlie's mother was around the same age as my grandmother, but she had crossed over soon after giving birth to Pearlie. Mama Nall raised Pearlie almost from birth. Now, G. C. and his brothers' father was named Thomas. Thomas got in a whole lot of trouble with white folks in Livingston because he was straightforward with them. He had his own blacksmith and shoeshine business, and he did very well, pulling in business from both white and Black folks. But when a relative of one of the affluent whites in Livingston opened up a blacksmith business, they tried to run Thomas out of town.

Thomas refused to go, and as a result they tried to intimidate him. Thomas simply stood up to those very same whites who were trying to destroy him, but soon after, word got back that the local Klan had placed a target on his back. Mama Nall and Pearlie begged him to leave town. Miss Ruby Tartt, a reputable white woman in Livingston and a famous writer, hid him until she was able to sneak him out of town one night on the doodlebug freight train heading north.

Prior to Thomas's marriage to Pearlie, he'd dated a woman who folks around Livingston said was crazier than a fox and twice as scandalous. She and her parents had moved to Livingston from New Orleans. This woman was so smitten with Thomas, she'd been overheard on many occasions claiming she'd kill, cheat, or hurt any woman who came close to him. She was said to have a mean streak the size of the Mississippi River, and most folks knew she and her mother dabbled in the blackest of magic, otherwise known as casting spells or putting down what country folks called the "roots."

This belief was widely accepted throughout the South, though a small minority considered it folklore or country superstition. I'd always heard that if the roots were applied properly, the person they were placed on would become ill, die, or wish they were dead.

For her part, Grandma Lula wholeheartedly believed in the spiritual realm and thought that if someone put the roots on a person who possessed a strong belief in the Lord, believed in the power of prayer, or had one of her quilts of souls, those things would counteract the impact. She felt that her quilts acted as talismans, because they held the peaceful souls and kind spirits of those who'd passed on. She also thought that the Lord had placed angels in our lives to protect us and ward off evil. I'd watch as she'd say a silent prayer over each quilt after she'd finished it. Then she'd tell me, "Close your eyes, chile, 'cause I gots to hand this quilt over to the Lord."

Now, Thomas recognized early on the cruelty and posses-
siveness of the woman who was in love with him, and he heard
her threats about putting the roots on folks. As a result, he left
her before their relationship could get off the ground. After,
she threatened him to no end. About a year later, Thomas and
Pearlie married. The woman was visibly upset and vowed that
she wouldn't rest until she'd made their lives pure hell. She
declared openly that she'd make sure of it, and Mama Nall said
that this curse was the cause of her grandbabies passing on.

Grandma felt that if she could take the clothes of G. C.,
his brothers, and old fabric from Grandma's loved ones, it
would fend off any spells this woman would try to cast on little
Backus, the only remaining child of Pearlie and Thomas. The
good spirits in the quilt would protect Backus and keep him
from harm. Again, my grandmother wholeheartedly believed
that roots or spells could be cast for good or for bad, but that
evil spirits could be prayed away or contained with the appro-
priate talisman. Her quilts of souls were a salve for many.

The rest of that day was spent working on the quilt. As
evening began to roll in, Grandma said she could hear Grandpa's stomach grumbling. It was time to start gathering our
things. Grandpa was sitting in his usual wood-backed rocking
chair inside the screened front porch, contentedly waiting on
Grandma to warm up his food from yesterday's leftovers. In
the middle of stuffing strips of clothing back into the sack,
Grandma told me to stop what I was doing, go in the house,
and get one of her small Mason jars. When I returned, she took
my hand and led me down to my special place.

"Chile, I wants you to take the top off that jar and scoop up
some of them tadpoles."

I looked at Grandma with gigantic tears in my eyes. I just
couldn't do it.

"Grandma," I cried out loudly. "They ain't hurting nobody.
Please, Grandma, don't make me put these little babies in the
jar. They ain't hurt nobody and they ain't got nobody. I can't

take them away from their mamas. Please, Grandma, don't make me put these babies in the jar. They can't breathe. They can't breathe, Grandma."

"Shush, chile, it's gone be okay. You see, we gonna just take a few and bring them to the big pond and let them find a mama 'cause it plenty of them in the big pond. G. C. gonna be smilin' down on you when he sees them tadpoles."

When she said it, I couldn't do anything else but believe. After we gathered the tadpoles, Grandma hugged me tight and held one of my hands as we walked. My other hand clutched the Mason jar, holding it to my chest like it was an infant. When we reached the pond, Grandma looked me in the eyes and said, "Now we gone praise the Lord and let them tadpoles free."

I opened the jar, and the tadpoles wiggled out, disappearing into the clear waters. I could see them as they jetted off. A part of me felt alone and heartbroken. Watching them swim downstream, I felt as though I'd lost twice that day. I'd lost G. C. and I'd lost some of my tadpoles. The spring was their home, and they'd been taken from that safe haven. They were strangers in a new environment, dropped off and abandoned—just like me, not so long ago.

Watching them, I was four years old again, a little girl yanked from her home, not knowing whether I'd ever return. Back then, I was young and vulnerable and didn't possess a voice, just like my tadpoles. My only perception of them was as helpless victims who couldn't or wouldn't be able to take care of themselves. That day at the spring when G. C. and I had fought, I couldn't understand why he couldn't see that, why he wanted to confine them to a small jar or use them as bait. Imagining my tadpoles dangling from the end of a fishing pole, hurt and fighting for their lives, made me sick to my stomach. I felt it was up to me to protect them.

But Grandma showed me in her own way that there were folks out there in this big old world who loved me. Just like the tadpoles, I had been placed in larger waters with other mamas.

As we left the pond that day, a sense of calm engulfed me. Once again, Grandma had taken what I'd considered a solemn event, added a pinch of reality, and explained it in a way a child like me could easily grasp.

Dark skies began to move in. I sat in my favorite swing on the front porch beside Grandma and Grandpa in their rocking chairs, eating cornbread and buttermilk. All I could hear was the metal spoons raking up against the glass Mason jars. The sound of their smacking temporarily canceled out the singing of the crickets and katydids.

"Come here and get these jars, chile. Rinse them out and put them in the cupboard. Grandma gots a surprise for you when you get back."

I scampered down the long hallway to the kitchen. With breakneck speed, I took the dipper from the bucket outside, rinsed her and Grandpa's jars, dried them, and returned both to the makeshift wooden cupboard. When I got back to the front porch, Grandma was holding the leftover scraps from G. C.'s and his brothers' clothing. When she told me that she'd be placing these pieces in my quilt, I couldn't do anything but smile and put my arms around her waist. I think I cried. Knowing that G. C. would be there each time I wrapped myself up in my quilt of souls filled me with joy. This was a way in which I could once again be close to him.

My "little red riding hood" look: eleven years old,
standing in the dogtrot of my grandparents' house

9

Two Peas in a Pod

GRANDMA WAS OVER SEVENTY-FIVE years old but, oh my goodness, did she still exude an enormous amount of energy! She'd grab and pull pea pods from their stems as if her hands were a machine. I couldn't believe a woman of her age could outdo a child as young and spry as me. Grandma would take a row at one end of the field and I'd take the other, and we'd reap that field until we met somewhere in the middle. Sometimes I felt lost, almost buried, among the tall rows of crowder and black-eyed peas. We'd been in the patch since five in the morning, pulling pods from the long, skinny brown vines and filling our cotton sacks to the tip-top. We were trying to beat the sun before it got midway in the sky.

It had only been a day since we'd started working on G. C.'s quilt. Even though I was apprehensive, I was anxious to see it completed. But I knew it wouldn't happen until we'd finished picking and shelling the crop of peas. It wasn't quite noon, and I'd already filled up six sacks. I was sure Grandma had more.

Morning turned to early afternoon. My bare feet acted as a thermometer, allowing me to gauge the rise in temperature. When the scorching dirt burned the bottoms of my feet, I knew it wouldn't be long before the air became hot as Hades from the thick Alabama humidity. As Grandma inched closer to midfield, her singing grew louder and louder. Singing and working in the fields were as common to her as sun to shine. Her lusty alto voice resounded off the trees:

Bringing in the sheaves,
Bringing in the sheaves.
Here we come rejoicing,
Bringing in the sheaves.

I could see her bright red head scarf bobbing up and down as she steadily pulled and packed the peas into the cotton sack draped across her waist.

"C'mon, chile, we almost at the end of these here rows before we take it on back to the house. Grandma needs to rest these ol' bones for a spell, then we can finish that lil boy's quilt. We gonna get it knocked out before Mama Nall come from up yonder to fetch it. Yo' grandpa is goin' into town Sat'day. I suspect I'm gone send you with him. Then we gone put a mess of peas aside for Mama Nall. We got way more than what we need. It's a sin to have all these extra peas jus' sittin 'round here when you got folks starvin'. So we jus' gone put some extra bags in the smokehouse for folks who ain't got none. You hear me, chile?"

"Yes'm, Grandma."

"You got chores to do before I let you get on outta here on Sat'day. So we best make haste."

"Yes'm."

Through all the hard work and sweat that Grandma left in the field, many times she had hardly anything to show for it. With a wink and a smile, she'd give most of it away to any and every one, leaving just enough to tide us over until the next crop. A part of me had a feeling that Grandma used the early morning pea excursion to ease my mind about the passing of G. C. The night before, I'd had nightmarish dreams of him wandering in total darkness. I felt his soul was looking for peace but couldn't find it.

In the bedroom, only a small amount of floor space separated my bed from Grandma and Grandpa's. Grandma slept on the side of the bed facing me. Last night, I'd put the covers over my head, leaving a small slit in the opening of the quilt so I could watch her watching me. I felt safe, knowing she'd keep her eyes on me until I fell asleep, but I couldn't stop tossing and turning. My stomach was balled up in a thousand knots as I thought about G. C.'s clothes in the croker sack in the smokehouse. Each time I closed my eyes, I saw him the way he'd looked the last time we were together.

The moonlight shone brightly through the only window in the bedroom, illuminating Grandma's face. As she looked at me, her eyes told me that she felt every inch of my restlessness, pain, and hurt. "Don' worry, chile, it's gonna be alright in the mo'nin'. Grandma gone see to it. Trouble don' las' always. Grandma wants you to rest now, 'cause we got a whole field of peas to pick by noon tomorrow."

Grandma was right; I needed my sleep. Getting up before daybreak after having such a bad night, then having to pick a field of peas on top of that, was grueling. Now, all I could think about was finishing up and heading back home, where we'd sit on the back porch, shelling the peas. I hoped I'd be able to keep my eyes open.

I loved shelling peas with Grandma. As my thumb glided down the center of the pod's hull, peas would rush up, and the noise of them hitting the bottom of the black metal pot was symphonic. Each pea that fell made a special ping-pong sound. I was almost as proficient as Grandma in using both hands to find the quickest way to open the shell and allow all the peas from the pod to drop simultaneously.

Between our shelling and Grandma's humming, the combination nearly lulled me to sleep. I caught myself a few times before my face fell into the batch of peas. Thank God we only had one more sack to finish. My fingers felt like they had blisters the size of watermelons.

"Edgar, Edgar, come on out here and help us sort out these peas."

Grandma had to scream at the top of her lungs for poor old Grandpa to hear. I heard him making his way from the bedroom and crossing the linoleum kitchen floor to the back porch. His arthritis caused him to shuffle when he walked. The shoes he had on were almost two sizes too big for his feet. His son, Uncle Po-Boy, had given them to him last year, and Grandpa had balled up a couple sheets of newspaper and stuffed them in the toes to make them fit. I guess he liked the way the shoes looked, or he didn't have the heart to tell Uncle Po-Boy they were too big.

At this time of day, Grandpa would take his suspenders, which held up his blue khaki pants, off his shoulders and let them hang down to the side. I'd often wondered why Grandpa wore his pants pulled up so high. I swear, if he'd pulled them up any more, the waistband would have touched his chin. Down in the country, old men wearing suspenders was as common as old women wearing aprons.

"Yes'm, Miss Lula, I heared you callin' me so loud, thought somebody done 'ceased back yere."

"What you talkin' bout, Mister Horn? Been callin' you pert'near longer than it takes to skin a pig and clean it. You are slower than pourin' molasses out a bucket in the wintertime. Now, I wants you to finish up this last sack of peas so me and this chile can work on Mama Nall's lil grandboy's quilt. You can sit right here. When you finish, you can put them in this here sack for Miss Sugar, Mama Nall, and Miss Jubilee—you know how they like peas from my patch. The rest of them, just put them in the smokehouse."

"Yes'm, Miss Lula."

After listening to Grandma give Grandpa instructions, I left to take care of the prequilting duties. These chores never changed. Grandma had to have her bottle of snuff, because she loved dipping when she sewed. I'd draw a bucket of cool water from the well out back to fill her favorite Mason jar. Lastly, I'd bring three spools of white thread, which she'd place in her lap, and six stitching needles that she'd stick in the bib of her apron, just in case the one she was using broke or fell in the dirt.

During the week, Grandma would sometimes make enough dinner to last for two days—leaving us more time to quilt. Now all I had to do was wait for her to tell me what quilt we'd be working on that day.

"Gone, chile, and fetch that bag of clothes out the smokehouse that gots G. C. and his brothers' clothes in it. We jus' gots a few more clothes to put in it 'fore we done."

I hated going in the smokehouse. The cracks in the wood were the only source of light. Some days I'd have to fish around forever, searching through twenty or more bags of used scraps of clothing, to find the bag of rags Grandma would be working on that day. These quilts were all done, and she'd given them to the recipients, but had held on to the excess material. She said it was bad luck and disrespectful to throw this fabric away.

I loved watching her take bags of leftover clothing and marry them up with quilts she'd make for others, especially when she didn't have enough material for that one quilt. Or she'd use them to make what she called piece quilts, taking those spare pieces of clothing and combining them into one complete quilt we'd keep for our own use. Sometimes she'd use the extras to patch up holes in Grandpa's khaki trousers and shirts, or even make an outfit or two for me. The bags of rags had a multitude of uses.

I'll never forget when Grandma made me two patchwork dresses from swatches of clothes. They were very colorful indeed, and consisted of various types of material, from corduroy to wool blends. The first day I wore one of those dresses to school, oh, how my classmates laughed and teased me! I wasn't too upset by their ridicule until one day, when we were all outside during recess, Mary Lee recognized pieces of her grandmother's dress and apron in my dress. She started crying like she was being beat to death. She just stood there, pointing at my outfit, screaming at the top of her lungs, "That's Big Mama's stuff all over your dress!"

I just stood there, dumbfounded. The other children left whatever outdoor activities they were engaged in and began pointing and laughing. When Miss Clay heard the commotion and came running out the schoolhouse, I gave her a blow-by-blow description of what had happened.

"Grandmama made me this dress with clothes from Mary Lee's Big Mama, who done passed on. When she see my dress, she just starts a yelling and screaming and pointing and everything! I didn't do nothing to her, Miss Clay, I swear. But Big Robert and Clarence and Leah and them start making fun of Mary Lee. I told them to stop, but they just keep on."

Brenda added her two cents. "Yep, Clarence was the one pulling on Phyllistene's dress, and then he run away, then he come back and pull on her dress some more. He made up this dumb song 'bout Mary Lee's Big Mama. It say Phyllistene kilt her and put her in the cloak closet and then Phyllistene ran away with Big Mama's clothes. He just a stupid big-head boy."

"Thank you, Phyllistene and Brenda. I can always count on you two to tell me what I need to know."

Then Miss Clay screamed at the top of her lungs for everybody to get back in the classroom. After she scolded the entire class for how "ign'ant" they were acting and told them how disgusting it was to laugh at folks' clothes, she lined up about twenty kids against the wall. One by one, she put the wood paddle on each one of their backsides until she brought the tears. For the rest of the day, everyone was quiet as a church mouse, as Grandma would say. Only Mary Lee, Brenda, and I were spared.

To make matters worse for my classmates, Miss Clay sent a note home to their parents. Back in those days, all you needed to do was let a couple of parents know what their children had done and believe me, every family within a ten-mile radius would find out. The next day at recess, it was the talk of the schoolyard how their parents tore up their asses.

I never told Grandma what happened. There was no need to, because she was also a recipient of the pipeline of information passed from one family to the other. Grandma never made me outfits out of the used clothing of folks who'd gone on to glory ever again.

After toting the bag of clothing belonging to G. C. and his brothers to the front yard, dread overwhelmed me again. Maybe it was my fear of the unknown—I had no idea what had really happened to him and wasn't sure what new information Grandma was about to reveal. I thought about Ella and how her story had ended. In a way, when Grandma placed her dress in my quilt, I gained at least a semblance of closure. But this was not the same. G. C. was someone I saw almost every day. I could talk to him and he'd respond. He was no older than me, and now he was gone. I'd thought that death only happened to someone old, someone who'd lived on this earth for much longer than me and G. C.

Many times, Grandma told me that no child should have to pay for the sins of their mama and papa. That day, I knew she was speaking about G. C. and his brothers, that she meant it just wasn't right for those three boys to suffer to that extent.

Mama Nall had tried the best she could to help her great-grandbabies, who Grandma referred to as two-time grandbabies. And still those boys left this world because their fever was so high, their insides burnt up. All of them—G. C. too. The day he passed, Mama Nall had come by when I was at school to tell Grandma that he'd taken sick in the middle of the night. G. C. had a light complexion, but due to the fever he'd turned almost as dark as me and Grandma. He hadn't eaten anything in over four days, and Mama Nall said he'd started having conniptions like he was possessed. She immediately hitched her two mules to the buckboard and put him in the wagon. It wasn't any use taking him to the white doctor in Livingston, because they didn't want to see anything Black coming through their door. So, she did the only thing she knew how: she took him to Miss Jubilee.

I tried to visualize Miss Jubilee working desperately to keep G. C. alive. She and Mama Nall did all they could do. However, it got to the point where nobody could save G. C. but the Lord. I guess the Lord wanted him more, because he took him on home to glory that night. Grandma worried about my deep concern for G. C., including the awful dreams I had. She assured me that she wanted me to not think any bad thoughts about him, because he was in a better place now.

As she spoke, she cut out a large piece of his overalls and placed it right in the middle of the quilt. Then she took the shirt Mama Nall said he'd had on the night he went to glory and sewed it in next to the overalls. Grandma cut the shirts and pants that had belonged to G. C.'s brothers into strips and put them all around G. C.'s clothes, as though they were watching over their little brother.

I can't explain the exact moment I felt relief. I suspect my old folk's soul realized something that my nearly nine-year-old mind had difficulty accepting or believing. It saw the quilt in its completeness: three lives bound together by pieces of their clothing, woven with a needle, thread, and an abundance of love. That quilt became a living symbol that all three brothers were at peace.

Grandma stood up and held it wide. We admired the gentle colors and the warmth it generated. I couldn't help but wrap myself up in its fullness. When I closed my eyes and caressed the cloth, the smell of G. C. emanated from the fabric, a scent I remembered from the last time I'd seen him, when we ran down to the spring, barefoot and carefree. Standing there, I realized he wasn't gone at all. On those days when the fog would roll in and engulf the spring, I'd take solace in knowing it was G. C., inviting me to come take a dip in the cool waters. I hoped that one day, I'd feel his spirit pass through me to let me know he was all right.

As we began putting away the quilting for the day, Grandma sat in her chair in silent contemplation. Then she said, "Gone, chile, call your grandpa. Put a few chunks a wood in the stove, so we can get supper warm. Grandma be inside direc'ly."

Before I opened the screen door, I turned around to say something, then decided not to. She sat in her chair, covering her face with her apron. This was her moment, and she needed the space to grieve in her own way.

The waters that flow from the dreaded Conkabayou Bridge

10

Mama Nall

EARLY THE NEXT MORNING, I woke to the sound of a wagon in the distance. The metal clanging of the reins echoed off the trees so loudly it was as though a team of mules was right there in our bedroom. Grandma was already up, feeding the chickens and slopping hogs. I slipped into my overalls, ran to the back porch, threw a dipper full of cold water on my face, and grabbed a pinch of baking soda for my teeth. I made a brief stop in the kitchen, long enough to pop one of Grandma's sweet buttermilk biscuits in my mouth. Another one I held in my hands, to eat as soon as I could swallow the first one. Grandpa said he was feeling poorly and there was no need to fix him anything to eat right then. Poor Grandpa. Between the asthma, arthritis, and the rheumatism, I don't know which he suffered the most.

In no time flat, I got to the front yard. There was Mama Nall, sitting high in her wagon. She was the only person I knew who owned mules with large gray spots all over their hides. Grandpa called them "bino" (albino) mules. I opened the front gate for her, and she took her time climbing down from the wagon. I don't know what came over me then, but before she came inside the yard, I put my arms around her waist and hugged her real tight. Even though it was already hotter than hell and, as always, she was dressed in a hundred pounds of clothing, I might as well have been hugging a block of ice.

Once I let go, she looked at me through that crooked eye and said, "What ya doin', chile? Don' ya worry 'bout Mama Nall one bit, ya hear me? You jus' git on in that house and git yo' grandma. I can't be waiting here fo'ever."

"Yes'm, Mama Nall."

Truthfully, she scared me to death, and all I wanted to do at that moment was get as far from her as I possibly could. It never crossed my mind that G. C.'s passing had probably brought back painful memories of her other two great-grandsons, who'd died the same way. Like a hurt puppy, I whimpered away and retreated under the house, where I could listen to her whispered conversation with Grandma.

Once they were alone, I waited for Mama Nall to cry out. Having seen so many grieving people wail and scream at the top of their lungs, I was convinced this was the way most folks processed their grief over losing a loved one. I wanted to see tears flow from Mama Nall's eyes, to know that she too was hurting over the passing of my friend. Grandma laid the quilt in her open arms. I waited for Mama Nall to embrace it and feel the spirit of her grandsons flowing through it. Children no older than me, whose lives ended suddenly and tragically, one after another, after another.

Mama Nall just stood there, holding the quilt like it was the sack of unshelled peas we had set aside for her. In fact, she seemed more emotionally attached to the peas. She climbed back on her buckboard and clicked her teeth to signal the mules to begin their slow trot up the hill. Grandma stood at the front gate, waving.

I couldn't wait. I came barreling out from under the house, taking only a few seconds to shake the dirt off my overalls. By the time I made it to the front yard, I was out of breath and barely getting my words together. "Grandma, she didn't cry or nothing—what's wrong with Mama Nall? Don't she miss G. C.?"

Grandma was taken aback by my outburst, I think. But as I recall the time I spent with her, I realize how impassioned and inquisitive I was. And after hearing the stories of Ant Ella and Miss Cooter, part of me knew a larger story lay within the soul of Mama Nall.

And I was right. That afternoon, I learned that Mama Nall and her entire family had been sold right before the surrender. Mama Nall "jus' had a rough row to hoe," Grandma told me, because she and her family were sold to one of the evilest slave-owners this side of the Mississippi, a man who often had his way with Mama Nall's mama. Growing up, Mama Nall saw one of his overseers strip a baby from her mama's arms right after the child was born—they never saw that baby again. Another overseer stomped a newborn baby to death just because it had crooked feet and would be unfit for the fields. That overseer said he would not put food in the mouth of a "nigger who ain't no good for the fields or the house." After witnessing these dreadful deeds, Mama Nall swore that she would never allow anyone to beat her down. That's why she had a mean streak as large as heaven and earth, my grandmother told me. She'd seen an abundance of killing and maiming before she was knee-high.

Mama Nall left that plantation soon after marrying Mr. Nall. She was only a young girl of fifteen or so. They settled down on a little piece of property not far from Livingston. And in time, their six-year-old granddaughter Pearlie came to live with them. When Pearlie married Thomas, she was barely seventeen. From that point on, it looked like she was having babies every year. Pearlie ended up with all boys; three girls came along in between, but they all passed away before their first birthday. This pained Mama Nall tremendously. I'm certain she experienced flashbacks to the deaths of infants she witnessed when she was a young child.

The wild speculation as to why Pearlie kept losing her girls didn't help. Gossip ran rampant that the roots had been put on her. Some even said she was "getting rid" of the girls and choosing to keep the boys. The country grapevine was well known for circulating more gossip, heresy, and wild superstitions than fleas on a hound dog, as Grandma would say.

Every year, Mama Nall and her husband, Cletus, harvested two large cotton and corn fields. Between Mr. Nall's good friend Mr. Walt, Pearlie, and Thomas, they worked and sweated, bringing in a good amount of crop that sustained them financially. All was going well until Mr. Nall was brutally murdered. That was a dark day for all Black folks up and around Livingston, because Mr. Nall was well respected. He was killed right before Pearlie moved up North.

Mr. Walt and Mr. Nall were closer than two peas in a pod, my grandma told me. They lived in close proximity, and Mr. Walt eye-witnessed a group of white men on horses forcibly removing Mr. Nall from his home. You could hear Mama Nall yelling, the grandchildren screaming and crying, but their fearful cries went unheard by the posse that took Mr. Nall.

Mr. Walt said he knew they were taking him down to nearby Conkabayou, because that's where they took Black folks they planned on hanging or maiming. What those white men did to Mr. Nall that night was unbelievable. Mr. Walt witnessed a white man tie Mr. Nall's feet, then another white man jumped on his horse and dragged Mr. Nall around in circles until he wasn't moving. Mr. Walt told Grandma that he hid out in the woods, watching the entire incident unfold. He was afraid to move; he knew if they found him, he would be their next victim. He just hid his face in his hands and cried, he said. He'd never felt that helpless in his life.

Some of his church members helped Mr. Walt haul Mr. Nall's body to the undertaker. Folks said that poor Mr. Walt went to his grave soon after that incident. It took a considerable toll on him physically and mentally. For her part, Mama Nall was so broken up over what was left of him that she became almost mute, and very rarely spoke. Mama Nall told Grandma years later she was all cried out. The white men had taken everything from her that wasn't nailed down.

The backstory behind what transpired prior to the killing of Mr. Nall I found out by eavesdropping on my grandparents' conversation with Cuttin Jeff. Apparently, white folks'd had it out for Mr. Nall all along, because they said he'd started an uprising in the late 1930s, right before Grandma ended her working days for Dr. Murphy. Whites and Blacks in the town of Bellamy, which was a stone's throw from Livingston, started a ruckus after a white farmer cheated Mr. Nall of the money he owed him for the cotton he'd picked.

Mr. Nall said the cotton weighed a certain amount, but according to the white man, it came in lower than what Mr. Nall saw with his own eyes as the cotton sat on the scale. Mr. Nall let him know about it too. I guess that white man had time to think about how Mr. Nall spoke up for himself, and he probably told some of his friends that Mr. Nall had sassed him. Before you knew it, the whites had burnt down one of the Black churches. Black folks were madder than a bed of fire ants, so they went and burned down some barns belonging to some of the white citizens and killed some of their cows.

These tensions had been simmering for some time. In the late 1950s, Sumter County, Alabama, was the origin of the lesser-known Voting Rights Act of 1957. African Americans began peaceful protests in Livingston and other small towns throughout the county in order to register to vote. This was years before the organized sit-ins and bus boycotts that occurred throughout the South. Yes, tiny Livingston, a small community not far from the Mississippi line, was at the forefront of the movement, but the county received no local or national attention. Its Black residents just quietly went about trying to exercise their right to vote. One periodical I saw later in life listed Sumter County as the place the civil rights movement forgot.

Some Black residents did end up successfully voting. My great-grandfather, Josh Horn, was one of three Blacks allowed to vote in Sumter County from the early 1900s to 1940. During the 1930s and 1940s, more African Americans lined up in front of courthouses, refusing to move, standing in the Alabama heat all day if necessary in their attempt to register to vote. Again, this was long before Rosa Parks refused to give up her seat on the bus or John Lewis's stand at the Edmund Pettus Bridge. And the retribution was fast and fierce. Hooded white men rode on their horses of white supremacy, and Black folks were hunted down like animals, maimed, and killed.

To this day, my assumption is that this is why so many Black folks were lynched in the area near the Conkabayou Bridge. During the 1920s and 1930s, there was more lynching in Sumter County than anywhere else in the South. I imagine that the Black people who resided in the area got fed up with their families being brutalized and began fighting back. Hence, the riots of the time. By then, the county was sitting on a powder keg. Both whites and Blacks were injured in the melee, which went on for over a week.

Things finally calmed down, but no one forgot the incident. Years had passed, yet tensions continued to boil. Mr. Nall was a marked man, I heard my grandparents say. It wasn't a coincidence that the man who was said to have pulled Mr. Nall out of his house was the same one Mr. Nall said had cheated him. He was also the brother of the only lawman in Livingston.

I heard old folks speak about those turbulent times while they sat in my grandparents' front yard. Things had gotten so bad that some sympathetic whites would sneak Black men out of town to save their lives—just like with Pearlie's Thomas. After Mr. Nall's death, Pearlie and her children moved north, too, and Mama Nall had to spend all her waking hours farming, even on Sundays. Mr. Walt and his sons, who lived nearby, would come over and help out until Mr. Walt passed on. Mama Nall didn't go to church much because of all the chores she had to do just to get by. Grandma and Miss Jubilee would only see her every now and then.

I began telling Grandma that all I'd wanted to do was hug Mama Nall and tell her how much I missed G. C. But Mama Nall had recoiled. That's when Grandma explained to me how difficult it is for somebody to take in love if they've never experienced it themselves.

"You got to give to get," she said, looking into my eyes. "Poor Mama Nall. Them grandbabies was the closes' she comes to caring 'bout somebody. I can tell you this, chile: when Mama Nall by herself, she got tears enough to fill up that pond down yonder. Grandma knows this. I don' s'pect Mama Nall much longer for this here world. That lil two-time grandboy took the last bit outta her. Grandma knows how it is when your family get took from you. You just sick. Too sick to cry, and if you do, you gone get sick. Mama Nall beens through a lot, baby. Everything she get close to, it get took away."

Grandma spoke frequently about how difficult it was for her own mother to overcome the tragedy of losing three children while enslaved. Her mama would cry out at night when she thought about her babies, and Grandma said she never forgot those cries. She spoke longingly of not having any known family members until her children and grandchildren came long, and for the hundredth time, told me that she never wanted me to forget the stories of her mama, papa, and Ella. We would pray for Mama Nall, she added. She never wanted me to forget Mama Nall's story, either. Grandma always told me that we mourn when no one's looking, in the quiet of the night, no one there with you but your thoughts. That's when I imagined Mama Nall, who lived all alone in her three-room shanty, filled up two silver washtubs of tears.

Grandma spent the last hours before sundown sewing pieces of clothing from G. C. and his brothers into my quilt.

Scraps of denim overalls surrounded by black-and-red checkered shirts fit neatly into two large squares. The shirts sat diagonal, with strips of the overalls acting as dividers. I loved the way this clothing blended in below Cooter's yellow dress. The bright and dark colors complemented each other. Grandma even smiled at her work.

After his death, I used to imagine G. C. wandering in a clear space, looking for someone he could romp and run with. When Grandma sewed his brothers into the quilt, it felt like he was no longer alone. The brothers didn't live long on this earth, but now they were forever together. Their fabric, those pieces of corduroy, wool, and denim, were arranged throughout the sides and middle of my quilt of souls. Then Grandma put a strip of G. C.'s gray britches along the left edge. Looking at it, I imagined him running down to the spring to romp and splash around, and I smiled.

11

Miss Jubilee

IT WAS A SATURDAY in 1962, and I'd turned nine. Grandpa and Cuttin Jeff had just dropped me off at the small path that led to Miss Jubilee's house. That day, I was carrying a special gift for her.

As I leapt from the truck and trotted the two hundred feet to her shanty, I saw her at the door. Miss Jubilee was almost as tall as the old oak tree in our front yard, and like most old women down South, she wore long cotton underpants and thick stockings, even during the hot Alabama summers. Hers had lost all elasticity, so they just fell and gathered around her ankles. She stood, one hand on her hip, the other one waving good-bye as the truck carrying Grandpa and Cuttin Jeff took off down the road. The Alabama red dirt and dry underbrush crackled as it rubbed up against the pale gray metal of the truck's underbelly.

Miss Jubilee towered over me, moving her lips, no sound coming out. Then she smiled, revealing a single tooth, like a lone tree in the middle of an meadow. Her lips quivered, which they often did as she searched for words, before they began pouring from her mouth like water from a faucet.

"Miss Jubilee sho nuff glad to see you, gal. It get mighty lonely out yere in these backwoods, but I swears, you a sight for sore eyes. Now I betcha gots somethin' in them sacks for ol' Miss Jubilee. You know I can justa smell Miss Lula's tea cakes miles away. Lawd, Miss Lula know she can make some mouf-watering tea cakes, even betta than my mama."

Miss Jubilee had a hypnotic glare. Her eyes sat deep in their sockets, leaving a small platform below her bottom lids. I could lay a penny in that space and leave it there all day. I always longed to know the story behind her eyes. Sometimes I wanted to look away, but she possessed a strange magnetism that drew me in and wouldn't let me go, no matter how I tried.

After placing the cookies my Grandma had sent her on the table, I reached into the croker sack and pulled out the quilt of souls Grandma had made for her. It was as bulky as it was grand and double-stuffed with cotton I'd picked from my grandparents' small field. Its faded blue, red, and green hues, dominant stripes, and checkered patterns flowed into one another. Grandma had washed it thoroughly and placed it on the line out back to dry in the Alabama sun for three days. Still, those pieces of tattered clothing, produced sometime during the mid-1800s, held the musty smell of long ago. The baked-in odor from Miss Jubilee's past refused to be washed away.

As I handed it to her, Miss Jubilee's eyes got as big as the sinkhole in her backyard. With trembling hands, she took the quilt and began caressing it like a newborn baby. Then she brought it to her nose. Her inbreathing was a haunting yet beautiful sound, like the song of a woman who'd just found the lost object she'd been searching for her entire life. She motioned for me to follow her down the hallway to her screened-in back porch. She flopped down in the straw-bottom rocker, still clinging to the quilt, and then it happened: tears welled in her eyes and began flowing like an April shower.

I stood looking at her as she rocked. A sadness came over me like I'd never felt—I didn't know how to respond.

"Dis yere my mama's and papa's clothes, and my baby sis' blue dress that yo' grandma puts in this quilt. Ain't seen them clothes in yars. I keeps they few clothes in dat ol' croker sack that I gave yo' grandma. Never open that bag in I don' know when. Lots a pain an' mis'ry tied up in that ol' sack a clothes, gal. Put them in that sack after my folks gone. I was a lil gal when they's sold. I jus' 'members cryin' and runnin' after that wagon that carry my fam'ly way from me. Ol' man Hitch and his wife Cilla grab me, they says it be okay. Theys gone be my mama and papa now. The bes' thang I ever did, sendin' they clothes to yo' grandma."

Miss Jubilee's entire body shook with grief. I wanted to do something to try and ease her hurt. Grandma had just told me yesterday how my "nine-yar-ol' body haves a ninety-yar-ol' spirit." The nine-year-old in me said run. The ninety-year-old said show wisdom.

I didn't know what possessed me to ease up behind Miss Jubilee, grab a handful of her hair, and begin braiding it, just as Grandma did for me when I was feeling sad. But I did, and I started humming a tune, too, the one with no name that Grandma always sang. Miss Jubilee seemed so grateful. She sat breathing in that quilt and gently rocking in her chair. "Thank ya, chile," she said. "My mama and papa sees you. You know I sees them 'bout every day now. They say they comin' soon to take me home, to be wit' them in glory."

I couldn't put a name to what I was feeling; I was confused, yet unafraid. My entire four-foot frame felt like it was being draped in cobwebs, and I tried but failed to move. I stared at the palms of my hands, stretching my fingers apart, wondering what had come over me. Miss Jubilee's hair was beautifully done, with what looked like a hundred braids. But I didn't even have a comb.

In her rocker, Miss Jubilee was quiet as a mouse, still clinging to her quilt. Watching her, I didn't hear Cuttin Jeff blowing

his truck horn to signal he was near. I didn't hear the dogs barking, or Grandpa and Cuttin Jeff as they beat their way through
the bushes and weeds that led to Miss Jubilee's front yard.

"Hey, Miss Jubilee," Grandpa shouted, "me an' Jeff been
callin' y'all. Y'all act lahk ya mo' def den me. I almos' break
m'damn neck in dem weeds getting up here. We comes for da
chile so we can head on back down de road. Looks lak dat storm
pert'near on us. What wrong wit' y'all? Ya looks lahk y'all done
seent a ghost."

Miss Jubilee suddenly stood and took a small silver
container from her apron pocket. She pulled her bottom lip
down and set a speck of brown powdered snuff inside, then
offered some to Grandpa and Cuttin Jeff. Cuttin Jeff shook his
head, but Grandpa said, "I reckon I jus' might. Much obliged,
Miss Jubilee."

The only thing I could do was sit and stare at Miss Jubilee's beautiful braids, spread neatly over her head, a work of
art performed by my little hands—a quality job I didn't even
remember happening. Now Grandpa too was taken aback.

"Gal, ya did all dis yere braiding?"

What was I to say? Miss Jubilee proudly responded, one
hand on her hip. "Yea, she did, Edgar. The gal gots old folks'
soul. Make sho to brang her back next time y'all down this way."

"Yes'm. C'mon, gal, we be burning daylight; look at dem
black clouds over yonder. I be seeing you, Miss Jubilee."

"Come here, chile, and gives Miss Jubilee some sugah and
a big ol' hug."

I grabbed her at the waist as she bent her tall frame, bringing me close. When I closed my eyes, I felt the world spinning on its axis. I felt the intensity of her embrace, and I never
wanted to turn her loose. If I did, I feared she'd drift away and
I'd never see her again.

I still hadn't spoken a word since that spirit came over me.
I think Miss Jubilee knew what had happened and how I felt,
because she winked at me with those deep-set, all-knowing eyes

of hers. I couldn't help but turn around and gaze at her as I backpedaled away from her house, past the bushes that separated us. It must have been those same spirits that reached out and prevented me from tripping as I walked away.

This time I climbed in the front of Cuttin Jeff's truck, pulling all seventy pounds of me up and onto the torn seat. The ripped leather and cotton stuffing that had burst from the seams poked me in the back of my neck, so I decided to lay my head in Grandpa's lap. I was so consumed by my thoughts that I couldn't smell the stench of snuff coming from his mouth as he kept up a lively conversation with Cuttin Jeff.

Before I knew it, Cuttin Jeff's monotone voice lulled me to sleep. I was still thinking about Miss Jubilee—her hair, the gigantic sinkhole in her backyard, and whether she was a living being or one of those kind spirits Grandma always talked about. Questions swirled in my head like the planets in the solar system. I wouldn't ever forget what I'd heard and felt that day, nor the horrific tragedy that had befallen Miss Jubilee's family.

That night, Grandma and I sat in the front yard. We loved sitting there together, especially after sewing, savoring the symphony of crickets and katydids and the warmth of the setting sun on our faces. The sweet smell of sap emanating from the Alabama pines when it hit the almost-night air made us breathe in a little deeper. It was the perfect time to tell Grandma what had transpired with Miss Jubilee. I tried to gather my thoughts, then said, "I gave Miss Jubilee her quilt just like you tell me, and I braided her hair and I don't even remember it, Grandmama. She told me her mama and papa see me, but I ain't seen them. I got scared, that's why I comb her hair."

Grandma peered through me as though I were glass, and I felt she was seeing straight to my soul. After all, I'd delivered the quilt to Miss Jubilee, and I guess Grandma knew that Miss Jubilee would share with me both the joys and the sorrows of receiving such a special gift.

"You knows Miss Jubilee gots a healin' spirit. Folks go to her all the time 'cause she knows how to heals most what's ailin' folks," Grandma said. "She gots the Lord's favor too. Been knowin' Miss Jubilee for a long time now. She been 'round almost fo'ever. Mos' folks don' knows how old she is. I suspect Miss Jubilee gives you her story 'cause she don' ever wants you to forget what happen to her fam'ly. You the one who gone carry it with you. You hear me talkin' to you, chile? You the one gone tell it; you gone tell all of it one of these days."

12

'Twixt Laurel and Livin'ston

THE STORIES I HEARD from old folks like Miss Jubilee, who were born and raised down in the country, supplied my mind with enough history to fill a library two times over. Five years in Alabama had made me a walking repository of local superstitions, ghost stories, and tales of slavery. Whether I was sitting in the front yard with Grandma, eavesdropping on grown folks' conversation, or sitting with Miss Jubilee and the other elders, I always listened intently.

I was especially thirsty for more of what I called Grandma's "Miss'ippi stories," the ones about her life in Laurel, Mississippi. Grandma had passed on a wide assortment of information about others, but I longed to know more about *her*, both before and after marrying Grandpa and having children. I never tired of hearing about her relationship with the Murphy family, whom she'd started working for in Laurel when she wasn't much older than me.

A family photo of the Murphy family sat on the mantelpiece, tucked in between the many pictures of my grandparents' children and grandchildren. Doc Murphy was dressed in a grayish suit that looked too small for his frame, a starched shirt, and no tie. A long-faced woman sat snuggled beside him in a dark wing-backed chair, and two children stood in front of them: a little pasty-faced boy with two missing front teeth, and a little girl with pigtails and ribbons tied into crooked bows. I thought the picture frame was much prettier than the folks in the picture.

In her grandmotherly stern voice, Grandma immediately responded to my thoughts: "Chile, I don' never wants to hear you talking mean 'bout folks. Pretty is as pretty does."

Every chance I got, I'd go through the black-and-white photos in the chifforobe with, as Grandma would say, a fine-tooth comb. Eventually, she told me the identity of each person in the twenty-five or so photos. Sometimes she'd spend hours describing how each one walked, talked, and dressed, with a snippet of their life thrown in for good measure.

Of all the pictures in her collection, a photo of a woman named Evelyn most captivated me. Evelyn was the daughter of Grandma's best friend, Miss Missouri, and she looked regal. In the photo, she sat on a lovely flowered sofa, legs crossed, a long cigarette holder clutched between two fingers. I felt her eyes drawing me in. Whenever I looked at her picture, I saw the same look in them that I saw in Grandma's and Miss Jubilee's eyes. They possessed a quiet strength, but at the same time, a heartache from years of grieving. A painful story lay behind Miss Evelyn's stare, and I wanted to find out what it was.

I longed to know, too, the reasons Grandma compared me to Miss Evelyn. She would often tell me, "Chile, if you ain't the spittin' image of Miss Evelyn, lookin' at you whilst you sittin' over there with your nose in that book, I don' know what. When Evelyn was a youngun, every time I see that gal, she gots a book plastered to her face and always using them fancy big words."

I also loved learning elaborate vocabulary and could barely wait for Miss Clay to give me my assigned fifty advanced words every Monday. I'd look them up in the dictionary, enunciate them, then use each one in a sentence. I had an expansive vocabulary and, believe me, I used those cherished words at every opportunity.

My classmates thought I was unusual because sometimes I'd isolate myself, sit on the school steps, and read the encyclopedia front to back, rather than joining in a game of tag or baseball. A few times Miss Clay was so concerned by my lack of involvement with the other kids that she put a lock on the bookshelf during recess. I overheard her talking to Grandma about these tendencies, but Grandma would only say, "Well, this chile jus' gots old folks' soul, that's alls I can tells you, Miss Clay."

On that day in 1962, the sun had barely shown its face. I lay sprawled out on the cotton feather bed, listening to the early sounds of morning. I heard Grandma in the kitchen, banging pots and pans, singing "Danny Boy." She seemed to sing from a distant place and time, for the people who were no longer in her life. I could feel the contentment in each note—I knew it was for those who were no longer here or near. I could've melted like butter and soaked right into the mattress as her voice trailed off in the distance.

When I peeked out the screen door, I saw that Grandma had already set a bag of clothes out in the front yard for quilting. By the time Grandpa and I had eaten breakfast, she was in her favorite rocker, selecting pieces of clothing. I pulled my straight-back chair close enough to count every mole on her forehead. But before I had a chance to open my mouth and ask about the quilt, Grandma spoke. She told me that she'd dreamed about my mother, who was named Evelyn, last night, which in turn reminded her how much she missed her friend Evelyn. It was as though Grandma was saying that she'd raised two Evelyns, one by birth, the other like a surrogate daughter.

She said the Lord put it on her mind to tell me an important story of her days in Laurel, and began by telling me how she'd ended up working for the Murphy family in the late 1890s, not long after losing Ella. I had a feeling that behind her tiny gray-blue eyes, a heaping cupful of sadness was waiting.

By the spring of 1926, Grandma had had her third and fourth child. This was the year my mother, Evelyn, and her twin brother, Edward, came barreling into the world. It was a difficult birth, because my mother was trying to make her presence known by coming out breach: butt first. If it wasn't for Old Miss Callie, a midwife said to have delivered most all the Black children within a twenty-mile radius of Livingston, I can't imagine what would've happened. Fortunately, Miss Callie lived over on Moore Place. Grandpa couldn't get the two mules hitched fast enough to retrieve her.

My mother was named after the daughter of Grandma's friend Miss Missouri. Grandma's other children, Sarah and Edgar, were almost teenagers by the time my mother was born. Her son Charlie was born two years after my mother, and my aunt Phyllis, the baby of the family, was born six years after my mother.

"Direc'ly after your mama was born, me an' Edgar starts callin' your mama Sista. Your grandpa starts callin' her that first; 'fore you know it, all of us callin' her Sista. I name Edward after Edgar's brother, who was killed in the war. Edward come outta me right after your mama. He jus' a big pretty baby: black as night, eyes big and roun' like saucers. Bottoms of his hands and feets pretty near dark as the rest of him. The purtiest thing you ever wanna see; skin smooth as corn silk. So I call him Beauty 'cause I don' want him to never forget how purty he is. Till this day, everybody I know call him Beauty."

Missouri's daughter Evelyn was much younger than Grandma, almost like another one of her children. When Evelyn became an adult, she taught at the only Black school in Laurel. She even turned her kitchen into a school, where she'd teach adult African American men and women to read and write in the evenings. On the weekends, she'd sometimes help Grandma out at the Murphy place. Grandma would constantly tell me what a hard worker Evelyn was, how she was able to rise above all the difficulties that she faced, including losing her mother at a young age.

Miss Missouri passed away when she was barely forty, and Evelyn was sent to live with her mother's sister, Glory, in Hattiesburg. Evelyn reportedly had an older sister, but her whereabouts were unknown. Why exactly Miss Missouri had sent her older daughter away was a big mystery. The question of where the child had ended up fueled wild speculation and grapevine talk. It was a fact, however, that Evelyn and her older sister didn't have the same father.

Grandma remembered well when Miss Missouri sent Evelyn's big sister away. Miss Missouri told Grandma that she'd sent the child to live with the little girl's grandparents because she felt she would be better off. A couple years later, Evelyn was born. The first time Grandma met Miss Missouri, they were children growing up on the Young plantation in Sandersville, Jones County, Mississippi. Miss Missouri had come down with cholera when she was younger than me. Grandma's mama, Emma, fed her heavy doses of herbs, which drove the cholera right out of her.

Grandma left Sandersville at thirteen to work for the Williams family as a nursemaid in Laurel, about ten miles north. When Grandma went to work for the Murphy family, she tried to get Miss Missouri to come with her, but Miss Missouri decided to stay right there in Sandersville.

It was a well-known fact in Jones County that Evelyn's papa was a white man. Folks also knew that this man was living off and on with Miss Missouri, almost like husband and wife, until the day Miss Missouri passed on. Evelyn was about ten, and losing her mother so abruptly hurt her to the core. She would talk about her mother constantly. Grandma would say that was why Evelyn worked so hard, to redirect her grief over her mother's passing.

I had an enormous longing to meet Miss Evelyn, especially when Grandma would talk about how she was the most God-fearing, foot-stomping, holy-ghost-riding, pipe-smoking, running-off-at-the-mouth woman you'd ever want to meet. When Miss Evelyn was talking, Grandma told me, you couldn't get a word in edgewise.

Now, Evelyn's father was Jim Mullens, but everyone called him Red. He was a first-generation Irishman, born in Ireland. His son, Evelyn's half-brother Donald, was married to Doc Murphy's sister Kathleen. When Evelyn was a young girl, Ant Glory would often bring her to the Murphy place. Evelyn would stay with Grandma most of the day, until Miss Glory returned to pick her up and take her back to Hattiesburg, a three-hour ride by horse and wagon.

Miss Murphy never had a problem with Evelyn hanging round the house. What was there to say? She was family and a spitting image of the rest of the Mullens clan. Jim Mullens's hair was as red as the crimson four-o'clock flowers that bloomed in my grandma's garden. His skin was white as cornstarch. In contrast, Miss Missouri was Blacker than coal. Evelyn inherited her father's red hair and freckles on both jaws. She was tall and big-boned, with honey-colored skin and a pointy nose.

But Lord—that mouth! Evelyn was assertive, Grandma told me, and could be very boisterous. Her self-image and the womanly confidence she exuded was overwhelmingly positive. She never wanted to hear about what she wasn't capable of doing or places she couldn't go. It was like talking to a brick chimney. She was determined to accomplish everything she set her mind to. This was why Grandma named my mother after her. Grandma wanted her girls to have their own minds and be able to shoulder the load, whatever life threw at them.

Jim, Evelyn's father, was known far and wide for his mean streak. He was stubborn as a mule, and, like Evelyn, he never allowed anyone to dictate his next move. Many of these attributes Evelyn came by honestly—passed down from Jim. Jim was also a man who never minimized his relationship with Evelyn's mother or denied that Evelyn was his child. Grandma told me he would sometimes take Evelyn with him to the old country for two weeks during the summer when she was a girl. She spent that time in Ireland as a seamstress for his wife, whom he married right after Miss Missouri died. That was how Evelyn learned about Irish culture.

Truth be told, Jim Mullens didn't want Evelyn working for the Murphys. He thought it beneath her. Evelyn's education was bought and paid for, her papa made sure of that. She went to the best school in upstate New York. When Jim and his wife hosted parties and large affairs, Miss Evelyn would attend and sing old folk songs that he'd taught her:

Casey Jones,
A mighty man was he.
Casey Jones runs his fine locomotive
With the cannonball special on the old I. C.

The faces of the whites who witnessed Evelyn's singing and dancing were postcard-worthy. Their mouths opened so wide, our mule, old Bob, could have walked through untouched. The only thing they could do was stare as she danced and sang..

Grandma would often snicker at the thought of Miss Evelyn's wise talk. She had a way of using Irish phrases like her daddy, then throwing in some "cullud-folk talk" for good measure. Grandma would get a kick out of trying to mimic her. I'd try my best to imagine how she sounded, but at nine years old, I had no idea what it meant to have an Irish accent or act Irish.

I believe Grandma's relationship with Evelyn relieved some of the stress she experienced while trying to balance care for her own family with that of the Murphy family. Miss Evelyn was

Grandma's catharsis; she entertained Grandma with her singing and dancing, her energy and humorous spirit. This must've
been a blessing during those years. Miss Evelyn's effervescent
personality offset the weight of worry from Grandma's travels
between Livingston and Laurel.

"Working for Doc Murphy got to be some kinda hard on
me and Edgar," Grandma told me. "Up and down that road,
'twixt Laurel and Livin'ston. It come a time I had six chil'ren
and Edgar was doing mighty poorly. But I had to make a way.
I want all my chil'ren to get proper schoolin', especially the
girls. So I had to work for Doc Murphy and see the chil'ren
when I could.

"I do thank the Lord he hired Cooter to help out. It sho nuff
took a load off me. Then Evelyn helpin' out when she can. But
by the time I'm carryin' your mama and Beauty, I can barely
walk by nightfall. Like I told you 'fore, I almos' met my maker
bringin' them two chil'ren into the world. They almost five
when I go to Doc Murphy and flat-out tells him, 'Doc Murphy,
I'm gonna have to turn you loose. My babies still young and
they needs they mama in the worst way now. Hurts me sorely
to leave my younguns, and Edgar ain't spry like he used to be.
And me going up and down that road 'twixt here and Livin'ston
in a wagon and two mules every Friday got me plumb tuckered
out most of the time.'

"Chile, that man look at me, then look at the floor, then
he look at me agin, jus' likes he wants to cry. He says, 'Miss
Lula, you've been good to me and my family. You helped me
bring all my children into the world. I'd do anything to keep
you working for me.'"

There was a long pause. A smile crossed Grandma's face,
and she inhaled deeply before spitting a chunk of brown goo
into the spit-can I'd made for her.

"Doc Murphy take a deep breath and tells me that if I
stay, he gone hire me a driver to take me to Livin'ston every
Friday mo'nin' and brang me back on Sunday evening. I looks

him straight in the eye and tells him, 'Doc Murphy, you a good man.' Then I tells him I jus' don' know how white folks gone act when they see a cullud woman ridin' back and forth 'twixt Laurel and Livin'ston in a fine-lookin' 'mobile like the one he gots outside."

Doc Murphy let out a wide, mischievous grin when she told him about her concerns. "Don't you worry one bit about that, Miss Lula," he told her. "You gonna be just fine. If you have *any* problems at all, I want you to let me know."

Grandma told Grandpa about Doc Murphy's offer, and he was happy; their daughters were getting older, and Grandpa would always complain about the "gals needin' they mama." But the kids weren't too pleased with the decision. They missed their mama and wanted her home all the time. Still, when Grandma gave me the backstory about Doc Murphy, it made me love him almost as much as she did. His parents had emigrated from Ireland to the United States in the late 1860s, when he was a child. His father was known by everyone as Papa Murphy. Papa Murphy had rosy cheeks, a robust laugh, and a big belly. Every time he laughed, his stomach shook like a bowl of freshly made Jell-O. He loved smoking his pipe, which was more a part of him than the clothes on his back. He went out of this world lying in bed with a pipe stuck in his mouth. The family didn't remove it. They buried him just as he was, pipe and all.

Papa Murphy was a preacher who could outpreach a lot of the Black preachers around Mississippi. Grandma said he was the only white preacher that ever preached at the church she attended. When the Reverend Papa Murphy started preaching, he'd set the pulpit on *fire*. All the women and half the men folk would be shouting to creation.

The Murphy family came from a huge, extremely wealthy Irish clan. Some of Doc Murphy's extended family members didn't stay in Mississippi upon their arrival in the country. Instead, they ended up moving north. Doc Murphy didn't need Mississippians' money. When he and his family came from across the waters, they brought a ton of money with them. They also invested heavily in American textile and manufacturing businesses. Doc Murphy attended the best schools and became one of the most prominent doctors in the South. Grandma would show me the yellowed newspaper clippings about him and his family, which she'd kept for years. One of the Murphy men started the first Black school in Laurel. Miss Evelyn taught at that very school.

By the summer of 1931, Grandma was in her late forties and by no means a spring chicken. Her twins had just turned five. And sure enough, as Doc Murphy had promised, he hired a Black man named Stump to take Grandma home every Friday afternoon and return her by early evening on Sunday. Their mode of transportation was a fancy-looking riding machine, a brand-new automobile used almost exclusively to take Grandma to and from her family.

"Sho nuff fancy, too," Grandma told me. "I used to sit back and watch the countryside go by. Di'n't take long at all to see my chil'ren. Better than a wagon and mule that took forever to get from Laurel to Livin'ston. Except for the times when your cuttin Jeff would take me back and forth. I sure did appreciate him for that. It gave them two old mules time to rest up, 'cause they on they las' leg, tha's why we had to stop more times than I can count. Bless Doc Murphy for makin' it so I can get home to spend more time with Edgar and the chil'ren.

"Well, one day we on the road somewhere 'twixt Laurel and Livin'ston, so quiet, won't hard to hear the crickets in the trees. The sun was shinin' bright, robins singin' themself to death. Outta nowheres, I looked up the road and see this big white fella standin' in the road wavin' his hands, jus' like this here. Look like he havin' conniptions. He got one of them 'mobiles like us. Stump stop that 'mobile so fast, I almost fell over on the floor.

"Now, Stump a big man, with the biggest hands and arms you ever seen in your life. He jus' as tall as that pine tree up yonder. Stump jus' sit there while the man walk up to the 'mobile where we sittin'. He got so close I can see that shiny tin star barely hangin' on his shirt with the sun beatin' off it. Like your grandpa, he chewin' on a toothpick. Stump tells him, 'Good day, Sheriff.'

"Stump the most proper cullud man I seen in my day. Not a word outta place. Sheriff leaned in that 'mobile like he huntin' for possum: eyes redder than this shirt I'm sewin' on right here, and he got on a red shirt matchin' his eyes. 'Where y'all on your way to?' he asks. 'Who this automobile belong to, boy? Why that nigger gal in back there? Well, speak up, boy; you got a tongue, dontcha?'

"Me and Stump both sit straight up like an arrow. Stump says, 'Sheriff, this is the house and nursemaid for Doctor Murphy of Laurel, Mississippi. He pays me to take her home every week to see her husband and young children and return her to Mississippi by five every Sunday evening. Can I answer any more questions for you, Sheriff?'

"That Stump, he bright as they come, and Doc Murphy like him might'ly. Sheriff look at me sittin' in the back of that 'mobile and looks me up and down jus' like this here."

Grandma demonstrated how the sheriff eyed her, staring, eyes bulging like he'd never seen a Black woman in his life.

"I sit there quiet as a tick on cotton, just waitin' for him to go on 'bout his bizness. He says, 'Y'all gone now, 'fore I change my mind 'bout letting y'all through and haul y'all's Black asses to jail jus' 'cause I feel like it. But I'm gone be watching y'all niggers every time you come this way, ya hear? Jus' ain't right, you sittin' there jus' like you a white woman or something.'

"Every time we go 'twixt Laurel and Livin'ston, Lord knows, that mean sheriff get meaner and meaner. Sometime he jus' make us get out and stand in the hot sun till he feel like lettin' us go on our way. Sometime, if we lucky, he might let us sit down on the side of the road in a teeny bit a shade, 'cause Lord knows it's blisterin' hot. He always sayin' he wants to keep his eye on us; don' want us outta his sight.

"Now, chile, where do he think we goin' with him sittin' up there with that pistol on his hip? We don' want him to start shootin' while we on these back roads. He could bury us both back up in them woods and nobody never finds us. 'Scuse me, Lord, but he must think we fools. I watched him sittin' in his 'mobile, or sometimes he sit under a shade tree, drinkin' a jar of water while we sit in the boilin' sun. Then jus' like regular, he come over and, like every other time, he smart-mouth me and Stump. Don' even allow us to get a drank of water that we got sitting in the jar in the back of our 'mobile on the flo'.

"'I'm gone let y'all leave now,' he says. 'I'm gettin' tired of all this rigmarole you keep fillin' me up with.'"

"I takes out my clean hankychief from my apron pocket and wipes my face and tries to straighten my sweaty clothes up on me. I thanks that sheriff every time: 'An' you have a mighty good day, Sheriff; we don' mean to raise no ruckus; jus' goin' to see my babies, tha's all.' Chile, me and Stump so glad to feel that water goin' down our throat it wa'n't funny."

The distance between Laurel and Livingston was a little over a hundred miles. During that era, it could end up being a six- or seven-hour trip, especially traveling over dirt roads. Grandma and Stump would leave around nine in the morning and get to the country around three or four o'clock that afternoon. Sometimes they wouldn't get there until after dark. When you factor in a sheriff who spent hours humiliating them, I can't even begin to imagine how miserable it must've been, or how much extra time was lost.

"Sometimes he stop us comin' and goin'," Grandma said. "Sometime jus' when we headed to Livin'ston. I reckon he comes to know every time we comin' up and down that road. It got so where Stump would jus' roll his eyes like so. Stump a young man, so he despise dealin' with that sheriff's foolishness. Every time I gets in the back of that 'mobile, I close my eyes and take it to the Lord in prayer.

"Chile, I left so many prayers on that road 'twixt here an' Laurel. I pray that my family don' find us hung from one of them sycamores or jus' laid out in the middle of the road from that Alabama heat. I can't say nothin', chile, 'cause I don' want Doc Murphy to think I don' 'preciate what he done for me and Edgar. I figure I be better off jus' puttin' up with ol' sheriff and all his foolishness. I don' want to be worse off. I sure can't say nothin' to Edgar, else he gone worry his self crazy. He already doin' poorly and got them chil'ren to look after. Jus' had to turn it over to the Lord; that's much as this poor soul can do."

Late summer rolled in and the sheriff continued pulling them over almost every week. As I listened, I felt hostility building in my heart. It was a humiliating story, and I was powerless to ease my grandmother's past hurts. All the while she was unpacking the story, my mind drifted. I saw Grandma's predicament as her being trapped and not able to move, and in my youthfulness, I knew very well what that was like. I thought about how badly I'd wanted to ask the people in the car on that long ride from Detroit where I was going, and I imagined Grandma's situation being a hundred times worse. I wanted to take revenge on Sheriff Suggs. I wanted him to suffer for all my grandma had endured.

Later, I'd feel ashamed of these thoughts. But daydreaming was the way I managed feelings over which I had no control and situations I couldn't yet comprehend. With some stories Grandma told, I'd change parts in my mind, especially when people were hurt or feeling pain. I'd replace those pieces and craft a happier ending, and that's exactly what I did with Sheriff Suggs. I sent him to a place from which he could never return—and never do harm to anyone ever again. That was how I forgave.

I never told Grandma about these horrible thoughts. But I'd just finished imagining the sheriff's slow demise, and Grandma must've noticed my mind drifting. She stopped unexpectedly, right in the middle of her story, to chastise me.

"Now, chile, I don' ever want to see you hol' onto that, you hear me? 'Cause being cross will kill you; I see it in your face, in your eyes, and your spirit, chile. Grandma wants you to let that go right now; throw it right down there in that dirt and let the Lord carry it 'way from you."

I tried to do as Grandma asked and let the anger float down the hill from the front yard to the banks of my spring, to let the blue waters wash it away. But I wasn't yet ready.

If daydreaming was my way of escaping to a happier place, singing was Grandma's. The tale of Sheriff Suggs must have begun to take its toll on her, too, because she belted out one of her favorite songs, a hymn I'd heard her sing many times before when something lay heavy on her heart:

It's me, it's me, it's me, oh Lawd,
Standing in the need of prayer.
Tire and weary, but it's me, oh Lawd,
Standing in the need of prayer.
Not my mother or my sista but it's me, oh Lawd,
Standing in the need of prayer.

Our hearts beat simultaneously, in rhythm, as the song rolled from her lips.

There were times when Grandma would stop in the middle of a story and tell me I needed to learn to walk in someone else's shoes. For years, I took that literally. I'd slip my feet into Grandpa's hunting boots and tromp around the farm like a soldier going to war. When I visited Great Ant Tudney, I spotted a pair of her shoes and slid my bare feet into them. She looked at me like I'd lost my mind. I'd even walk around with a stranger's shoes on, to try to capture what Grandma was trying to tell me.

Once, when I went to town with Grandpa, he caught me wearing the shoes of one of the old men he was playing checkers with. The man had placed his shoes next to the fireplace, and when I spotted them, I couldn't help myself: I wanted to see how ol' Mr. Ned's shoes felt on my feet. But all I could feel were the grains of dirt that had settled in the bottom and a hole in the sole so big the cold floor touched my toes. I looked as goofy as could be.

"Chile, if you don' take Ned's shoes off yo' feet, I'm gone tan that hide. And if you ev'n look lak you gwine cry, um gwine give you somethin' to cry 'bout."

I knew Grandpa was just talking. He only whupped me once. Most times, I could just about do anything and he'd look the other way.

It would be a couple of years before I'd begin to grasp what Grandma was trying to say to me. But as I reflected on what she'd endured on that road 'twixt Laurel and Livingston, I could almost feel the sweat rolling down her back as she sat in the hot sun. I was there, too, waiting with her alongside that road. In the farmhouse yard, she eyed the quilt in her lap and smiled. And I longed to understand her depth of forgiveness.

"I gets so tired," she told me. "Went through a heap of trials and tribulation in them times. I felt right poorly for Stump. He so proud 'cause he got proper book learnin'. It jus' wa'n't right for that boy to put up with that kinda mess. I pray so hard that I could jus' make things right 'cause that boy ain't done nothin' to nobody. I always try to take some of the load off him 'twixt him and that sheriff, 'cause that boy sho nuff had a rough row to hoe. Lord knows he did.

"So, I always talked to him while we sit there, 'cause I see his spirit gettin' rile' up, lil by lil. I spot it in his eyes. He ain't say much 'bout it; he knows he can't, neither. So he jus' try to stay quiet. I jus' don' know how long I can keep him like that. Don' want nothin' happenin' to that boy; don' know what I'd do. I calls him to pray with me while we sat there in that hot sun. He minds what I say. I was glad 'bout that. That sheriff one sorry fella, but Lawd, did I pray for him too, both day and night, 'cause I don' know how long this gone go on. But he still sit there and watch us from his 'mobile, and when he get a-hankerin' for us to go on down the road, he comes waddlin' over: 'Y'all get.' I thanks him, then Stump starts the 'mobile and we on our way.

"It was getting on late in the evenin' one day while we tearin' down the road tryin' might'ly to get to Doc Murphy before nightfall; we runnin' way late. By the time we make it to Doc Murphy, we run smack into Evelyn sittin' on the back porch with the chil'ren. She smokin' and suckin' on her pipe so hard like it gone be her las' time smokin'. When she see me and Stump, we just drippin' sweat likes a boar hog. She looks me straight in the eye and says, 'Miss Lula, y'all three hours late. Matter fact, don't think I haven't noticed how you've been late almost every other week.'

"Chile, Evelyn commence to goin' on and on 'bout us being way late. She jus' ain't gone leave well enough alone. I done already explained to you jus' how Evelyn is when she gets onto somethin'. She ain't gone give up for all the tea in China. So I says, 'Gone Stump, gone home to ya fam'ly while me and Miss Evelyn talk.'"

Grandma said it wasn't no use trying to hide anything from Miss Evelyn, because she had a nose for trouble.

"'Begging your pardon, Miss Lula; but can you please, ma'am, tell me what's going on? Can't let you go no further; *I must know*. When I look at you and Stump, both of you standing there soaking wet like you all been dipped in a creek. I know it's Sunday, and I also know that neither of you went to a baptizing this evening.'"

Grandma felt that she had no choice but to tell Miss Evelyn everything. She ended up telling her the long, drawn-out story "from the rooter to the tooter," all about the sheriff and how he'd been hounding them since spring.

"Now summer *almost over*! It's been that long, Miss Lula? Lord have mercy!"

Grandma rose from her seat to show me Miss Evelyn's reaction to her story.

"Evelyn like a mad, wet hen, flappin' 'round like so. Them frecklies on her face look like they slidin', ready to jump off. She done took that pipe she smokin' and throws it 'cross the yard; madder than a bull who jus' sees red. Miss Evelyn's I'ish talk commence to comin' out now: 'Miss Lula, my papa told me that folks who do evil, dat cat need to eat dem and then let the devil eat the cat.'"

Miss Evelyn and Grandma sat in Doc Murphy's kitchen, talking for hours. The next morning, Miss Evelyn peeped her head in the back door of the Murphy house, smiling like a Cheshire cat, dressed up in her ruffled dress with its high collar and a matching bright blue hat with lace and feathers jutting from the headband. Grandma loved the way Miss Evelyn dressed. Whether she was going to market, church, or to teach, her clothes were immaculate. When she walked down the hill to the Black school, she was the envy of every person in Laurel.

"'Good morning, Miss Lula; I'm on my way to school right now—running a little behind, but my students can wait. I wanted to drop in on you for a minute to make sure you're alright this morning. You and Stump looked awfully tired last evening. Miss Lula, I also want you to know that you won't ever have to worry about your predicament with this sheriff anymore. Now, that's my final word'."

Doc Murphy returned from his out-of-town business trip later that day. As always, he came right to the kitchen, rifling through the pots Grandma had on the stove. He absolutely loved Grandma's cooking and would always go on and on about missing her food whenever he was away. It wasn't unusual for Doc Murphy and his wife to talk to Grandma about the kids, food, and how all the folks who worked for them were doing. The Murphys thought of Grandma as part of their extended family and never hesitated to tell her that.

It was early Friday morning, around seven-thirty, and Stump came by earlier than usual. Normally, he picked Grandma up for her trip to Livingston about ten. This time, when he came to the kitchen door, he told Grandma that he wouldn't be driving her anymore. He said Doc Murphy had hired another man to be her driver, because there was other business he wanted Stump to take care of. He told Grandma how sorry he was he wouldn't be driving her and left.

This caught Grandma by surprise. He'd been driving her back and forth for the past six months. But she didn't want to question Stump. He looked sad enough as it was.

Grandma was still reeling from the shock as she prepared for her trip home. It was late morning, so, as usual, she cooked up enough food for Doc Murphy and the children to tide them over for the weekend. Doc Murphy had left town again, so Grandma didn't get a chance to see him before she left. But recently, he'd hired a woman named Dora to help with the cooking and cleaning on the days Grandma was gone. Miss Evelyn pitched in during the late evenings after Dora left for the day. Grandma thought the world of Dora, because of the abundance of energy she brought to the household, not to mention how much she resembled Ella. She was more capable of chasing the Murphy children around the house, too, because she had young legs.

That day, Grandma grabbed the cookies she'd made for her children and rushed out the back door to the car. As she adjusted her hat, she almost walked into a smiling white man with the biggest grin you'd ever seen. He stood there, holding the door open for her.

"Good morning, Miss Lula," he said. "My name is Paul Lee and I'm here to take you to Livingston. I'll be back by noon Sunday to pick you up, if that's alright by you. You 'bout ready?"

Grandma was so glad she didn't have snuff in her mouth, else it would have spilled out all over the front of her clothes. She couldn't move. The man had to come over and take her arm to escort her to the automobile door. What would that sheriff think when he saw this big white fella driving a Black woman through Mississippi?

As the car made its way down the road, right before crossing over into Alabama, as sure as night turns into day, there was the sheriff's automobile parked on the side of the road. He stood there, waving his hands.

There was a twinkle in my Grandma's eyes as she described what happened next. She took a deep breath and spit into her snuff can. If I moved an inch closer to the edge of my seat, I would've fallen onto my ass. The anticipation was killing me.

"When that ol' sheriff get near, I see his face beet red; looks like he seen a ghost when he sees Paul Lee climb out that 'mobile. 'Hi,' Paul says, 'how you doing, Sheriff? My name's Paul Lee. Sure do look like rain. Hopes it's enough to water my crops, because we only got a smidgen yesterday.'

"That sheriff still ain't open his mouth. He ain't pay Paul Lee no mind. He commence to comin' 'round where I'm sittin'. Chile—that man took his hat off his head and gives me cordials. 'Hi you, Miss Lula?'

"'I'm a kickin', Sheriff, but not high—how you this mo'nin'?' You shoulda seen that man, he just a standin' there skinnin' and a grinnin' wider than that road 'twixt here and Laurel. I thought I was gone pass out.

"'I'm doing fine,' the sheriff said. 'Doing just fine, Miss Lula. Just want to make sure y'all alright. Now, Miss Lula, I hears from folks who live in Livingston and about that you makes the best tea cakes and pecan candy in the whole damn South. I'd sho be obliged if you could make me a taste next time you come through here. I hear your vittles and fixins some kinda good, too. Makes a hound dog beg for possum.'

"'I sure will, Sheriff. Gonna make sure you get some next time I see you. Now, Sheriff, you know my candies made from black molasses—you gotta watch how much you eat of that molasses, you might just get the runs, but will keep you reg'lar, though, and you don' have to worry 'bout gittin' no piles.'

"'Yes, ma'am Miss Lula. My missus can barely cook a lick 'cept for flapjacks. I love to smother them cakes in molasses and butter. So I knows what you talkin' 'bout, 'cause I love any kind of molasses. I'm mighty grateful, Miss Lula, if you can bring me some. Now, y'all better get on your way, 'cause wouldn't want you to get caught up in the storm that's comin'—look at them storm clouds rollin' in. It's sho nuff gone pour down.'"

I couldn't believe what I'd just heard. Did Grandma mean to tell me the sheriff went from "nigger this" and "nigger that" to sharing recipes? My mind blazed. Grandma seemed to understand. She said, "The Lord softened his heart, chile. Wa'n't nothin' but the Lord. Sometimes you jus' don' know what you don' know. Then sometime the Lord gone put somebody in your path for a reason. Don' never doubt what the Lord can do, you hear me, chile?"

I was still learning what the Lord was capable of doing. For the life of me, I couldn't understand how He swooped down and turned that devilish sheriff into an angel so quickly. But Grandma claimed that from that day on, Sheriff Suggs became one of the nicest men you'd ever want to meet. She continued to be driven back and forth between Laurel and Livingston for years, and the sheriff continued to meet their car on the back roads to talk. He even invited Grandma to his home to meet his wife, Miss Mollie, who fell in love with Grandma and her quilts. Every now and then, when Grandma was on her way back to Laurel, she'd peek in on Miss Mollie for a spell. Before long, Grandma was making Sheriff Suggs and his family quilts for his wife's folks who'd passed on and giving Miss Mollie her recipes for pies and cakes.

Miss Mollie told Grandma that her mama had been very sickly and had died when Mollie was only fourteen. Her mother never had the opportunity to teach her to cook. By the time Grandma finished with Miss Mollie, she could cook like a pro.

In the early 1940s, Grandma left Doc Murphy for good. Miss Mollie cried like a baby when Grandma told her she wouldn't be working there any longer. But my grandparents' youngest daughter, Phyllis, was ten years old, and my mother, Evelyn, was close to finishing high school and had been accepted into Alabama Teachers College.

Grandma had worked for years, saving for her children's college education. Her three oldest children had married and moved north, and Grandpa had gotten bad off with his asthma and rheumatism and was laid up quite a bit. Grandma just didn't feel right leaving him in his worsening condition. Even after Grandma left Doc Murphy, Miss Mollie would come to the country and visit with her. They'd sit in the front yard while Grandma worked on her quilts and hummed.

Sheriff Suggs passed away a couple years after Grandma stopped working. Ironically, Miss Mollie ended up bringing all of his old clothes for Grandma to make into a quilt of souls. Miss Mollie explained that she wanted Grandma to sew the quilt instead of her, because she wanted Grandma's hands on it. She asked her to please remember him the way he ended up, rather than the way he used to be. She said she wanted to sit with Grandma when she was ready to work on the quilt and tell her the whole awful story of Sheriff Suggs's childhood while Grandma stitched. She said, "You'll understand then, Miss Lula."

Grandma agreed to wait. But she was eager to hear his story. After Miss Mollie left, she reached her hand into the bag of clothes and picked up a few of the pieces. She could feel Sheriff Suggs's spirit and knew he was at peace. To me, she spoke of the red shirt he was wearing that day in the summer of 1927, the first day she ever laid eyes on him. There was anger in his eyes and evil in his heart that penetrated through the shirt.

Later Miss Mollie returned, just like she said, and as Grandma turned his clothing into a beautiful quilt of souls, Miss Mollie revealed to her the entire ordeal of Sheriff Suggs's life. And that's where Grandma stopped and returned the unfinished quilt to the croker sack. Significant pieces of Sheriff Suggs's story remained untold. I likened it to the missing pieces in my quilt. Grandma was incredibly selective in her placement of fabric. Certain sections she worked around instead of filling in.

Like those gaps, I knew this wasn't the end of the life stories of Evelyn, Miss Mollie, or Sheriff Suggs. Grandma would revisit them—she always did. And if I tried to ask her before she was ready, she'd just say, "In due time, chile. In due time."

In silence, we sat in our front yard, feeling the warmth of the setting sun on our faces. The luscious smell of Grandma's four-o'clock flowers made my heart sing. And quietly, Grandma started singing her version of "Danny Boy." I'd later learn that this was a song often sung by Evelyn. The words were profound, and Grandma sang with precision and grace. Each note sent chills down my body. I saw myself in each stanza, because today I'd traveled down that road with her 'twixt Laurel and Livingston.

> But come ye back when summer's in the meadow
> Or when the valley's hushed and white with snow.
> I be here in sunshine or in shadow;
> Oh Danny Boy, Oh Danny Boy, I love you so.
> But if you come, and all the flowers are dying,
> And I am dead, as dead I well may be,
> You come find the place where I'm a lying
> And kneel and say an "Ave" there for me.

So much was left unsaid. I breathed in and exhaled the larger story that waited, close by. It had begun to grow; soon it would blossom and take shape in the shadow of the sun. I felt it so strongly I could have burst into a thousand pieces.

13

Bessie's Wrath

IT WAS FRIDAY MORNING, and I was up extra early. The day before, Grandma had told me that the fabulous Miss Sugar would come by right after school and take me to spend the weekend with her. My time with Miss Sugar was the only thing I loved as much as sitting with Miss Jubilee. Grandma reminded me not to dawdle on the way home because Miss Sugar wouldn't wait. "When Miss Sugar's ready to go, she's ready to go," with or without me, as Grandma made perfectly clear.

This would be the first time I'd gone to Miss Sugar's house on a Friday evening. Occasionally, she'd pick me up on a Saturday and drop me back at Grandma's on Sunday afternoon. But an extended period with her was a brand-new experience. Ever since Grandma told me, I couldn't think of anything else. The sound of Miss Sugar's car and the feel of climbing onto the warm leather seats hung in my consciousness. I could almost smell the fumes.

The long day allowed my mind to ramble over how I could get home faster than usual. I wanted to be there when Miss

Sugar pulled up to our door. I didn't want to miss her grand entrance, which was always priceless. At that moment, I decided to take the shortcut. This was such an elaborate, clandestine operation that it had to be carried out with precision. I didn't even tell Brenda, because if she slipped up and told her grand-mama, it would get back to my grandma through the country grapevine. As much as I loved Brenda, sometimes she could be prone to diarrhea of the mouth.

My dilemma was this: There was one path Grandma demanded I travel to and from Bethel Hill, and that was the long, out-of-the-way southern route. It was a straight, narrow dirt road, totally devoid of adventure. It took me over an hour to walk to and from school using this path. The Conkabayou route, however, was due west, through the woods, and took half that time.

My classmates didn't have to go anywhere near the Conk-abayou to get to their houses, because they only lived a hop, skip, and jump from Bethel Hill. I actually had to bypass their homes to reach this shortcut, crossing the dirt road in front of the school and zipping through the Moore Place community. If I went this way, in no time I'd be stepping foot inside my grandparents' backyard. But I'd also pass Ant Bessie's house, which sat about a mile from my grandparents' place and another mile from my school. The only thing that separated her property from our pasture was Grandpa's fishing pond. Since my grandpa and Ant Bessie were siblings, this stretch of land was jointly owned and considered "Horn" property.

The low-lying Conkabayou Bridge itself sat off the sparsely traveled Highway 28. A dark, brush-filled swamp about fifty feet below the bridge ran parallel with the road for nearly three miles. A stretch of this area, called "the Bottom," was murky marshland, shadowed by dense woods. At a certain point it transformed into acres of prime farmland. This path ran near Ant Bessie's property and was in the opposite direction of the path Grandma mandated I take to school every day, rain or shine.

One of the reasons Grandma didn't allow me to go this way was the violence that had once occurred there. All along the Conkabayou Bridge, African Americans had been lynched and brutally attacked and left for all to see. Sporadic incidents were still said to happen in the Bottom, and over the years I heard many folks, young and old, talk about the area with dread. I'd heard of bodies swinging from trees, being removed and buried right there. The area was supposedly scattered with unmarked, makeshift graves of people who'd died under excruciating and unimaginable conditions.

As my grandparents' friends and family sat in our front yard, discussing these atrocities, I'd lie under the house, listening. I'd heard the cries of men and women who came to our home to tell my grandparents about their loved ones, dragged from their houses in the middle of night, terrorized by members of the Klan or those the men called nightriders. Grandma would hug and pray with them.

The old folks spoke of the lost spirits of those who'd been murdered. At night, those spirits would roam the swamps of the Conkabayou, looking for peace. This kind of talk was pervasive in Livingston and the surrounding area. But I can't remember whether I was more saddened by the lonely spirits in search of closure or the hopelessness in my grandparents' eyes whenever someone talked about a family member who'd met their death below the Conkabayou. I could only imagine the despair these poor souls experienced—alone, afraid, and screaming from the end of a noose.

Even though heinous acts had been committed there, Grandma told me the Bottom was sacred. It would be disrespectful to trample over those poor souls' graves. Still, I was deeply curious. In addition to my thirst to know more, traveling this route would shave off fifteen minutes of walking time.

That Friday, for the first time in my life, Grandma and Grandpa's talk didn't deter me from taking the route through the Bottom. The thought of getting home early blacked out all fear, all shame. My greatest challenge and only concern was evading Ant Bessie's eagle eye. The path would take me extremely close to her little shanty, and it seemed she lived for catching me—or anybody else, for that matter—doing something they had no business at.

Still, my mind was made up. If caught, I would deal with the consequences later. I tried desperately to resist looking at the schoolroom clock, which stood high on the pale wall in the back of the class. That day, as I sat, trying to will time to speed up, I swear it had the world's loudest tick. I closed my eyes, hoping something magical would happen to move its black metal hands along.

Finally they landed on the three and twelve. Miss Clay hadn't gotten a chance to utter her usual "Have a nice weekend, children" before I took off over the hill. The last word I heard come from her mouth was "have." I ran faster than a gazelle, blazing a path through the Moore Place homestead and across Buzzards Creek. Adrenaline took over. I barely saw what was in front of me, and in an area of the Bottom that ran parallel to Ant Bessie's property, I ran full speed into what felt like a bed of spiderwebs.

My arms flailed wildly. I couldn't flee, and the smell was awful. I was trying to escape from something I couldn't see but could certainly feel. In the middle of a cotton field, I was all but frozen, wrestling with the air, crying frantically because I couldn't move anything but my arms and hands. Then, out of nowhere, I felt myself being lifted off the ground and tossed about twenty feet. I landed on top of a large mound of freshly picked cotton, stacked at the end of a row, and sat there, legs sprawled. Spit flew every which way as I cleared crisp strands of cotton from my bottom lip and tongue.

Just as I was about to launch myself up out of the stack, I saw Ant Bessie staring me straight in the face. I was caught, plain and simple. Instinctively, I knew there was no reasoning with her. At first, she just stood there, leaning on her five-foot walking stick, with her signature part straight down the middle of her scalp and two long metallic gray braids, one on each side. Her body was draped in her day-of-the-week apron, the one with the squirrels and nuts spread over the bib and apron pocket. It was her Wednesday apron. Her Monday apron was all red except for the bib. She never deviated; she'd never wear her Monday apron on Tuesday or her Thursday apron on Saturday.

"Git up from there and come right chere in front of me so I can get a good look at you. Now, I know Ma Lula don' bit mo' know you over this way than a man in the moon, do she?"

"No ma'am, Ant Bessie."

"So what you thank you doin' cuttin' through this yere pass? Ya know better. A chile's got no bizness down yere. Hell, that hi yalla nigga I had pickin' my field of cotton jus' left this big pile of cotton right yere, jus' took off. Tha's why these hi yalla niggas ain't worth a damn. No wonder Papa told me if um gone hire somebody's to work for me, don' never hire no hi yalla: ya find the Blackes' man you can, 'cause they works hard. Now you jus' get yoself rat on up to Ma Lula's. We gone see what she gots to say 'bout you bein' up in yere."

The only thing I could do was hold my head down while Ant Bessie led me to Grandma's like I was a prisoner on a chain gang. I made up my mind that day: Ant Bessie was two times eviler than Satan himself, and I feared her more than any living being that God put on this earth. I remembered Grandpa saying, "If you cut Bessie down the middle, if you waitin' on blood to come outta her, you be waitin' a long time, because the only thing gonna come out of her is ice water." I never understood until that day.

As we got closer to my grandparents' house, Ant Bessie took the lead. I dreaded facing Grandma and was terrified that the old tattletale would make me miss my trip to Miss Sugar's. The combination of going through a scary experience in the cotton field, missing my getaway, and disappointing Grandma—and, on top of all that, Ant Bessie's nasty attitude—weighed on my small shoulders like a bale of hay. I couldn't help but let the tears fall. I went right back to my days of cry-talking. "I'm sorry Ant Bessie, I won't cut 'cross your place no more. Please don't tell Grandma on me. I don't want no whupping...bahhhhh... please don't tell Grandma, bahhaaaaaaa..."

Again and again Ant Bessie turned, yelling at me to shut up or she'd "slap the Black off" of me.

We finally reached the backyard and, through tear-stained eyes, I made out Grandma coming down off the back porch. The screen door slammed loudly, which meant she was *really* concerned. Having heard my ear-piercing crying, she'd forgotten her own edict, which she'd uttered to me many times: "Chile, if I gots to tell you one more time 'bout lettin' that door slam! You won't born in a barn."

That day, Grandma didn't ask any questions. She just grabbed me up in her long arms, hugging me like she hadn't seen me in a hundred years. All the while, Ant Bessie's mouth went on a mile a minute: "This yere lil Black gal, I finds her layin' on a pile a cotton in my field over yonder near the Bottom. She justa wailin' and actin' like she got the conniptions or somethin'. I knows she been down there at the Bottom; tha's how she end up in that field. I knows you don' 'llow this gal to go that way. She knows she spose to go 'round Jeff Martin's prop'ty. She ain't spose to be nowheres near that place, Miss Lula."

I stood there, holding onto Grandma for dear life. Ant Bessie wouldn't shut up for nothing.

"She jus' actin' grown, like one of them fas' tail gals. I can tell you, that's what wrong with these yere chil'ren these days: they think they growner then they mamas and papas, and they don' think they shit stink. What they needs is a good strap on they backsides. I had to knock mine on they rump a few times, for that matter. Miss Lula, I thanks ya needs to send that chile rat on back up nawth to her mama and daddy, 'specially since she gettin' ol' now. Looks like to me, she don' wants to mind. Next thang you know, she gone come up pregnant."

"Bessie, I'm gone stop you right there. This chile hard-headed sometime, but she got ol' folks' soul and a heart of gold. She a special chile, jus' like my sista Ella. Now, Bessie, I wants you to go on in the front yard wit' Edgar, sit a spell, an take a load off. Bless yo' heart, you look like you gone fall out from chasin' this here chile. I be on direc'ly. I gots a piece of coconut cake on the little table off the kitchen; you welcome to it. Go on now, let me sit with this chile for a minute or two."

"Thank you, Miss Lula, I'm sho gone get me that piece a cake."

I was *so* glad to see the back of Ant Bessie's dress walking away from us. Grandma stood there, hugging me until every tear dried. When I began telling her what had happened, she said:

"Shush, chile. Grandma already know there spirits down yonder. You prob'ly got tossed by one of them. I tol' you 'bout your old folks' soul. You been casted. If spirits wanderin' anywhere 'round, you feels them, chile. They sho nuff 'round you, especially when you down there where all them cullud folks been kilt. Tha's why Grandma don' wants you down there; it's too much for a little bitty chile like you to understand, you hear me?"

As always, Grandma's voice of reason soothed my aching spirit to the point where I almost forgot why I'd gotten into such a mess in the first place. With Ant Bessie, as with Mama Nall, Grandma tried her best to make me see how it felt when a person is devoid of love, never hugged, when all affection has been and continues to be missing from their lives. I tried to imagine being without Grandma's hugs—it was inconceivable.

This was the summer of 1963, and in a couple of months I'd be turning ten. It was a period in my life when I was trying to learn how to manage disappointment and forgive-ness simultaneously. I'd try to understand Grandma's lessons and set myself in Ant Bessie's shoes. But it was as difficult as trying to squeeze my size five feet into a toddler's bootie.

Grandma always told me that each person I'd encounter along my journey, good or bad, would provide me with a learning experience. As I'd recounted to my classmates when telling them Miss Daisy's story, Grandma said that some leaves fall when the wind blows, but others stand strong, even through the most wicked of storms. She encouraged me to be the leaf that refused to fall.

Miss Sugar never showed up that day, which left me feeling dejected—until Cuttin Jeff arrived with a message. Miss Sugar had called him on the telephone party line to say she'd be there bright and early Saturday morning.

14

No Sugarcoating

THE NEXT DAY, breakfast was a stack of Grandma's famous flapjacks, smothered in molasses. It was like biting into a cloud of airy dough, and delight exploded in the pit of my stomach. Grandma's food was so good the taste lingered in my mind hours later. I was ecstatic because soon I'd be leaving to spend the weekend with Miss Sugar. I couldn't wait to see her reaction to the bag of peas Grandma and I had picked a few weeks ago. Miss Sugar loved fresh peas. Whenever she'd drop by for a visit, she'd always remind Grandma to save a bag for her at harvest time.

I was dressed in brand-new overalls and my first pair of Keds tennis shoes, which Grandma's youngest daughter, Ant Phyllis, had brought me from Birmingham. They were beautiful, as white as cooking flour. My plan was to keep them like that so I could show them off at school after summer break. Since I spent almost half the year barefoot, shoes always felt funny when I put them on. Grandpa would tell me I'd better learn to wear shoes because going barefoot would make my feet grow long. He'd tease me about not being able to find a boyfriend because "No boy wants to court a big-footed gal." I'd blush, then we'd both bust out into belly-aching laughter.

That Saturday, I took my favorite spot, sitting on the ground between Grandma's legs, and she began loosening the old braids from my hair to plait new ones. I loved when she combed, brushed, and braided my hair. Her fingers possessed a certain magic. It felt especially wonderful when she'd scratch and lift my dandruff. Afterward, she'd slowly start from the top of my head, making tiny parts with the comb. She would put a drop of castor oil on her fingertips in order to saturate each section, gently rubbing it in until my entire scalp was done. Then she'd take her fingers and massage. I always wished that she'd never stop.

I thought my hair looked particularly cute today because I had bangs, which she unfurled after she finished my braids. The things my Grandma could do with newspaper! She didn't need fancy hair rollers or hot curlers. The night before, she'd tear off a piece of paper, separate a clump of hair, roll it around the paper, then concoct a way to prevent it from unraveling during the night. When I woke the next morning and she took it out, the curl in my bangs was tight as a slinky. Beautiful, coiled, and bouncy.

I often used "hair-fixing" time to ask Grandma to finish a story or start a new one. Today I asked her, "Grandma, please, please tell me 'bout Miss Evelyn. Was she pretty like the ones in the pictures in the chifforobe? Did she have pretty hair? Where she at now?"

"Shush, chile, do you want to hear this story or not? I tell you, you just as fidgety as that ol' hen over there in the chicken coop. You full a questions. Just hold on to your horses while yo' Grandma sets her mind straight."

Grandma began to tell me how she was always after Miss Evelyn to find a husband and settle down. She tried playing matchmaker with some of the available men at her church and almost got Evelyn married off to Nebulon Chaney, a farmer and preacher that lived in Laurel.

"Miss Evelyn gave that man fits. She jus' a strong-willed woman, set in her ways. When she get that way, you can talk to her till you blue in the face, you might as well be talkin' to that brick chimney over yonder. I remembers makin' dinner for Doc Murphy and the chil'ren one evenin'. Evelyn comes a stormin' through the back door madder than a wet hen. Her light skin turn beet red. She says, 'Ma Lula, that Nebulon Chaney—ain't no way in heaven I'm going to marry that man, period. I have my own mind and I can full well take care of *meself.* Don't need no man tellin' me what I am and what I ain't gonna do. I 'magine he thinks I'm one of them young, fast-tail gals he been seen courtin' before me. Them poor gals don't know no better, but Ma Lula, I'm a grown woman. I gots my own money, my own house, and my own mind, and don't need none of his. Don't need a man who think their only job is takin' care of me and tell me what I'm gone do. I'm not going to hang my brain on no coatrack, then acts like I got good sense. He tells me he jus' wants to feed and buy me anything I wants so I never have to worry 'bout nothin' but havin' a bunch of his chil'ren.'

"She says, 'Ma Lula, if that be the case, I might as well put a muzzle over my mouth, cotton in my ears, a dishrag over my eyes, and lay down every night and open my legs real wide.'"

When Grandma said this, my eyes got big and my mouth gaped wider than our barn door. My curiosity had begun to run amuck whenever there was talk of boys and girls and what they did when they got together, especially when no one was watching. That's when I felt Grandma's greasy hand on my chin. She turned my face around to see whether I was paying attention. She was almost finished with the last braid and, believe me, I didn't want this story to end.

"Evelyn says she tell Nebulon the good Lord don' make her to walk 'round the house for the rest of her life like a skunk lookin' for a bottle of perfume. 'No ma'am, Ma Lula; no way, no how,' she said. 'He might need a woman to do all these things for him, but it jus' won't be Evelyn Deavers.'"

Miss Evelyn went on for hours, nonstop. After she spoke her piece, Grandma let her know that not every woman is meant to have a husband. There may be something else in store for them.

I could tell by the longing in Grandma's voice how much she missed Miss Evelyn, and I wished she could relive those days of the two of them doing what they did best—enjoying each other's company. But just like Grandma, Miss Evelyn had seen a lot of bad things happen during her time in Mississippi. That was one of the reasons Grandma thought she might have left the area, never to return in this lifetime. Miss Evelyn would defy most every law meant to hold Black folks in servitude. One time she got caught using the white bathroom in downtown Laurel. At, out of all places, the Laurel courthouse. White folks nearly lost their minds when they saw Miss Evelyn strutting out of that bathroom, head held high. If it hadn't been for Doc Murphy, she might have ended up hanging from a nearby syca-more tree.

But Evelyn was a determined woman who wouldn't kowtow to anyone. As far as she was concerned, they could put up all the "Colored" and "White" signs in the world; nine times out of ten, Evelyn would ignore them. The incident with the white bathroom wasn't the only time Evelyn pushed the racial button in Laurel and Hattiesburg. She became known as a malcontent who'd one day get what was coming to her for being uppity.

Yet she never did. After all, she was a Mullens, and a Murphy too. Evelyn would always say that she would not walk into anyone's back door *ever*, and she would sit where she pleased. Grandma told me she would get letters from her all the time, but when Grandma and Grandpa moved to their new home in Brewersville in 1941, the letters stopped coming.

I sat on the ground, squashed between Grandma's thighs as she put the finishing touches on my braids. It was as though I could feel her heartbeat emanating from the dirt beneath me.

"I sure do miss that gal," Grandma said. "If I don' see her on this here earth, Lord knows I sees her on the other side. That Evelyn one special gal. Gots a hole right here in my heart where Evelyn used to be."

The sound of an automobile horn, along with the wailing of an engine through the trees, interrupted her. Miss Sugar would be here in a matter of minutes. Grandma hurriedly snapped on the last barrette as I held up the mirror, admiring my new coiffure—a part down the middle of my head with four braids on each side and a blue butterfly barrette on the end of each one. I loved turning my head fast, so I could hear the click-clack of the butterflies hitting each other.

"Stop, chile," Grandma said. "'fore you break your neck or one of them barrettes. You jus' gone kill them butterflies."

Miss Sugar was the most outspoken woman I'd ever met. As Grandma said, "That Sugar always look like she jus' stepped out of the picture book, chile. She don' mince words atall, and she smart as a whip too. I loves that gal jus' like she my own flesh and blood."

When I finally saw her, she didn't disappoint. From her wild and colorful clothing to the various shades of bright lipstick carefully applied to her lips, Miss Sugar was incredible. The spattering of curse words she used was even more colorful than her outfits. She was especially infatuated with the word "ass" and used it with absolute impunity.

Grandma had met Miss Sugar in Livingston years ago, after she finished working for Doc Murphy. They met during a Sunday church service, and Miss Sugar took to Grandma immediately. Grandma reminded her of her grandma Pie, she said, and from that day forward, she became a regular visitor to my grandparents' little house in the woods. She'd come by to check on them regularly and bring a gallon or two of her freshly made buttermilk.

Most every word that came from Miss Sugar's mouth was humorous. Especially when she cussed. She'd try not to use profanity around Grandma; if a bad word or two slipped out, she'd immediately apologize. She knew Grandma hated profane language of any type. But whenever Miss Sugar was describing a situation to Grandpa that got her dander up, if Grandma was out of earshot, she'd cut loose. Her voice would rise an octave and she'd begin talking much faster than normal. Before I knew it, the "shits," "assholes," "dammits," and her favorite word of all, "Black ass," would come out with lightning speed. I'd be under the house, listening and grinning like a chessy cat.

That Saturday, I spotted Miss Sugar's luxurious, canary-yellow Buick Electra 225 convertible at the top of the hill, just below the tall pine tree. Glistening in the noonday sun, it was a beauty to behold. Miss Sugar bragged about her car being one of the finest ever to drive the streets of Livingston. She even gave it the name *Yalla Gal.*

Miss Sugar didn't have an ounce of modesty. Her favorite saying was "I ain't no stranger to bragging, and anybody that don't like it can kiss my Black ass." Folks around town were said to be envious of her not only because she had money but because she was brazen and bold, and never suffered any repercussions from white folks as a result of her behavior.

Today, Miss Sugar was wearing a tight red dress that fit every which way but loose, as Grandma would say. Her signature red lipstick matched the blush on her cheeks. The rest of her makeup was flawless—not an eyelash out of place. It was over ninety degrees, yet the heat didn't faze Miss Sugar; she had on long white gloves that came up to her elbows. She was the only woman I ever saw who wore long gloves in the middle of summer. On her head sat a small, crimson-colored hat, cocked to the right. The black fishnet attached to the brim barely covered her eye.

Miss Sugar didn't rise from the car. She glided, almost floating, as she lifted the latch to the front gate. Every time she visited my grandparents was like the first time; her different looks, her grand entrance, the glamorous outfits—it was all beyond amazing. To witness her grand entrance, I'd gladly have paid an admission fee. All I could do was stand there with my mouth hanging open as she reached down to give me a quick kiss on the forehead.

"How's my little Tight doing?"

"I'm doing, Miss Sugar," I said. I guess I was feeling grown, for I responded the way I'd heard my grandparents do so many times before.

"Tight" was the name Miss Sugar gave me the first time I met her, and it had stuck. Grandma would sometimes twist my hair into small balls. I'd have twenty or so of them all over my head. They'd be so tight, you could see my skin pull each time I laughed or talked. I remember Miss Sugar asking me, "Aren't those knots too tight for you, gal?" And ever since, she'd called me Tight.

Miss Sugar had a booming voice and a thunderous laugh. She could belt out songs so loud, you'd swear she was wearing a microphone. And Lord, could she sing. The first thing she'd do before she sat down was sing a few lines to a song that she probably made up:

That man so doggone fine,
He jus' turns my Kool-Aid into wine.
If he comes down to the night spot,
Things gonna get pretty hot.
Ooooh hoochie coochie

"Now, Sugar, you know that's the dev'l's music," was all Grandma would say.

Miss Sugar would reply, "That's why I'm keeping it short and sweet, Ma Lula."

Whenever Miss Sugar would come by, Grandpa would get an extra pep in his step. He loved to hear Miss Sugar sing, and he didn't mind her singing the blues at all. He'd sit there and tap his feet as though he was trying to keep time. Miss

Sugar's singing rivaled her dancing. She'd jump and dance all over the front yard, waving her dress around like a fan. All the insects would run for cover whenever she got to carrying on; otherwise she'd have a whole bunch of them caught up in the hem of her dress.

Miss Sugar was married to Mr. Tank, who was small in stature, gentle, and extremely good-looking. He had straight, thick black hair, an olive complexion with a tiny goatee, and a super-thin black mustache. His eyes were greener than Kentucky bluegrass, and to top it off, he dressed as fine as Miss Sugar, in dark suits with large, multicolored ties and a pocket watch that dangled from a long gold chain. He was sharp as a tack, and his family history was full of mystery.

He and Miss Sugar looked as opposite as days are long. She was at least 5'11" in heels, and Mr. Tank barely reached her chest. Once, I saw her pick him up off the ground like he was a toddler and plant a big kiss on his lips before putting him back down. She and Tank laughed like it was the funniest thing that had ever happened to them. The only thing me, Grandma, and Grandpa could do was laugh as hard as they did.

I'd often wonder how Tank put up with Miss Sugar's bossiness. She'd bark out orders like an army general: "Tank, do this"; "Tank, do that"; "Stop, Tank"; "Pick that up, put that down"; "Slow down, Tank"; "Hurry up, Tank." And she wasn't ashamed to tell him to kiss her ass. But after all that hoopla, I'd watch as she'd lay a kiss on his lips so ferociously, it felt like the ground moved under them. It was obvious that she loved him dearly, even though she'd constantly poke and prod and pull at him about what to do and how to do it.

I overheard Grandma saying that Miss Sugar had desperately wanted children, but after all those years being married to Mr. Tank, none had ever materialized. Since she couldn't conceive, she put all her energy and time into developing and building her own butter, cream, and milk business. After she stopped cleaning and raising white folks' children, she became a self-made woman who started out with a couple of cows and two churns.

For years, Miss Sugar would churn milk until her hands were raw. Then she'd hitch up her two mules and travel to Livingston and all the surrounding towns, selling milk and butter. I couldn't imagine the grueling day-to-day job of churning milk. I remember the days when I'd milk old Josie for about an hour to get two pails. Then I'd sit on the back porch, churning half the day just to squeeze out a couple pounds of butter. Miss Sugar had to be tenacious and hard-working in order to turn her milking into a profitable business.

It probably helped that she'd worked for the most powerful judge in Livingston prior to starting her milk venture. Miss Sugar would brag about how the judge and his family couldn't do "a damn thing without her." She claimed to have had them eating out of her hand. The judge and his wife had thirteen children, including two sets of twins. She'd joke about how the judge's wife had more "chil'ren than she had bloomers." Most were stair-step children, and Miss Sugar said there were so many younguns running around that house she'd take a few of them home with her just to give the judge's wife a break. She was close to both sets of twins, and the judge would tell all the other judges about what a great caretaker Miss Sugar was for his children.

Before she knew it, Miss Sugar was traveling to the homes of various judges from Livingston to Hattiesburg to provide childcare services. She was networking before it was called that. And those same folks had a hand in helping set her up in the milk business. The judge, who had influence with the local banker, also had a hand in the purchase of her beautiful home, which sat on twenty acres of land in Gainesville, just a few miles north of Livingston.

Instead of opening the front passenger door to Miss Sugar's car, in my excitement I hopped over the front door, landing feet first on the beautiful white leather seats. I figured that since

Miss Sugar had the convertible top down, it was okay to take the plunge. Grandma and Miss Sugar both stopped talking midsentence and looked at me like I'd lost my mind. It didn't take but a second for me to realize I'd messed up and maybe jeopardized my weekend getaway.

"Get outta that car right now and git over here," Grandma said. She was always calm; even when she was frustrated or angry, her facial expression never changed. Her eyes, however, gave her away.

"Now," she said, "I want you to go on back over to that car and get in there like you got good sense. You know I ain't raised you to act like a heathen."

"We're going to go now, Ma Lula," Miss Sugar said, "before this child get too carried away."

I didn't open my mouth, just shrugged my shoulders and looked sideways at Grandma and Miss Sugar to make sure I was still on good terms. I felt so bad about what I'd done. Impulsively, I ran back to where Grandma was standing inside the fence and began hugging her like it would be the last time I ever saw her.

"Chile, you know Grandma love yo' heart and yo' liver too. Now, you be good—don' want to get no bad reports from Sugar."

I didn't want to get my Keds dirty, so this time I gently tiptoed back to the car, trying to avoid the sand by stepping on the grassy pieces of road. As Miss Sugar pulled off, I looked back at Grandma, standing next to the gate, watching until the car disappeared. It had been years since I'd left Detroit, yet, even through my excitement, sometimes when I'd leave the safe confines of what I now called home, I felt a tinge of fear at the thought of not returning, of never seeing Grandma again. My heart would sink. A part of me wanted to bail out of the car and run back to the safety of her arms.

The first night I'd spent away from Grandma had been brutal. The horrible dream from my first nights in the country had returned. After my third overnight visit to Miss Sugar's, the nightmares subsided, but I still felt a sliver of fear and insecurity at being away. Miss Sugar's way with words and her bubbly personality gave me comfort. Even with her sometimes gruff talk and the curses she'd sling around, being in her presence was very soothing. She had a commanding voice and she was unafraid to use it, but she could also be compassionate and sympathetic. Whenever I'd have nightmares, I'd wake up and find her sitting on the side of my bed, rubbing my forehead and telling me that everything would be okay. With her, I felt safe.

Her choice of words, specifically the curse words and country slang, was different from the other old folks I met during my years in the country. Every time she'd say "your little Black ass" I'd bust out laughing on the inside. I'd never met anyone like her, and I knew she loved me in her own Miss Sugar way.

Miss Sugar's place sat way out in the country, a beautiful two-story white frame house with a white wooden picket fence. She had flowers of all kinds: white, yellow, and red roses; chrysanthemums; daisies; and black-eyed Susans, all encased in separate beds. Right before the three steps that led to her front porch were six large elephant-ear plants, three on each side of the walkway.

Inside the screened-in front porch sat four green metal chairs with flower cutouts in the back and a large rocking swing that matched the chairs. Unlike my grandparents' wooden swing, which hung high from the ceiling, Miss Sugar's sat so low my feet would touch the floor. It automatically swung back and forth as I sat down. I think her front porch was larger than my grandparents' entire house. It reminded me of the houses I'd seen in those *Fun with Dick and Jane* books I hated so much.

Miss Sugar and I spent the rest of the day and into early Saturday evening churning the milk she'd squeezed from her

177

dozen or so cows. During those days, for some reason folks didn't worry about food spoiling if it wasn't refrigerated. Miss Sugar kept her milk in aluminum tubs in the coolness of her smokehouse for an entire day, each tub covered with a lid to prevent insects from getting in. When it was time for us to start churning, she used the tub handles to grab one side of the container, and I'd hold the other side. We took one silver tub of milk at a time to the back porch, then gently poured the milk into two churns. One tub was enough to fill up both churns to the tip-top, with only a small portion left over. Miss Sugar fed this to her six cats.

To make clabber and buttermilk was a different process. Lots of folks in the country loved the taste of clabber milk, but I'd gag just looking at it. Plain and simple, it's spoiled milk. After a few days in a heat-controlled environment, it ferments and turns into clumps. Then it begins to smell like the underarms of someone who's worked in the fields all day. My grandma loved to use this kind of milk for baking cakes and pies. Some folks would drink it straight from the glass. Miss Sugar's customers lived and died for the way she prepared her clabber milk. She put a lot of love and care into her product.

After we finished churning, Miss Sugar used a funnel-shaped cone to pour the milk into gallon jugs. We separated the plain milk and buttermilk, then toted them out to the icehouse in the backyard. The milk we separated for the clabber customers we'd set in the small room in the back of her house until fermentation.

Miss Sugar was probably in her early fifties, but to me she didn't look a day over thirty-five. Through the grueling job of churning milk and making butter, she never removed her makeup, earrings, or high-heeled shoes. She didn't wipe the sweat from her face; she patted it. Then she'd announce, "Miss Sugar still look damn good, don't she, chile?"

After a long day of churning, I'd smell milkier than the entire pasture of Miss Sugar's cows. I couldn't wait to submerge myself in a tub of soapy water. For my bath, I'd be using real soap and relaxing in a real tub, where I could control the water temperature. At home, my grandparents had no running water, so Grandma would warm up large buckets on the wood-burning stove until they boiled. Then she'd pour the water into a ten-gallon silver washtub filled with cold water. I couldn't create much lather from Grandma's homemade devil lye soap, which smelled like a forest fire in the thick of Alabama's smoldering heat.

At Miss Sugar's, I didn't have to use recycled bath water, either. At my grandparents' house, bathing took place twice weekly, usually on Wednesdays and Sundays. Grandpa always bathed first, then Grandma. I went last. By that time, the water would be cruddy from the sweat and grime residue from my grandparents' bodies.

Whenever Miss Sugar showed off a new product on my visits, my eyes got saucer-wide. The first time she showed me a bar of Dial soap, I was floored. The smell stayed in my mind for a long time. Nothing topped it—until she surprised me with a plastic bottle of "Fuzzy Wuzzy" bubble bath: I thought I'd gone to heaven. I poured so much of the rich pink liquid into my bathwater that bubbles covered every inch of my almost five-foot frame.

I lay there soaking until I heard her coming up the long, tiled hallway yelling, "Tight, you better get your little Black ass outta that tub 'fore you turn white. Dammit gal, you gone make me miss my seven o'clock Saturday evening funnies on this television tube messing around with you. Now I'm gonna count to ten, and I better hear some feets hitting that floor, and the only thing I wants to see is your bare Black ass coming around that corner putting on them night clothes. We still gotta eat supper before my show. I don't miss my funnies show for nobody, you hear me? God bless my grandma Pie who left for glory years ago, and Lord knows I love her to death. But if she raises up from the grave and wants to talk to me at 6:59, I'd tell her she better go back where she came from 'cause she's shit out of luck till my Saturday funnies gone off. I be damn."

I heard Miss Sugar chuckle loudly. Once she got on a roll about not missing her favorite show, I knew she was dead serious. I hightailed it out of that tub so fast it would've made your head swim.

Watching television was the grand finale before we retired for the night. I'd watch Miss Sugar as she stared at the television screen. She'd laugh so loud at the animated *Beanie and Cecil* cartoon, I thought she'd choke. She'd already taken out her false teeth and placed them in a glass half filled with water, which sat beside her rocking chair. I too enjoyed the funnies, but not half as much as I loved Miss Sugar's reaction to them. I spent more time ogling her toothlessness and imagining what was going on in her mind than I did looking at the black-and-white TV screen.

During my visits, Miss Sugar never deviated from her Saturday evening schedule. She told me she fell in love with the TV set from the moment she bought it four years before. Even so, it was as though she was looking at the television for the first time whenever she turned it on. She'd whoop, holler, clap, and laugh so loud I thought the house would collapse.

I slept in what Miss Sugar called her guest room. It was elegant, with pink and green wallpaper and four "whatnot" shelves in each corner. Each one held glass figurines of elephants, birds, small vases, and framed pictures of different people. A dresser that sat close to my bed had nine glass and wooden music boxes on its top. I'd wind up each one before jumping into bed. Then I'd close my eyes and visualize Miss Sugar. On closer inspection, I could see the age lines that crossed her face, which I was sure represented wisdom. Each line chronicled the various trials of her life. I could never fully imagine the difficulties she'd faced just for being the daring Miss Sugar in 1960s Alabama, but I tried.

My admiration for Miss Sugar grew each time we were together. Her strength of heart, ambitious nature, toughness, assertiveness, and business savvy clung to me like wet clothes on a dry body. Just being in her presence, my confidence in what I could one day accomplish in this big world began to grow. Miss Sugar was a monolith I envisioned standing strong in the middle of an ocean. The floods came, but she was immovable, solid as a rock.

A house in Gainesville, Alabama, that looks eerily similar to Miss Sugar's

15

The Big Reveal

THE NEXT DAY WAS A GORGEOUS SUNDAY. Basking on Miss Sugar's front porch with the morning sun on the side of my face, I took in its beauty. It wasn't quite nine, but both Miss Sugar and I were yawning like it was midnight. After yesterday's hard work, it was hard to keep our eyes open. On Monday, folks from all over Gainesville, Livingston, and the surrounding area would make their trek to Miss Sugar's house to purchase their milk. She told me she had a slate of regular customers and no plans to take on any new ones.

"I ain't no spring chicken no more, so I ain't gonna work my ass off not one more day. Now, there was a time when I'd have to saddle up my two old tired mules and off I march, going door-to-door delivering milk. Jumping up and down from that wagon, my feet feel like they been poked with a hot iron. Feet so tired, might as well be walking around on just legs. Don't deliver no more. They got to bring their asses on down the road to my house if they wants it. Guess what, Tight? You better believe they here often and early every week to get their milk and butter.

"You know I didn't have to work like a slave just getting off the boat, because Tank gots plenty of money. But, chile, Miss Sugar wants you to remember: when you grown and finds yourself a husband, you make sure you have your own, because a man can walk out on you anytime and you ain't got nothing but maybe a pair of his old stanking-ass shoes to show for it, but he's gone. Now tell me, what you gone do with them shoes? You ain't gone get a damn dime for them, and you sure enough can't wear them. So mind what I tell you. I done seen that happen so many times before. A whole lotta women running around here chasing some sorry-ass man who ain't worth piss."

As much as I loved Grandma's stories, Miss Sugar's descriptions of people, and of relationships between men and women, were exciting. I stood at the cusp of adolescence, and this kind of talk fed my curiosity. Like that morning, I think Miss Sugar sometimes forgot I wasn't that old and treated me like a peer.

"You know, Tight, I was a baby when my real mama sent me away to Livingston to stay with my papa's folks. They had some money, so they gave me everything I wanted. Ain't seen my mama no more. I was a young gal when she passed away. Didn't even go back to her home-going. Grandma Pie says she ain't done nothing for me no-way.

"My papa was a real tall man with big eyes like mine. I looked so much like him, Mama Pie said that every time she looked at me, she may as well been looking at him. He left Livingston when he wa'n't even eighteen. The white man he worked for chopped off two of my papa's fingers because he said my papa stole from him. I was half grown when Papa told me this story and how he beat that man like nobody's business with only one hand. He left his plow in that white man's field and never looked back. He hopped train boxcars some, then he'd run some, bleeding like a chicken who just got they neck chopped off. He said if it wa'n't for this old colored man that he ran into on that boxcar, he bleed to death. The man stopped the bleeding and saved my papa's life.

"Grandma Pie and Grandpa Nate used to send me up North to New York every summer to stay with my papa. He had a nice little house up in Harlem. Mmmmm, I loved that place, with so many finely dressed colored folks. My papa got a porter job on the New York railroad. You shoulda seen the way him and them other colored porters hide me out from the white man, because I ain't supposed to be on that train. It was like playing hide-and-seek.

"I loved my papa to death; he was a good man, Tight, and he sure enough took care of me. To this day, I think my papa pass on 'fore he hit fifty 'cause all that bleeding caught up to him by and by. Now let me tell you this, Tight. When I meets that fine hunk of prime beef, my Tank, in New York City, I was just seventeen. I was sitting right there on the front steps, minding my own business, when I see him, and Lord have mercy." As she spoke, Miss Sugar's face lit up like a Christmas tree. "After summer, I come back home to Livingston and told Mama Pie about Tank. I bet you won't guess the first word that comes outta her mouth? She says: 'I hope he ain't one of those po'-ass nawthern niggers. Don't want you to be marrying no man who ain't got a pot to piss in or a window to throw it out of.' She say a man likes that can give you one or two things. Guess what that is? Well, I'll tell you—she say, 'They can give you the clap or they can give you the blues, and they might just give you both.'"

I thought Miss Sugar was going to fall out of her chair laughing. I had no idea what she was alluding to—her choice of words was colorful and couldn't be found in any of the books I'd read. Still, I waited on the edge of my seat.

"Both Grandma Pie and Grandpa Nate were color-struck as hell," Miss Sugar said. "They told me I better not walk in that door with no man darker than that brown cow out there yonder in that pasture. Truth be told, Tank coulda been black as tar; it was just *somethin'* about that man. But I ain't gone lie and tell you that his olive color and them green eyes like an alley cat didn't have nothing to do with me falling head over heels for that man. Tight, *ooooh-weeee*. I coulda just scooped his little short ass up and lay him 'twixt two pieces of light bread and gobble him up like a ham sammich. And to top it all off, he dressed up like he got a million dollars in his pocket.

"When he sees me, he comes a-prancing over to where I'm at with one hand in his pocket, rattling his coins, and a toothpick hanging from his mouth, grinning like a wide-eyed chessy cat. The first thing that came out of his mouth was: 'You mine.'

"I reckon that was over thirty years ago, and I ain't looked back since. I do a bunch a trash talking about finding a man who's gonna give me a baby, but I'd be a fool to leave that man. But you know what, Tight, much as I love Tank, if he leaves me today, I'm gone miss him, but you better believe I'll be able to take care of myself. You see this house here? Well, I bought it and almost everything in it. I wanted Tank to know right off the bat, I don't need one penny of his money. He pitched a bitch, but I said, 'No, no, no. I gots to have my own.'

"Gone tell you something else 'bout my Tank: his papa name Lorenzo, an old 'talian man who fell hard for Tank's mama, Cleora. She was a high-yalla colored girl passing for white. Yes, Lord, she was light, bright, and damn near white. Cleora never told Lorenzo how she was mixed until after my Tank was born. Chile, my Tank say he was born light-complected, but I can tell you this: he was a far cry from being white. I seen a picture of him when he a little something, he had a wide pug nose and black curly hair. He say right after he was born, Cleora ended up telling Lorenzo about her Black mama and her papa a white slave-owner from Alabama. Tank said his papa wasn't mad at all. He never did marry Cleora, but he made sure that he spent a lot of time with my Tank and his mama didn't want for nothing."

Lorenzo ended up telling his parents about Cleora and Tank, too, Miss Sugar explained.

"They shitted bricks when they found out they having my Tank, a little niglet grandbaby with 'talian blood. But lo and behold, chile, when Lorenzo brought Tank to see his grandparents, they loved him from the moment they laid eyes on him, but wants nothing to do with Tank's mama. Up to the day she died, them 'talians still ain't talked to her. Them 'talians sure enough knows how to hold a grudge. They acts like it's all his mama's fault. One thang for sure: she ain't had that baby by herself. You got to watch yourself, chile, when you starts messing with boys. For as long as you can, you needs to keep your dress down and your drawers up, because women always the ones who gone get the short end of the stick, even though it takes two to tango, baby."

I smiled to myself as Miss Sugar spoke. The more she talked, the more it sounded as though she was trying to take flight from the rocking chair she was sitting in. As the story became more intense, the wooden legs went faster and faster.

"Tank felt so bad for his mama, because they won't let his papa have a thing to do with her. Tank said if his papa married her, he'd leave all that 'talian loot on the table. Lorenzo knows what side of his bread was being buttered. Course, he didn't marry her; instead he chose the money. He said his mama never married nobody. She left outta this world a young woman. Tank said he think she passed on because her heart just broke in two. My Tank was only nineteen."

Here, Miss Sugar stopped and scooted her chair so close to mine that when she opened her mouth, I could see her tonsils staring at me like two cherries hanging from a vine. She looked around to ensure no one was listening. The funny thing was, no one lived within miles of Miss Sugar. The only living things that could have possibly heard her were insects, birds, and the cows out back, and maybe Mr. Tank, who was dead asleep. The window to the bedroom he and Miss Sugar shared was barely open, yet we could hear him snoring louder than a freight train.

Still leaning close, Miss Sugar picked up right where she left off. "You know them 'talians quick to send your ass outta this world. You don't see or hear of any of these crackers around here messing with me or Tank, do you?

"Hell, back in the day, lots of folks 'round here knew about that liquor Tank's boys used to cook up in them backwoods. My man had colored and whites running liquor like a damn race-horse coming up on the finish line. Things pretty dried up now with the moonshine and rotgut, but back in the day, baby, Tank was the man, and you better believe them 'talians rewarded him mighty finely. Them crackers down here to this day know they better not even look at Tank sideways, because my Tank gots a long memory. He knew every cracker that took part in gulping down that rotgut liquor. White folks back then knew: no Tank, no liquor. Meaning nobody would be getting drunk around these parts. And everybody knew how these white folks loved getting liquored up seven days a week and twice on the weekends. Tank was a lifeline to all the booze coming in and out of Sumter County. How you like that?

"Me and Tank walk 'round Livingston with our nose so high in the air it ain't funny, because folks know better than mess with us. They knew if they did, them 'talians would open up a can of whup-ass on them. White folks around here may be a tad bit crazy, but they ain't that damn crazy."

I looked up at her, eager for more. But Miss Sugar's eyes had locked in on her watch, with its colorful band that matched her outfit, and she jumped up from her seat like she'd sat on a half-dozen thumbtacks.

"Woo, Lord, look at the time. Been sitting here talking my ass off. My sista gone be here sometime 'fore ten. She sent me a letter last week, saying she gone be here. We gots the same mama, but different papas. Mama Pie told me after my mama died that I had a baby sista who my mama kept. Mama Pie explained it the best she could. But I still had empty feelings about being given away. I carried that burden on my shoulders like I was dragging around a tree trunk. Papa never say one word, good or bad, about Mama or my sista. Mama Pie hated

Mama with a passion, but she always wanted me to know my baby sister. For as long as I can remember she'd tell me, 'It ain't your sista's fault she born; she didn't choose her daddy, either, and it damn sure won't your sister's fault your mama chose to give you away.' Before she passed on, she made sure I knew exactly how I could find my sista in case I wanted to write and seek her out. It just took me longer than I thought."

As we sat on the front porch, waiting, I closed my eyes to see if I could conjure up a visual of who her sister might be. I couldn't imagine anyone as outrageous, charismatic, or funny as Miss Sugar. The noise of a car horn came blaring and echoing through the trees. Miss Sugar and I jumped up and walked toward the road in front of her house.

"Lord, Lord, here comes my sista," Miss Sugar said, and started straightening her clothes for what felt like the hundredth time. She wore a body-hugging bright yellow dress the exact color of her Buick, with matching shoes. Her makeup, as always, was done to perfection. She must've looked in the mirror fifty times to make sure she didn't have a hair out of place.

"Fix them overalls up on you, chile. Come here; let me do something with them butterfly barrettes—they all crooked. I should've took them braids out your hair and put you a couple of ponytails to go with your bangs; that be much better. I swear, Miss Lula need to get you out of these overalls and get you some clothes that fit better on your narrow behind. Lord knows you ain't got no meat on that little ass of yours. Gots to get you cuted up 'cause you gone be courting pretty soon."

Then she did the most unimaginable thing. She stuck her thumb in her mouth, got it real spitty, and wiped both corners of my eyes. I could feel the wetness hanging on my eyelid. I wanted to throw up. I couldn't *believe* Miss Sugar had just given me a spit bath.

A hilly slope overlooked Miss Sugar's house, which sat down in a valley. This made it easy to see the sleek, cherry-red car as it came into view. It barreled down the hill like the driver was trying to escape the police. Most folks eased their cars down the steep incline so sand wouldn't fly all over. This car was going so fast, all I could see was a cloud of smoke. Both Miss Sugar and I stood there, spitting sand out of our mouths, as the car came dangerously close to where we were standing. It was going so fast it bypassed the house by a quarter of a mile. Then came the deafening sound of squealing brakes as it backed up over the sand.

I could tell Miss Sugar was boiling mad. Her bottom lip quivered like a flap in the wind. The curse words began to fly as she stood there, wiping sand from her face with her hand-kerchief. Desperately, I tried not to laugh. But when the car came to a complete stop, Miss Sugar's expression changed from hostility to puzzling calm. A tall, voluptuous woman dressed all in white emerged. She was majestic, and as she lifted herself from the car, I swore I could see a crown sitting on top of her head. She made Miss Sugar's entrances look elementary. Her two-piece outfit hugged her frame like it was painted on her body. Her hair was almost as red as the dress Miss Sugar had worn the day before, and her hat was purple, dotted with little emeralds and white pearls. Her high-heeled shoes were tall and pointy, making tiny holes in the dirt as she made her way to where we were standing. She was graceful in the way she strolled; she didn't stumble, not even a bit.

As she moved toward us, smiling, I saw a set of deep dimples in her cheeks, just like Miss Sugar's. Never had I seen Miss Sugar speechless—until now.

"Oh, my Lord, you got to be my sister," the strange woman said. "You're a sight to behold. I'm so sorry about driving so fast and kicking up all that sand. It came up on me so quick. I have to get used to driving in the country again."

She winked at me, then grabbed Miss Sugar, who seemed to be in a state of shock. They both started sobbing uncontrol-lably. At one point, Miss Sugar's sister pulled away and took the back of her hand and wiped the tears from Miss Sugar's face. Miss Sugar called her "Bay Sis," which down South means "baby sister."

"Now, who's this cute little girl here, Dot? You're a pretty little something, aren't you?"

Hearing this woman tell me how pretty I was caused goose pimples to ripple up and down my arms. I felt special. The only thing I could do was stand there and stare. It felt as though I'd seen her before, but for the life of me, I couldn't place her.

"This is Miss Lula Horn's grandbaby. She comes 'round here every now and then to keep me company and help me out with my churning."

Oh my! The look on her sister's face, and the twinkle in her eye, as Miss Sugar went on and on praising me. Then the most incredible thing happened. The woman bent over until she was eye-level with me. The next thing I knew, she hugged me so tight I struggled to breathe and buried her face in mine, sobbing.

"Let me take a good look at you. Dot, you mean to tell me this really is Lula Horn's granddaughter? Lord, is this the same Ma Lula that worked for Doc Murphy in Livingston for all those years? Lord have mercy."

"You mean to tell me that you know Miss Lula, Bay Sis?"

"I sure do. I consider Ma Lula my second mama and a friend. After Mama passed away, Ant Glory, our mama's sister, took me in. Even though Ant Glory lived in Hattiesburg, she still made sure she brought me over to the Murphy place in Laurel quite regularly. I'd help Ma Lula with the children whenever I could. After I was grown, I got a job in Laurel as a teacher. The school was right down the hill from the Murphy place, so when I finished up for the day, most times, I'd head right over there and talk to Miss Lula for a spell."

The gears in my head came to a screeching halt. My Lord, Miss Sugar's sister had to be Miss Evelyn. The face, the clothes, knowing Grandma from Doc Murphy's place, a teacher! You would've thought I'd died and gone to heaven. I didn't know whether I wanted to cry, laugh, or jump up and down. So, I did the only thing I could, the thing I'd been doing for years.

I listened.

Quickly, I found myself immersed in Miss Evelyn's talk of her days in Laurel as a schoolteacher. It reminded me of the stories Grandma had told about how cultured and well-dressed Miss Evelyn was. She still looked like she'd stepped out of a glamour magazine. The sound of her voice was so fluid and precise that my entire body shivered like a single feather was brushing against my skin.

"Miss Lula loved Doc Murphy and his family, but I think they loved Ma Lula even more, if you can imagine that. I've never seen white folks go out of their way for a Negro woman like the Murphy family did for Ma Lula. Then again, Ma Lula treated them like they were her blood family. Them Murphy children doted on Ma Lula. Every time she turned around, there they were, tugging on her apron strings or propped up in her lap. That youngest lad would get mad as a box of frogs every time Ma Lula went back to Livingston to see her own children. So funny hearing Miss Murphy call that lad Ma Lula's child, and that she just happened to birth him. We'd both fall over laughing.

"Ma Lula just had a way with grown folks and children, too. Never seen nothing like it. Heap of times when I got flustered and wanted to go into town and cuss out white folks, she was the one who talked me down. You know I was just a hot-headed Negro-Irish gal, so I came 'cross this temper of mine honestly. No one, I mean *no one*, could shake me back to reality but Ma Lula."

Miss Evelyn paused. With her eyes lowered, she began rubbing the front of her dress with the palms of her hands, like she was wiping away lint. Deep anguish lined her face. "I couldn't wait to finish teaching school," she said, "just so I could stop by the Murphys' and sit on their front porch and listen to Miss Lula sing. Lord knows that woman had a voice on her. I swear, I could hear the robins and blue jays in the trees singing right along. Ma Lula just had a way about her. Didn't matter where you went in Livingston, nobody ever had a bad thing to say about her. I sure did miss her when she left Mississippi."

She turned to Miss Sugar and asked, "So Dot, how did you meet Ma Lula?"

Miss Sugar cleared her throat as she began to describe her first encounter with Grandma. "A long time ago, I went to Zion Hill church. It was my first time there, and my last. Don't know what possessed me, but I sits right down next to Miss Lula in the first pew. I never like going to church on time, 'cause I *love* walking in the door late just so them church folks can put they noses up in the air. I know they gone talk about me like a dog later on 'cause I'm dressed to the nine, do you hear me talking to you? I likes going in there right before it ends just to rile them hypocrites up a bit. They sitting there in church knowing damn well I just seen some of them crawling outta the juke joint across the road from me, drunk off they asses. Then they got the nerve to be sitting on the front row in church a few hours later, screaming and shouting louder than Jonah did when he got stuck in the belly of that whale. They ought to be 'shame' of they selves, pointing their fingers at me.

"I was gone cuss out every thang that moved that Sunday morning in that church. Even though we in the good Lord's house, I was getting ready to get in they ass like a fly on buttermilk. But before I knew it, Miss Lula smiles at me and grabs my arm and damn near drag me outta that church, sanging, 'It's me, it's me, it's me, oh Lord, standing in the need of prayer.' I never had nobody treat me that way since Mama Pie. When she talked to me that day, her eyes look so far into mine, I couldn't move a muscle. I just stood there like a lamb getting ready for the slaughterhouse. But baby, let me tell you, the words she told me that day will stay with me for the rest of my life. She say, 'Now, Sugar, don't you go looking at the bad in folks and work backward; you make sho you look at the good in folks and work frontward.' You know I still got a lot of shit with me, but Miss Lula's words kinda changed the way I look at folks. That says a lot coming from an old sinner like me."

Miss Evelyn nodded and said, "I'll never forget sitting on the Murphys' front porch when Ma Lula told me about how you can fill an empty heart with someone you care for deeply. But before I left for Chicago, I ran into an elderly maid who worked for old man Tom Millen, who told me Ma Lula had passed on. I figured that's why every time I wrote her, the letters came back.

"When I made it to Chicago, I promised myself I'd never come back down South unless I had my own transportation. Against my better judgment, I returned a year later on the bus, because Lord knows I missed seeing my kinfolks, but that ride was more than enough for me. I've never felt so degraded. Sitting there in the back, it stank so bad and wasn't fit for swine. I knew things couldn't do nothing but change down here sooner or later. That's why I left and didn't come back until now, because now I can drive myself."

So many times, Grandma had told me about Miss Evelyn— how she would always speak her mind and never allow herself to be treated as inferior. Listening to her describe her independence only increased my admiration. She and Miss Sugar exuded confidence in a way I'd never seen before, and over the years, I came to see that they were both advocates for civil rights, just by being themselves. They refused to be taken down by a society that judged them based on their race and gender. I'm sure other Black women and girls who came into contact with them felt the same way I did. They spoke their mind in a time where not only was there blatant racism, but sexism as well. Observing their behavior gave me a blueprint for how I would and would not be treated as a Black girl and, eventually, a Black woman.

In those days, I'd dream about being just like the three women I admired most: Grandma, Miss Sugar, and Miss Evelyn.

Sometimes I'd adopt Grandma's gait, the way she walked, or try to mimic the focused attention she put into making quilts. But most of all, I knew from a young age that I wanted to tell stories. Grandma planted this seed. Over the course of my years with her, I can't begin to count the times she told me about Ella. She spoke about my great-aunt so often that I felt I knew her intimately. But while I couldn't see myself doing anything in life other than being a storyteller, it was Miss Sugar and Miss Evelyn who gave me the ambition, fortitude, and abiding strength to execute this plan.

"I thought about you all the time, Dot," Miss Evelyn was saying. "I had to find out from strangers that Mama had you. I felt so guilty that Mama kept me but gave you away. When I got older, it was hard to face you, knowing what Mama did. So I didn't even try to contact you.

"I have a few good memories of Hattiesburg and Laurel— and a lot of painful ones. Those, I tried to forget. I never told anybody about the awful times, not even Ma Lula. I got much stronger over the years, and now I think it's finally time to talk. Dot, let me tell you, our Ant Glory was one of those old folks who was secretive about everything that went on in our house. She'd always tell me, 'Don't be going around telling folks about our business this, and our business that.' I got so tired of hearing those two words I wanted to throw up every time they came out of her mouth.

"It's about time that I share 'our business' with Ma Lula. Now, if you tell me she's gone on to glory, I may pass out right here in your yard. If you tell me she's alive, I may still pass out."

"Well, you better grab onto something, Bay Sis, because Ma Lula just as alive as I am and living about thirty miles up the road. She gone be so surprised when she finds out me and you sistas. She probably gone hit the ceiling and Mr. Edgar gone raise the roof for her."

Both women busted out in side-splitting laughter. In their adulation for my grandmother, I felt a gratitude headier than the jasmine perfume Miss Evelyn wore. That sweet aroma filled the yard as I sat between them, soaking up their every word.

"I ain't told nobody about you, Bay Sis," Miss Sugar said. "You was my well-kept secret."

"Well, I'm here now, Dot, and I'm not going anywhere. I promise I'll never lose touch with you. The Lord is good, because he put us back together after all this time. There's only so much the devil can do to mess up what's right. Ma Lula told me that." Miss Evelyn smiled and looked at me. "I can't get over that Ma Lula is still in Livingston. Just wait until she sees her Evelyn come walking through the door!"

There it was! I knew from the moment she'd started talking about Laurel and Grandma. But it wasn't until she said her name, Evelyn, that I felt sure. I couldn't believe I was in the presence of the pretty lady from the pictures in the chifforobe. She was much younger in those photographs and had put on weight; the girly smile was gone, but yes, this was the lady that Grandma compared me to every chance she could.

We stood in Miss Sugar's yard, the sisters deeply absorbed in conversation. Finally, Miss Sugar said, "Would you look at us, Bay Sis, we been standing here so long these high heels are killing my dogs. They're howling like they done seen a pack of deer. We need to go and sit down somewhere before I fall down. Woo, Lord!"

The three of us walked slowly toward the front porch, Miss Evelyn still holding my sweaty hands while she talked to Miss Sugar. She plopped down in the green swing, and I sat so close to her I was almost in her lap. I was mesmerized not only by her beauty, but by how refined she was. Pieces of her were Miss Sugar through and through, like their identical laugh and the confidence they exuded. In a shy way, I felt honored to be sitting in the presence of these strong-willed women, listening to them carry on without being chased away because grown folks was talking. Questions boiled over in my mind. The next thing you knew, there I was, pulling on Miss Evelyn's beautiful white dress.

"What is it, baby?"

Miss Sugar interrupted before the first word rolled off my tongue. "Tight, now you know Ma Lula would be upset as hell if she knew you busting in on grown folks' conversation. You know better than that. I think you 'smelling yourself', gal."

"Let the child speak, Dot. We spend so much time these days trying to stop children from having their say. Now go on, child, speak your piece; Miss Evelyn is listening to you, baby."

I'd never seen anybody shut Miss Sugar down that way except for Grandma. As soon as I opened my mouth, words began flowing like water from a busted dam. There was no way to contain them. I asked about Stump and Grandma's run-in with the sheriff, the sheriff's wife and his daughters, and what did Doc Murphy do to change the sheriff's evil ways?

"Well, child, you are just full of questions, aren't you? What's your name, child?"

"Phyllistene, but Miss Sugar and other folks call me 'Tight.'"

"Tight! Tight! Sugar, you need to stop calling this child out of her name. I swear, colored folks are constantly naming their children all these crazy names. I run into children named Jelly, Butter, Thursday, and Peanut. I even ran into a woman up in Chicago that named her daughter Doo-Doo. Now, why in God's name would you name a child Doo-Doo? Can you imagine what that child must go through in life? What made it so bad is the parents put it on that child's birth certificate. The folks down at the courthouse need to have their asses kicked for allowing them to get away with that. But I guess there's not much they can do, in that case."

Miss Sugar blurted out in defense of her name: "Well, my name is Sugar, even though Mama named me Dorothy. Mama Pie said she hated the name Dorothy worse than a hog at hog-killing time. So she start calling me Sugar. Mama Pie said she named me that because I was such a sweet lil thang. Now you can just kiss my sweet, sugary ass, Bay Sis. I mean, Evelyn," and she laughed hard to herself.

"Your name may be Sugar, but the family you never met knows you as Dorothy. I guess I'm just as bad, because I shortened your name from Dorothy to Dot. Now, hush up, let me finish talking to Phyllistene." She turned back to me and said, "Booker, who folks called Stump, was my Ant Glory's only child. He lives in Chicago now. He was one of the first Negro doctors in the area. Booker had seven boys, all of them doctors, lawyers, dentists, and businesspeople." To Miss Sugar, she added, "Dot, you need to meet some of your kinfolk on Mama's side. I wish I could live my life over, because it wasn't right for us never seeing each other."

Miss Sugar's mouth fell into a heavy frown. "Mama Pie never let it go about Mama giving me away, either," she said. "I used to pick up on grown folks' gossip, how Mama Pie was steaming mad about Mama not wanting to marry my papa. They said my mama too busy catting 'round with that white man, your daddy, Bay Sis. But trying to get extra information out of Papa's two sisters was like pulling teeth. You know how some old folks carry stuff to the grave. They just wasn't trying to tell you shit."

Miss Sugar chose her words carefully, but I could see her frustration. The veins were sticking out of her neck. She scooted her hips closer to the edge of the chair and raised her dress up right above her knees. The next words she spoke with conviction and a tinge of anger.

"Another reason why I ain't say nothing about you, Bay Sis, was because you know how nosy folks are when you tell them something. The first thing they want to know is: why your mama didn't want you? Or why she gives you away? All that would do is make me mad as holy hell, and I know I'd end up cussing somebody the hell out or slapping a mud hole in their asses. Just didn't want to think about it at all. Shoot! Me and Tight here, we knows how it feel when you ain't with your real mama, got to be some kind of reason."

"I'm so sorry, Dot," Miss Evelyn said. "I tried asking Ant Glory why you were sent away, and she started stuttering and avoided my question. I did talk to Booker, but he knows just as much as I do about stuff. Plus, he's five years younger than me. Speaking of Booker, he's always asking about you. We never forgot about you, Dot—just never seem' the right time to right this ship. Just wait until I tell him I seen you; he's not going to know what to do with himself—and when I tell him about Ma Lula, he's probably going to be down here so fast, it will make your head swim."

I sat there, wanting so badly to get back to the questions I'd asked Miss Evelyn. The last thing I wanted the sisters to do was continue talking about being separated from mamas and papas. Miss Evelyn must've recognized my angst, or maybe she was as eager as I was to change the subject.

"Now, Phyllistene, I didn't forget about your questions, baby. Let me see here—Doc Murphy had a lot of white folks in his pocket in Mississippi, and he definitely had something to do with that devilish sheriff's change of heart. He put the ball in motion. But I think it had more to do with an old Negro woman who showed up on the sheriff's doorstep, a ghost from the past. Now, Doc Murphy knew what he was doing when he sent word out to find that woman. I'm sure your Grandma Lula will tell you more of that story one day."

I sat, mesmerized, as she leaned down to me and added, "Miss Evelyn is going to tell you something else that I want you to carry in your heart and mind for the rest of your days upon this earth. I want you to promise me right now."

I nodded my head up and down furiously.

"Don't ever let white folks tell you that your history is not connected to theirs, and never let Black folks tell you their history is not connected to white folks'. My papa was Irish. My mama was pure African and as dark and beautiful as the Nile. During slavery, the slave-owner made more overnight trips down to the slave quarters than Carter got pills. There were as many half-white babies running around those slave quarters as there were chickens in a chicken coop. Most of their white papas didn't even own up to these children that carried their blood, even when they looked like they'd just spit them out. A whole lot of my friends in Chicago don't have any idea of who they daddies are. And it ain't that hard to figure out why. It's because they were the result of old masta creeping."

Miss Sugar shook her head. "Bay sis, this child too young to hear all that history stuff you talking."

"She needs to know, Dot. I'm only teaching history that she won't be learning in school, and *definitely* not if she's going to school down here in the sticks. That's why I became a teacher, because children need to know about their history—especially Negro children. Whites got a head start, Negros don't." Miss Evelyn looked down at me and smiled. "I'm glad Ma Lula told you about her life, family, and the struggles she had to endure. I want you to make sure you listen to every word Ma Lula tells you about the past, because she lived close to slavery days. She learned piecemeal, mostly by listening and opening her heart."

As Miss Evelyn spoke of my grandmother, she flashed a golden smile that was picture-postcard worthy. I not only felt the deep admiration that she had for my grandma; I saw it.

"I get so bitter when I see Negros being abused and mistreated and not being educated the way white folks are," she said. "It makes me sick. I think our people suffered more than any living thing God put on this earth. It was your grandma who taught me about human suffering. She'd tell me: 'Don't matter whether you colored, white, yellow, brown, or polka dot—we all cry wet when we hurt.' I can't wait to see my friend again. She's going to fall out when she sees me. Lord knows I loved my poor mama, bless her soul, but Ma Lula have a special place in my heart."

Mr. Tank appeared on the front porch then, all dressed up and looking like a million dollars. Miss Sugar gestured to him and said, "Come here, Tank, so you can meet my Bay Sis."

It took everything inside of me to contain my laughter, looking at Mr. Tank. The two women towered over him like trees over a blade of grass. But he wasn't deterred at all. He grabbed Miss Evelyn just above the waist and gave her a big hug.

"Now, Dot, this is one good-looking man you got here. How did somebody like you pull somebody this fine? Smells good enough to eat, too."

Mr. Tank stood there blushing himself into a boyish grin and basking in the praise. "I'm so glad y'all family again, Miss Evelyn," he said. "Sugar, I'm gone go on down the road and take care of that business we talked about."

He leaned into Miss Sugar and kissed her long and hard for what seemed like eternity. Miss Evelyn and I just sat there staring. After they finished carrying on, Mr. Tank let out a heavy sigh, came over to where I sat, gave me a wet peck on my forehead, then turned and walked down the steps. I could hear the metal taps on his shoes hitting the concrete as he went.

"Well, Dot, me and Phyllistene could've gone to Ma Lula's and back before you and Tank finished all of that kissing and carrying on over there."

We all fell out laughing.

I pause beneath a huge tree after a recent visit to the family cemetery where my grandparents, great-grandparents, and several of my grandfather's siblings are buried.

16

Reunion

EVEN THOUGH MY GRANDPARENTS' PLACE was only about a thirty-minute drive from Miss Sugar's down Highway 11, I felt that today it would take forever because of my excitement. It was exhilarating, lying on the back seat of Miss Sugar's convertible, my back plastered to the warm leather, my eyes on the clouds above. I could barely make out what Miss Evelyn and Miss Sugar were saying; the gentle summer breeze muffled their conversation. So I just lay there, admiring the lovely sisters with their bright scarves tied across their hats. They each wore cat-eyed sunglasses with white rims. I felt special being in the midst of them. Even though they didn't grow up together, they were both influenced in profound ways by Grandma.

My mind drifted to years earlier, when Grandma had told me about her three older siblings being sold like loaves of bread. I could feel the anguish in her voice when she spoke. It's difficult for some folks to imagine the sense of loss after being separated from someone through abandonment, death, displacement, or any other situation over which you have no control. Life had placed me and Miss Sugar in similar circumstances, and the feelings that arose were all too familiar.

As the car weaved along the country road, I thought about how Grandma would react when she saw Miss Evelyn. My heart sank at the possibility of her being so overjoyed that she'd weep uncontrollably—without covering her eyes with her apron. She always used her apron to mask her tears, and I didn't think I'd be able to stand the sight of actual tears rolling down her face.

Miss Sugar rounded the final curve, and I'm sure Grandma heard the horn blowing. As always, before the car came into full view, she was standing at the front gate, waiting for me. The car made its way down the hill, and I popped up from my lying position like a jack-in-the-box, just in time to catch a glimpse of her white head scarf, which for some reason she wore only on Sundays. We drove past a stack of freshly cut wood and a few chickens who'd escaped from the fenced-in backyard. They were running and flapping their wings as the car slowed to a crawl.

Miss Evelyn had one leg out of the door before Miss Sugar even came to a complete stop. Grandma stood there, one hand on the wooden pole that kept the fence from falling, the other in her apron pocket. The sun was shining twice as bright as I'd ever known it to shine at that time of day. It had settled directly over Grandma's head, blocking out her features.

Grandma stood erect and unmoving, then reached out and unlatched the gate. She walked through it, onto the grassy knoll that led to the road. As she got closer, she cocked her head to one side. Miss Evelyn was still leaning against the car, one hand holding on to the yellow metal. Tears flowed down her face as she took her hat and scarf off her head and handed them to me.

"*Evelyn!*" Grandma screamed her name so loudly it was deafening. "Evelyn, is that you, baby?"

By now, Grandma stood directly in front of Miss Evelyn. Both women were in shock. No words were spoken. Grandma reached out and took Miss Evelyn's hand in hers, and they just stared at each other. Then it happened: for the first time in my young life, I saw tears flood Grandma's face. Loud, sobbing tears of joy, tears Grandma had stored away for many years. A higher force pushed me right into the midst of the two women, and before I knew it, I stood there crying too, grabbing on to Grandma's apron strings until they came undone.

Miss Sugar joined the fray; then we were four. We probably looked a sight, all of us huddled together, boo-hooing like nobody's business. Grandpa was deaf as could be, but even he heard the commotion and made his way from the outhouse in the middle of the cotton field out back, where he'd been doing his business. He responded in all-too-familiar Grandpa fashion: "What's gwine on out yere? Soun' likes all hell den broke loose. I comes up short from doin' my bizness 'cause all y'all commotion."

No one paid him no mind. He just shook his head and headed back to the outhouse.

It felt like it took forever for Miss Sugar or Miss Evelyn to speak. No surprise, Miss Sugar spoke first.

"Would you look at us. Ma Lula, I jus' can't get over you knowing my sista. I ain't never told you 'bout her. Lord have mercy, blow my ass straight to hell. Excuse me, Ma Lula, but I just had to cuss. I just want you to know, my jaw's so tight after I found out my mama keeps Bay Sis but gave me away like I wasn't good enough, like throwing out an old rag that ain't got no more use. That's how I feel for years. That's why I ain't told nobody 'bout her. I was mad. Take me a long time but I got over it and now I ain't mad no more."

Miss Sugar's pronouncement—that Miss Evelyn was her sister—sent Grandma into even greater shock. She looked at Miss Sugar, then Miss Evelyn. She was probably asking herself how she could've missed the physical resemblance and other shared characteristics between the two women. She began shaking her head east and west, still in disbelief.

"All these years I been knowing both you gals," she said. "Lord, Lord, Lord. Y'all's mama and me thicker then thieves. Who woulda thunk we all standin' here in my front yard and me lookin' at my friend Missouri's two gals. I remember like it was yestiddy when Missouri had you, Sugar. I was sho nuff there when you come into this worl', jus' as bald as that eagle I seen sittin' on that pole the other day. Ain't got a stitch of hair no where. I ask Missouri, where's that chile's hair? We laugh 'bout that a long time. Chile, you a sight to behold. Next time I sees Missouri, she say she send you away to your grandmama in Alabama.

"But I tells you right here and now, Sugar: you turn out jus' fine. Now, come on. Y'all take a seat under this here tree 'fore we all fall out like flies in this hot sun. Lord, Lord, y'all sistas! Bless yo' heart."

Grandma was holding Miss Evelyn's hand as if she'd fly away if she let go. Just when I was about to take a seat on a large tree trunk that me and Grandpa had dragged to the front yard, Grandma gave me the grown-folks-gettin'-ready-to-talk look. She didn't have to part her lips. Like always, I bolted away down the dogtrot and made a quick right at the kitchen. I walked so fast I heard the skillets rattling on the papered walls. On the back porch, I stopped to get a dipper full of cool water from the bucket. I slurped it down so fast I almost choked, then unlatched the back screen door, shooed the chickens out of my way, and crawled under the house.

Now I had a good view of the front yard. It would work as long as the cackling chickens didn't give me away. But they were familiar with my routine. I lay, listening, while Grandma talked about how much she'd missed Miss Evelyn. The three women seemed so happy, talking and laughing about old times. They went on for hours. Grandpa even pitched in about how much he missed Grandma when she worked for the Murphy family.

"Ma Lula," Miss Evelyn finally said, "I missed you so much after you left Doc Murphy for good. I never told anyone about what happened to me when I was a young girl—nobody knows but the Lord, McIntosh, and Ant Glory. You remember McIntosh, don't you, Ma Lula? He was my Ant Glory's sorry-ass, good-for-nothing husband.

"Well, it wasn't a good month after you left that Ant Glory ran him off. She caught him in the cornfield with that child they call Lil Bit. That man had some nerve messing around with that youngun. She couldn't have been no older than nine or ten. He couldn't deny his wrongdoing, because Ant Glory found him out there with her. He was butterball naked. She caught him as big as day and she ran his bare ass all over that cornfield. He was almost to downtown Laurel before she stopped chasing him. I know he's somewhere *still* thanking his maker the double-barreled shotgun Ant Glory was toting misfired, otherwise they'd still be picking buckshots out of his Black ass.

"I guess Ant Glory finally said enough was enough. I heard after that incident, he left Mississippi and went up North somewhere. Until this day, I don't know why Ant Glory took so long to come to grips with McIntosh's indiscretions. I sort of felt sorry for her and what she went through to hold on to his sorry self. Ma Lula, please beg my pardon, you know I never use cuss words around you unless I'm mighty upset.

"I haven't told a soul about the times he forced himself on me when I was only twelve years old. I should have told you, Ma Lula. Today, I truly regret not being honest with you back then. I remember the times when Ant Glory dropped me off at the Murphys and you used to ask me why I looked so sad."

No one said a word, as though her words had pierced Grandma's and Miss Sugar's hearts. In the silence, I could see the pain on Miss Evelyn's face. Miss Sugar moved her chair closer, and Grandma grabbed Miss Evelyn's hands and cupped them in her own.

"It be alright, chile, you gone be jus' fine. Miss Lula right here and she ain't gone nowheres."

"Ma Lula, I wasn't knee-high to a duck's behind, not much older than your granddaughter, the first time he came after me. It started out with him wanting me to sit on his knee while he made funny little animals with his fingers. I'd laugh and giggle innocently, not realizing this was only the beginning.

"I remember the first time he messed with me like it was yesterday. Ant Glory would go into town every other Saturday morning to get groceries. I was barely awake when I heard the sound of footsteps coming down the hallway toward my bedroom. Remember, Ma Lula, how he'd drag his feet when he walked, almost shuffling along? I sat up, rubbing my eyes, to see him sitting on the side of my bed, smiling, showing that big gap in his teeth. He always had a habit of sticking his tongue in that open space, moving and wiggling it around. I thought it was hilarious, and I burst out laughing.

"Then something unimaginable happened: he grabbed me by the back of my head, pulled me to his face, then stuck his entire tongue in my mouth so far it almost touched my tonsils. I couldn't breathe; everything started spinning. It felt like I was going to vomit and pass out. He crawled on top of me. Ma Lula, I kicked that man between his legs with my bare feet so hard, he rolled off me onto the floor. Scared me to death."

As I looked at Miss Evelyn's face, I saw the shock, as if this abuse had happened only yesterday. She clenched her fist like McIntosh was standing in front of her. If he was there at that moment, I'm sure she would've pounded on him.

"That was just the first time. From then on, I slept mostly every night with one eye open. I was too scared to tell Ant Glory or anybody because he always threatened to tell her that it was all my fault. And I believed him, because he was a grown man and Ant Glory's husband. Y'all know that most folks in the country think children don't suppose to have a voice. That's why he had me thinking that nobody would believe a word I said anyway. Lord, the stories that man would come up with—I remember the times I'd be cleaning the house and washing dishes and he'd come out of nowhere, badgering me about not saying anything to nobody about what he been trying to do to me. He was always blaming the way he acted on me. That fool blamed me for having breasts and a nice little figure—like I could help it for what Mother Nature put on me at such an early age. Can you believe that?

"But I didn't know any better. I'd watch how he and Ant Glory would be hugging and kissing and carrying on just like he's the best husband in the world. She'd cook and wait on him hand and foot, kissing his ass every chance she'd get. Do you know that sorry bastard would wink at me while he was kissing all over her? I felt absolutely trapped. The only thing I could do was act like everything was okay, but I was hurting so much inside. I remember the nights when he and Ant Glory would get plastered and pukey drunk on moonshine. As soon as she went to sleep, here he comes, stumbling into my room. I'd fight that man so hard, and I'd usually win, because he'd be in a drunken stupor.

"Ma Lula, I swear, as sure as I'm sitting here, so many nights I'd take that quilt you made for me from my mama and grandma's clothes and sleep right in the middle of the cornfield where he couldn't find me. Some nights I'd lay there, staring up at the stars, praying for a better day. I can honestly say from the bottom of my heart, that quilt kept me safe and warm many nights in that cold cornfield. I could've froze to death.

"Lord knows, I was so glad to see summer come, because I knew Papa would come from across the waters. I thought long and hard about telling him what McIntosh was doing to me, but I truly believed Papa'd string McIntosh up and skin him like a deer. I didn't give a damn about McIntosh meeting his demise; I was only concerned about Ant Glory. It astounds me how, as a little girl, I was more concerned about protecting others' feelings than I was of protecting my own. I felt shame and dirty, and for what? I can't explain how I let all that hurt and bitterness fester inside me.

"I guess McIntosh got tired of struggling with me, especially as I got older. I definitely have Papa's mean streak in me, meaning I'm only going to put up with just so much, then you're going to have hell to pay. One night, lying in that cornfield, I made up my mind that I wouldn't shed one more tear because McIntosh wasn't worth the water sitting in the corner of my eyes, less long the streams that rolled down my face. I wasn't going to allow him to win this war, Ma Lula."

It looked as though the leaves on the branches of the oak tree that Grandma, Miss Evelyn, and Miss Sugar were sitting under hung lower, like they too were filled with sorrow. Even the chickens scattered about under the house were quieter than usual. I couldn't help but be drawn into the solemnness that overwhelmed the three women as they huddled together. I wanted to run out from under the house and embrace all three of them, to tell Miss Evelyn that trouble don't last always and wrap her inside my quilt of souls, like my grandma had done for me.

"Evelyn, that man jus' plain ol' vile and hateful," Grandma said. "The Lord gots a place for men like that. You hear me talkin' to you, baby? When you move to Hattiesburg with Miss Glory after your mama pass, can't keep an eye on you like I wants to, like your mama would want me to. But that didn't stop Ma Lula from prayin' for you day in and day out. I know my prayers got through, 'cause with all that going on, it wasn't nothin' but the Lord who pull you through. Sweet Jesus, you such a little chile and all that goin' on. Come here, chile, let Ma Lula hug your neck. I loves your heart and yo' liver too."

I listened as they wept enough tears to water Grandma's garden, Miss Sugar sobbing uncontrollably. All I could do was lie there with my face in my hands, absorbing it all. Silence reigned for what seemed an eternity. Then Grandma spoke.

"Evelyn, I remember what you tol' me when I was tryin' to get you married off: how you had your own mind. I knows right then, you gone be alright. All that mess you went through, chile—the good Lord brought you through the storm. Ma Lula wa'n't there with you, but the Lord was. Just look at you, chile, the prettiest thang I ever did see. It be your heart that shine through all that rigmarole. You a good woman, Evelyn, don' you *ever* let nobody tell you you ain't. I feels bad I try to get you married off to Nebulon after what you done gone through."

"Nebulon Chaney was a good man, Ma Lula. But what happened with McIntosh kept creeping through the back door every time we were together. McIntosh ripped out my soul and just destroyed my trust in men. Now, don't get me wrong: I wanted a husband and children, but every time men came calling and wanting to court, something inside me couldn't go no further. I spent so much time wondering what's wrong with me; just couldn't figure it out. When Nebulon and I were alone, all I could smell was McIntosh's tobacco breath. I felt the cold creeping up my back every time Nebulon touched me, just like those freezing blades of grass and cornstalks.

"It took a few years before Ant Glory saw I wasn't in my bed. She came looking for me one night and stumbled into me lying there in the cornfield, wrapped up in my quilt. Even through the darkness, I could see the concern in her eyes. It's funny how she never asked me what was wrong or why I was there. She just took me in her arms like I was a newborn baby.

"That's the last time McIntosh ever came near me. I'd see him every day like I always did, but when he saw me, he'd break his neck trying to head in another direction. Ant Glory must've put the fear of God in him. I've always wondered if she knew the whole time, but it took running into my shivering cold body sleeping in that field to slap her out of her denial."

I watched as Miss Evelyn folded her arms around her body, as though she was trying to shield herself from not only the pain but also the words she spoke of her past.

"I'd get so angry at Ant Glory, because it was though she refused to recognize what was happening to me. After I came to her when Mama passed on, even though I was sad about Mama's passing, I was still an energetic, playful child. A year later, I must've turned into the saddest-looking child you'd ever want to see. It had to be difficult for her not to see the change. You asked me so many times back then, Ma Lula, if I was okay. You probably thought I was just grieving my mama. But in truth, I was loathing what McIntosh was trying to do to me. A couple of times Ant Glory caught McIntosh flirting and making inappropriate remarks toward young girls no older than I was at that time. I'd hear her cursing to herself, but in the end, he'd always lull her into thinking he'd made a mistake and she'd end up begging for his forgiveness. Of course, he lied.

"After she found me in that field, Ant Glory told me to never mention what happened with McIntosh to nobody. She said he didn't know any better. She went on to tell me that this had to be our little secret. She said if folks got ahold of our business, they'd start talking about me being a fast-tail gal. Again, Ma Lula, I held it in my mind that it was all my fault for many years. Poor Ant Glory, she was the one who didn't know any better.

"Years later, I heard folks talking about how Ant Glory chased McIntosh through the same cornfield that was my hiding place for all those years. Lord knows I've always wondered about that chile Lil Bit and if she carried the same shame, guilt, and pain that weighed me down for so long. I lived up to the promise I made to Ant Glory about never saying anything. I tried to will myself to forget what happened, but McIntosh's cruelty never left me, especially at night. Well, I guess I'm what folks down here call a spinster, because I don't have a husband and I ain't looking for one, Lord willing. I'm just too broken. I'm sure no man out there wants to deal with all my problems, anyway."

Miss Sugar finally broke her silence. It had been too long since she'd added her two cents to the conversation, I thought.

"Evelyn, my Tank gots a friend and, chile—he be just right for you. You need a man who ain't gonna give you no trouble. His name is William, but most folks calls him Blue 'cause he blacker than the ace of spade, bowlegged as he can be, and finer then a cold glass of good wine in the summertime. Y'all fit like a glove. He gots one leg—the other one blown off in the war, but they put a peg leg on it. He's half blind in one eye and can't see out the other. I don't believe he can do the nasty, either. But he must've been something else in his day, 'cause I hear he got younguns spread out all over Miss'ippi. He just needs a woman's touch, make him feel a lil bit like a man every now and then."

"Dot! You ought to be 'shame' of yourself. I might be a little bit lonely, but I'm damn sure not desperate. Not one bit. By the way, if I just want something to keep me company, I got a German shepherd, a Scotch terrier, and a white collie. Now if I get to the point where I just want companionship, then I'll wait on the good Lord to put that person in my life. I refuse to go looking for love; I'd much rather let love find me. That's what's wrong with a lot of women these days, they settle for any man, just because they're a warm body to snuggle up with on cold nights. I want more, and I think I deserve better.

"For your information, Dot, I had a lot of suitors when I got to Chicago. I had colored doctors and teachers ask me for my hand. I politely told them that I didn't have time for a husband. I had so many propositions I started telling men I was married. Do y'all know, that didn't stop them jokers from asking me out anyway? Just goes to show you that men will still be men, except for my Booker, he was a different sort. Ma Lula, I know you remember my cousin Booker—folks called him Stump?"

"I sure do," Grandma said. At the mention of Stump's name, I imagined a twinkle in her eye so bright, it could light up a nighttime sky. "Them was some tough times when he drives me every week to see Edgar and the chil'ren. Jus' as bright as he wanna be. I think 'bout that boy all the time."

"Well, he was the main reason I ended up in Chicago. He'd write me letters every month, begging me to come up there.

He kept talking about all the opportunities for colored teachers. He said I could stay with him and his family long as I wanted. I kept putting it off; I didn't want to leave Laurel and my teaching post. Then one day, I ran into McIntosh in the five-and-dime store, after all those years. We locked eyes and I froze stiff. I could barely put one foot in front of the other. Do you know he had the nerve to come up to me to ask how I was doing? I don't know what came over me: the next thing I knew, I slapped the fire out of that man. Then I stormed out of that store and didn't look back.

"But y'all know what? I felt fifty pounds lighter. This time I fought him back with the strength of a woman. I wanted him to feel the sting of every little girl he ever abused; it was for Lil Bit and all those other girls that he had his way with that I don't even know about. That type of man preys on the innocence of the young until somebody stop them permanently.

"After that, I wrote Booker and told him I was on my way. A week later, I left for Chicago. Now, y'all want to hear something else that's funny? When Booker picked me up from that train station, I just dropped my bags and stood there with my mouth wide open. I wanted to run, but I talked myself out of it. I wanted to cry, but the tears wouldn't fall. Booker stood there jumping up and down, waving his hands all over the place, smiling from ear to ear. He grabbed me by the waist and picked me up off the ground, just like he did when we were teenagers after Papa Jim Mullens would keep me the whole summer. Booker and I were so close when we were growing up. I hadn't seen him in years, and I was in shock that day because he was the spitting image of his daddy, that dirty, stinking, no-good McIntosh. He has that round face, hair slicked back with a little bald spot in the crown of his head, big pointy ears, and that gap in his teeth. Funny thing is, Booker always had that gap, even when he was a kid, but I never really paid it no mind. Ain't that something?

"Booker ran his mouth like a runaway freight train all the way to his house. I don't even think he noticed how quiet I was.

A part of me felt like I did when I was a young girl running for my life, looking for a safe place so McIntosh couldn't hurt me. Every time I looked at Booker, I saw McIntosh. Ma Lula, I felt so ashamed for feeling this way. But these feelings were fleeting, as I only had love for Booker. He was more like a little brother to me than a cousin. I made up my mind that I wouldn't project my feelings about McIntosh onto him. It didn't take long for me to snap back to reality and realize that it wasn't his fault he was a spitting image of his father.

"When I got to Booker's house and he opened the door, all I could see was an anthill of children running all over. He and his wife made me feel so comfortable. I'll tell you all this: Booker is the most decent man I ever met in my life. To this day, I think that staying with him, looking at the way he treated his wife, children, grandchildren, and anybody coming in or out of his door put me on the road to healing. It wasn't nobody but the Lord that put me there with Booker and his family.

"After moving to Chicago, I started making a pretty decent wage as a teacher. I wore the most expensive clothes that money could buy, bought a new car every year, and purchased a three-bedroom house that would make the most modest person envious. I even joined one of those women voting groups. Truth be told, I was just a dressed-up garbage can for a long time. I have to tell you again that I hid my hurt pretty good, Ma Lula.

"I can't say for sure, but something told me that Booker had an idea of what his father had done to me. There were times where I'd get this sixth sense. I just couldn't put my finger on it. One thing I knew for sure: I'd never tell Booker about the misdeeds of his father, ever. That entire year that I lived with him and his family, not once did he mention McIntosh. It was almost like he didn't exist. We did, however, have the best conversations about his mama and how she'd beat our asses when we got caught in devilment. We'd sit around the kitchen table and laugh.

"One evening after supper, Booker and I got to talking, and you know what he told me? He said that Miss Lula is the one that taught him patience, love, and forgiveness. He explained how he'd watch you all those months when you all were traveling up and down the road between Livingston and Laurel. All that love in your heart was like the shade of a tree keeping him cool in the heat of those times. He has a picture of you right there on his mantelpiece, and every time he looks at it, it reminds him of your compassion. You meant a whole lot to Booker, Ma Lula."

Miss Evelyn sounded as though she was so relieved to finally open up. Grandma and Miss Sugar, I thought, were the only two people on this earth she'd feel comfortable revealing her experiences to. And I think she wanted Miss Sugar to know that she didn't have a great childhood, either, even though she remained with their mother. McIntosh shattered her innocence, and as a result she put up a wall, refusing to let anyone inside. Even Grandma.

What Miss Evelyn went through took on a deeper meaning as I got older and heard from other women who'd had similar experiences. They talked about how they too were ashamed to discuss the incident with others, out of fear of being blamed. I won't forget, either, when Mary Lee, one of my classmates at Bethel Hill, told me she was "doing the nasty" with a full-grown man. She was only ten, and, sadly, she probably thought this was okay because he made her feel special. She made me swear on a stack of Bibles that I wouldn't tell anyone. I can still recall the way she cuffed her hands against my ear and whispered her words. It was as though, deep down, it was too painful to talk about out loud. Her childish voice felt like feathers rubbing against my eardrum, and a tingling feeling went through me when she whispered that phrase—"doing the nasty." Then it was over, and she never mentioned it again.

One day soon after, I looked around for her in the classroom and she was gone. Poof! She disappeared just like that.

No one said anything of her whereabouts, and it was almost like she never existed.

I never told Grandma what had happened to Mary Lee.

On that hot summer day, as Miss Evelyn talked about her struggles, it reminded me of the stories I'd heard over and over. The names and faces changed, but the stories remained the same. People spoke about how some females brought it on themselves; that they were "fast girls" who couldn't keep their drawers up and their dresses down. Or excuses were made for the perpetrator, saying "He's just a man," "It was all that gal's fault that she got pregnant," and "What did you do to cause that man/boy to chase after you?" I can't tell you how many girls who were older sisters to some of my classmates were sent up North because they got pregnant. They'd stay until the baby was born—sometimes they didn't return at all. These girls were no older than thirteen or fourteen.

As I matured, I began to understand why Miss Evelyn felt powerless. Many folks during my grandparents' era believed that if a girl was raped or molested or ended up pregnant without a husband, it was all her fault. It didn't seem to matter how young she was, and there was no way to change their minds. Each day, I thank Grandma for being one of the few old folks who didn't shame the females who came to her about their problems. Instead, she listened to them, hugged them, and gave them encouragement.

That day with Miss Evelyn, I'd been under the house for hours, soaking up the conversation. Even though they'd comment here and there, the general quietness of Grandma and Miss Sugar stunned me. Maybe they wanted Miss Evelyn to bring them up to date on all the years they'd missed out on. Or were they in shock, after hearing about the terrible things she'd had to endure? I closed my eyes. I wouldn't move until I'd heard every word.

The road that leads from my grandparents' farm to the fork
in the road where my teacher, Miss Clay, would pick me
up and take me to Bethel Hill School

17

Broken

BUT MY THOUGHTS WERE INTERRUPTED by Grandma calling. I opened my eyes in time to see her heading toward the front door. That meant we'd be eating soon, and she was going to the kitchen to start warming up food. It was Sunday, and she'd cooked the entrees on Saturday. My job would be to peel and dice the Irish potatoes for her famous potato salad.

"Don' y'all move one bit," she was saying. "Y'all sistas gots too much catchin' up to do. I'm gone find that chile so we can get this food on direc'ly."

"Miss Lula, me and Dot can help you so you don't have to worry Phyllistene."

"Now, Evelyn, you know how I can't have more than one woman in the kitchen with me. My mama Emma usta say too many cooks spoil the meal."

Grandma barely got out the last word before I'd jetted out from under the house like one of Uncle Herman's hunting dogs was chasing me. Over the years, I'd developed impeccable timing on just how long it would take to shake off the dirt on my clothes. I thought I'd gotten pretty good at looking and acting oblivious. But deep down, I had a feeling Grandma knew I'd been planted under the house, listening.

Sunday suppers at my grandparents' house were always festive. Hardly did a Sunday go by that we didn't have at least one visitor. Most times it was Ant Bessie, Uncle Herman, or a friend or two who dropped in to check on the old folks. The best part of these gatherings was sitting at the dinner table, surrounded by grown-ups. The gossip that flew around the table was hotter than the steam from the pots of food lying in wait on the wooden stove.

Not only did Grandma have three, sometimes four, entrees spread across the white oilcloth-covered table; her different types of sweets made my mouth water. She'd bake blackberry or peach cobbler, caramel and coconut cake, and sweet potato or lemon meringue pies. Nobody left her house without carrying a bag of food away with them. Folks lived for Grandma's leftovers. Oftentimes, they'd bring an empty dish in anticipation.

Most of Sunday's food was prepared early Saturday morning, no exceptions. Grandma was a staunch Baptist who strictly abided by the biblical command to rest on the seventh day and keep it holy. The only things me and the grandparents did on Sunday that came anywhere close to work were washing dishes, light cooking, feeding the chickens, slopping the hogs, and making our beds. Anything else was considered sacrilegious in Grandma's eyes.

Even though our house was small, the dining room, which sat right next to the kitchen, was relatively large. Our dining table could seat at least eight to ten people comfortably. The table was flush against the wall, near the window overlooking the backyard, where you could see the chickens parading around. I'd prop a piece of firewood on the windowsill so we could feel the warm summer breeze. There wasn't any way of knowing how many folks would end up at our house for dinner on Sundays, so to be on the safe side, Grandpa and I would pull the table away from the wall and add the two spare chairs. The table was old and heavy, with two wobbly legs. I'd have to fold a couple sheets of newspaper real tight and put them under the legs to stabilize them.

With Miss Sugar and Miss Evelyn joining us, I knew there would be interesting conversation. At these Sunday gatherings, Grandpa always seemed to bring his best entertainment and stand-up—or, I should say, sit-down—routines. I don't think he ever met a conversation he didn't like. Since he was hard of hearing, everyone spoke really loud, and after all his years of being a bit deaf, he became good at lip-reading.

After washing my hands and face in the water basin on the back porch, I rushed in to peel potatoes and help Grandma set the table. I couldn't wait to run down the hallway and yell through the screened porch that dinner was ready. I didn't have to announce it twice; the aroma of Grandma's food seeping through the air, encircling the entire farm, was so good it made you want to slap your mother, as Miss Sugar would say.

After coming through the door, Miss Sugar and Miss Evelyn removed their shoes. During my years in the country, I'd see many women take their shoes off before they sat down at the table, and I often wondered whether this was tradition or superstition. Miss Sugar just said she couldn't enjoy her meal unless she took off her shoes. Grandpa took his seat at the head of the table, which was customary. He was the person who prayed over the food. If it was just me and him, his blessing was short and sweet: his usual "Jesus wept." On Sundays, however, he had an audience, and man, did he go for the long one:

"Lawd, I thank ye for all of us sittin' round this yere table this ev'ning, and fo' the food we 'bout to receive. Lawd, we wants to bless the cook, too, 'cause it be her hands that made this yere food. Thank you agin, Lawd, fo' brangin' us togetha to partake of these yere vittles. Thank you, Lawd, fo' jus' bein' so good to yo' chil'ren. Thank you too, Lawd, fo' brangin' these yere two sistas, Evelyn and Sugar, togetha this ev'ning to sit yere at yo' table. Lawd, we been waitin' long time for Sugar…."

Grandma cleared her throat so loud, Grandpa stopped in midsentence.

"Amen."

I'm sure if Grandma hadn't interrupted, he still would've been saying grace an hour later.

Miss Sugar, Miss Evelyn, Grandpa, and I began diving into the platters and pots of food. Today's fare was deer, fish, pork loin, chicken, and neck bones. There were also huge side dishes of Grandma's mouthwatering macaroni and cheese, potato salad, collard greens, and fresh hot-water cornbread.

As was typical with Grandma, she never claimed a seat at the table. She hung around in the kitchen just long enough to make sure everyone was satisfied with what they had on their plates, or she'd walk around pouring iced tea or lemonade into half-full glasses. I'd watch her run back and forth between the kitchen and dining room, pleading for everyone to eat as much as they liked because she had extra in the oven, keeping warm.

That day, right at the exact moment I was about to sink my teeth into a piece of hot buttered cornbread, I heard the familiar sound of click-clacking in the linoleum hallway. The sound grew louder and louder, until I could see Ant Bessie standing in the doorway.

"Well, Lawd, I know Sunday want be gettin' 'way from yere, less Bessie came 'round," Grandpa said.

"I 'spect I's jus' in time to sample Miss Lula's Sunday vittles." Ant Bessie stood there, leaning on her walking stick, her eyes glistening brighter than the one gold tooth perched in tho front of her mouth.

"'Tain't nothin' new, Bessie; you's here pert'near every Sunday, come rain or shine. If I don' see you on Sunday, either you's down in yo' legs or the good Lawd done took you on yo' way from yere. So I don' know why you tryin' to show off jus' 'cause we gots comp'ny, 'cause I know how you likes to eat and 'tain't never seent you turnt down no food."

As Grandpa talked to her, one of Ant Bessie's eyes locked on Miss Evelyn, the other on the food. Both Miss Sugar and Miss Evelyn stopped eating to pay proper respect.

"Hey, Miss Bessie, how you doin' this evening?" Miss Evelyn said.

Miss Sugar followed with "Good evenin', Miss Bessie."

It was just like Ant Bessie to frown and ignore their greeting. She glared at the two sisters like a bull seeing red. She was plain old mean. Sometimes I'd speak to her, and instead of acknowledging me, she'd turn and walk away like I hadn't said a word.

Grandpa broke in and said, "Gone over there and sit yoself down, Bessie. You see, we already pull out the table fo' you, 'cause I knows you comin' just sho as night turns to day. Never knows you to miss too many Sunday meals yet. One thang fo' sho: when the Judgment come, everybody gone be runnin' to the Lawd, but you gone be somewheres messin' 'round in somebody's bizness or somewheres eatin'. It gone be one or the t'other. Papa usta say how you eat more than all his chil'ren, cows, and hogs put togetha."

By this time, Miss Sugar, Miss Evelyn, and I were howling, almost crying with laughter. I was so tickled, I started choking on a bone from the fried fish. Miss Evelyn had to hit me on my back in order to clear my throat.

"I ain't stuttin' you, Edgar," Ant Bessie said. "What I wants to know is: who this woman sittin' next to Sugar?"

Miss Evelyn gently wiped her lips with her napkin before responding. "Good evening, Miss Bessie, how are you? Excuse me for my manners, but my name is Evelyn, Dot's—I mean, Sugar's—sister."

"Sugar, you ain't never told me 'bout havin' no sista."

"No, ma'am; nobody know. I only saw my sista one time in my whole life and that's when I was a young gal, but we together now, praise the Lawd. I missed her. Ain't nothin' but the dev'l keep us apart; ain't that right, Bay Sis?"

"You right as rain, Dot."

Miss Sugar and Miss Evelyn gave Ant Bessie just enough information to shut her up, at least temporarily. I knew my great-aunt well enough to know that it would only be a matter of minutes before she'd get started once again, digging for more dirt. Ant Bessie didn't like nobody, especially if their skin was dark like mine. Like Miss Sugar's grandparents, she was "color struck," or notorious for labeling people based on their complexion. Whenever she described a person, she'd say, "that yalla gal," or "that red boy," or "so-and-so is black as tar," or "white crackers." The darker they were, the more degrading she got. She always called me "lil Black gal," or told me I needed to stop being in the sun so much because I was getting Blacker and Blacker. Whenever she looked at me, I swear I saw two tiny pitchforks in her eyes, just waiting to jab and stab.

As I expected, it wasn't long before she began poking around. "You ain't from 'round here, are you?" she said, fixing her beady eyes on Miss Evelyn. "'Cause I never seent you befo'."

"No, ma'am. I was born in Sandersville, Mississippi, and worked in Laurel as a teacher. I live in Chicago now."

"Well, I wants to know how you and Sugar sistas. Sugar ain't never told me she lived in no Laurel befo'. Who's yo' daddy? I bet any 'mount of money yo' daddy a white man, whether you know him or not, 'cause you light, bright, and damn near white. And you got that straight white folks' hair. Sugar's hair nappy as a sheep's ass, so I know y'all both don' have the same daddy or the same mama—it's one or da other."

Miss Sugar and Miss Evelyn sat, looking at each other like they were wondering which of them would put Ant Bessie in her place. But Grandpa spoke first, pointing at Ant Bessie with a chicken bone.

"Bessie, eat yo' food 'fore you choke to death off that drumstick you puttin' in yo' mouf. You jus' talk too damn much for any use atall. I thank you talk mosta time 'cause you jus' like to hear yo'self talk. Rat now, I jus' want you to shut up."

"Well, Edgar, I don' thank it's right for folks to jus' sit here an lie to me rat to my face. Talkin' 'bout they's sistas."

"Bessie, you done took lost of yo' sense. You sittin' here at *my* dinner table. I ain't got to tell you a damn thang 'bout who come and go out my house."

"Edgar, I don' see nothin' wrong wit' me tryin' to figure out how this here woman gone jus' pop up and tells me she Sugar's sista. I been knowin' Sugar long time; she ain't never said nothin' 'bout no sista. So if this hi-yalla gal gone tell me she Sugar's sista, ain't nothin' wrong wit' wantin' to know how. So ifs somebody tells me what I ask, I jus' might shut up."

Ant Bessie had barely gotten out her last words when Miss Evelyn popped up from her chair. She rose so ferociously, the uneven part of the table started to shake, and some of the food platters slid downhill. We all had to push down on the table so it would stop rattling. When I looked up at Miss Evelyn, I remembered how Grandma had said her freckles seemed to dance around her jaws when she got mad. Well! She looked so angry, some of those freckles seemed to jump right off her face. I could've sworn that her hair turned from light red to a deep blaze of fire. Her eyes, normally round as fifty-cent pieces, became slits of rage. She stood directly across the table from Ant Bessie, looking her dead in the eyes.

"Look a-here, old woman: I don't know who you are and I'm going to excuse myself up front because my mama would roll over in her grave if she knew I ever talked to my elders like I'm getting ready to talk to you now. You lucky as hell that Ma Lula is out on that front porch, otherwise I would really give you a piece of my mind. First, you need to mind your own damn business and stay out of mine. Plus, may I ask, where are your children and husband? The way you talk to folks, you probably ran them off with your evil self.

"And for your information, I knew both my mama and my papa—now, do you know who yours are? If you do, so be it—that's all you need to know. If I was you, I'd sit back and enjoy this fine meal that Ma Lula has made for us and stop disrespecting this dinner table with all your foolish talk and shut the hell up 'cause you about to get on my last nerve. What you think Phyllistene think about how you talking? She's acting more like grown folk than you right now. So, I'm gonna sit back down and enjoy the rest of my supper and hope you act like you got good sense from here on out."

Miss Evelyn sat back in her seat graciously, but not before winking at me. Miss Sugar just sat there with a half smile on her face, nodding her head. Of course, Grandpa had to add his two cents: "Ha. I told you, Bessie, that you gone meet yo' match one of these days. Evelyn time enuf fo' you, ain't she?"

I couldn't resist sneaking peeks at Ant Bessie. She didn't look up once from her plate. Had Grandma heard any of the commotion? As usual, she'd taken a seat in her favorite rocker on the front porch. By the time everyone finished eating, she'd be in deep sleep or contemplation. She never sat down at the dinner table, even after cooking and cleaning for hours and preparing enough food for a king's feast. She'd always tell me she was happy just knowing that everyone sitting at the table got full as a tick.

Ant Bessie still hadn't said anything or made eye contact with any of us. It was eerily silent, except for the smacking of lips and the clatter of forks and knives hitting our plates. Then, from that silence, Ant Bessie erupted with a resounding, "Well, Edgar, y'all can thank what y'all want!" She was shouting loudly now. "I'm jus' gone go on back down the hill toward home. I done sit here at yo' table and been disrespected. I ain't got to put up wit' this yere mess. Can't enjoy Ma Lula's cookin' no way wit' all this mess goin' on 'round yere."

"Bessie, you ain't got nothin' left on yo' plate no way but spit. You done licked it clean. What you needs to do is stop puttin' on, 'cause you jus' full of ya know what. As sho as my name's Edgar, you ain't gone miss a day wit' yo' foolishment. You's jus' a mean ol' varmit."

If Ant Bessie was looking for pity from Grandpa, she was barking up the wrong tree. He wasn't the sympathetic type. She grabbed her walking stick, which was propped up against the window frame, fumbling it in her frustration. It fell on the floor, right next to my feet. I leaned down beneath the table and grabbed it, but before I could give it to her, she snatched it from my hand so hard, I thought she was going to take my arm along with it.

"Don' you dare touch my stick wit' yo' Black ugly self. Nobody ask you to put yo' hands anywheres near my stick. If I wants yo' help, I ask you, you heah me?"

Her words broke my heart in two. It hurt so badly it knocked the taste of Grandma's chocolate cake right out of my mouth. I couldn't even swallow. I don't think it was the word *Black* by itself that hurt me so; it was when Ant Bessie put *Black* and *ugly* together. I don't think it would've mattered if she'd called me white, yellow, or polka dot, and ugly; it was the combination of those words that stuck to my mind like flypaper. Embarrassment swamped me.

I think her behavior spoiled everyone's appetite for dessert, because Grandpa, Miss Sugar, and Miss Evelyn all excused themselves from the table, shaking their heads in disgust. Miss Sugar and Miss Evelyn both gave me a warm embrace and frowned at Ant Bessie as she sauntered toward the back door. Then Miss Evelyn released me and walked after her, calling Ant Bessie's name. I couldn't see the two of them from the dining room window, but I heard Miss Evelyn's raised voice.

Miss Sugar gave me another quick hug and a kiss on my cheek and said, "Don't you worry yourself, chile, everybody knows Miss Bessie is crazy as hell. And you know what? I wouldn't want to be in her shoes right now, 'cause Bay Sis is getting in her ass in that backyard. Even though she old and mean as sin, she still got to get her propers. That's just the way us grown folks handle our bizness."

I don't know how long Miss Evelyn was in the yard talking to Ant Bessie. All I wanted to do at that moment was put my mind on something else. As I began removing the dishes from the table, I could only think about Ant Bessie and her hatefulness. I placed the large silver bucket of water on the stove, heating it until it almost came to a boil. Then I took the dirty dishes and began scraping what little food was left on folks' plates into another bucket, which we used to feed the hogs.

I dropped a bar of Grandma's homemade lye soap into the boiling water, along with the dishes, and began using a rag to wash them before putting them aside to rinse. My hands were immersed in scalding water, but I didn't feel anything. I was numb, physically and mentally. The water didn't hurt as much as Ant Bessie's words. Somewhere deep in my spirit, I was screaming with humiliation and shame over the way she'd belittled me in front of Miss Sugar and Miss Evelyn. I wanted to escape, to run from myself.

After hurriedly finishing up the rinsing and drying, I fled into the woods. The only thing that could ease my spirit was the spring, with its calm waters. Lying there, the sting of Ant Bessie's words subsided, replaced by the chirping of robins and the melodious hum of hummingbirds. The sounds of nature drowned out the ugliness.

I don't remember how long I lay there, but I was lulled into an almost hypnotic state, mesmerized by my tadpoles, swimming back and forth, wiggling their little tails. Then I heard Grandma calling and I took off running up the hill, hoping that Miss Sugar or Miss Evelyn hadn't told her what Ant Bessie had said to me. I really had no way of articulating why. By the time I got to the front yard, Miss Evelyn was embracing Grandma in the same way she had when she'd arrived. "Don't you worry, Ma Lula," she was saying. "I ain't gonna be a stranger. You're going to see me a lot around here, so much I am going to wear out my welcome."

Standing there on the porch, looking up at Grandma, my hands felt like they were on fire. Tears of agony began to stream down my face. I stood, my fists balled up tighter than a spool of thread. The adrenaline rush had expired, and now all I could feel was physical pain. Grandma struggled to open my hands. When she did, my palms were bright, scalded red. "Grandma," I whispered, "I hurt so bad, they hurt so bad. My hands on fire, Grandma. I ain't do nothing to Ant Bessie, but she just poke fun at me anyhow. I didn't mean to put my hand in that hot dishwater, Grandmama."

Grandma held me tight, kissing my forehead. "Let me go and get you somethin' to put on them hands," she said, and walked hurriedly toward the kitchen. I saw the concerned looks on her, Miss Sugar's, and Miss Evelyn's faces. I was in so much agony all I could do was maintain a blank stare while hopping on one foot, then the next, trying to contain the pain. Miss Sugar sat down and pulled me into her lap. Miss Evelyn stood over me, rubbing my head.

When Grandma came back, she had a Mason jar filled with yellow stuff and a silver can of molasses. She gently unballed my hands and placed both of them in the cold bucket of molasses. The frigid wet stickiness felt amazing. I closed my eyes and took it in. After a time, Grandma gathered my hands from the bucket. She poured on globs of the yellow stuff, which I found out later was sulfur, and spread it evenly until it formed a plaster. My hands were as yellow as Miss Sugar's Buick Electra 225.

"Miss Lula, you sure you don't want us to stay here for the night to make sure Phyllistene's all right?"

"I think she's gone be jus' fine once that molasses and sulfa take hold; it gone take the burnin' out her hand. I 'preciate if y'all drop by Jeff Martin's on the way out to let him know I needs him to take this chile to Miss Jubilee's sometime tomorrow. She gone put some of her potions on them burns. Should be blisters, by then."

I was glad to hear I'd be seeing Miss Jubilee. I knew that she would heal my hands and maybe my heart, too.

"Miss Lula, I think Miss Bessie's nastiness was just too much for this child. It ain't right when grown folks make children feel less than. Come here, Phyllistene, let Miss Evelyn tell you something before I get on the road." Miss Evelyn reached out her hand and gently rubbed my face, then said, "You are the prettiest little girl I ever did see, do you hear me? Your rich, dark skin is the same color as the kings and queens of Africa. I don't want to ever hear about you being ashamed of your color, because you, my little one, come from who?"

"Kings and queens, Miss Evelyn."

"Don't you ever forget it, either. Now, give Miss Evelyn some sugar before I go."

Then it was Miss Sugar's turn. She leaned down and whispered in my ear so softly I had to close my eyes to hear. "The next time Miss Bessie call you out of your name, I know she old, but I just might have to take that stick and beat her ass with it. She a mean ol' heifer."

I laughed so hard, I thought the molasses and sulfur were going to fly off my hands. Then Miss Sugar and Miss Evelyn put their shoes back on and gathered up their hats and scarves. My heart sank, watching them leave. I stood with Grandpa and Grandma, watching and waving as Miss Sugar's car disappeared through the trees. When they were gone, Grandpa looked as concerned as Grandma over my burnt hands.

"You alright gal? Bessie didn't scare you none, did she? She jus' ain't been right since that ol' mule kicked her in the head a few years back. She already crazy as a juju bee even 'fore that. I jus' don' rightly know 'bout that Bessie."

Despite the pain, I was able to muster a slight grin. Then Grandpa walked away, shaking his head and mumbling something under his breath. I would venture to guess it was probably a few curse words.

"Come on now, so Grandma can get you out of this heat 'fore that molasses start runnin'. You don' need all this sun on your hands."

That was the last time I'd see Miss Evelyn, though she'd write Grandma frequently. I'd read the letters aloud to my grandparents as we sat in our rocking chairs on the screened-in porch. Miss Evelyn always had words of encouragement for me, telling me, "Phyllistene, don't ever forget who you are and what you can be, and never let anyone tell you any differently."

That day, the sun had almost set, which meant it was time for us to sit on the front porch or in the yard, breathing in the warm nighttime air. Grandma motioned me to take my familiar seat, so she could comb and braid my hair. As she worked, I told her about Miss Sugar saying that I should be wearing ponytails instead of braids all the time.

"Chile, don' pay Sugar no mind. You still ain't big as a minute, so we gone keep these braids and twists in your hair for the time bein'."

There was something so special about her hands on my scalp, especially after the incident with Ant Bessie. I guess they soothed some of my hurt. And I could feel Grandma knew exactly what was going on in my heart.

"Remember how Grandma told you before, I don' wants you holdin' bitterness in your heart, chile, not even for a minute. Nothin' get mad but dogs. The only thing you can do with a mad dog is shoot it. I told you, folks don' know what they don' know. Your Ant Bessie can't show no love if she ain't got it to give in the firs' place, and she never had it, chile. The slave masta beat it out of they mamas and papas, then they pass it on to they chil'ren. That's why it wa'n't a lot of huggin' goin' on at the plantation: 'cause ain't much to feel good about. My mama did a whole lotta huggin' on me and my sista Ella, though. She hold us every chance she get, 'cause she wants us to pass it on. When you done had three chil'ren almos' tore from your belly like Mama, she learnt to try to hold me and Ella tight as she can. That's why Grandma jus' hug you all the time; 'cause Mama shows me how.

"Your Ant Bessie gots to find her own way. The Lord will see to it. Like I tol' you before, your antee ain't seen much love in her poor life. She jus' like Mama Nall and pretty near lots of these country folks 'round here. They done seen so much killin' and carryin' on, folks dyin' all 'round, it hardens they hearts. So before you go to sleep tonight, Grandma wants you to say your prayers and say one for your Ant Bessie, too."

I felt much better with Grandma's fingers massaging my scalp. When I turned, I saw her removing the excess hair that had accumulated in the comb. She held it out to me and said, "Now, you take this here hair and throw it in the fireplace and set fire to it, 'cause you don' want the birds to get a hold of it."

Grandma believed that if you threw human hair on the ground and a bird found it and built a nest from it, the person to whom the hair belonged would experience excruciating head-aches for the rest of their lives. As I watched my hair burn in the fireplace, popping and sizzling from the castor oil, a thought flashed into my mind. Grandma would have been disappointed in me. But still, I began thinking that maybe, just maybe, I'd get up the nerve to ask Ant Bessie if I could braid her hair. I imag-ined myself gathering her hair from the comb, then tossing it on the ground. I'd wait for a bird to fly away with it. What a sense of satisfaction at that moment, imagining that Ant Bessie would suffer from horrific headaches for a lifetime!

That night, I lay in bed, full of bitter thoughts. Waiting to see Miss Jubilee was agonizing. Grandma promised me that her healing herbs would take away the blisters and my hands would "be jus' like new." She kept reminding me that when I saw Miss Jubilee, I'd need to do exactly what she said. I didn't know how to interpret that. What type of magic would Miss Jubilee be cooking up to heal my hands? My mind went back to the days of Sheriff Suggs and what had happened between him and Grandma. I desperately wanted to understand Grandma's depth of forgiveness, but no matter how hard I tried, I couldn't.

18

Fixed

MIRACULOUSLY, my hands made it through the night with just a tinge of pain. But the sticky residue from the jet-black molasses had begun to seep through the bandages. Folks down South called this syrupy stuff blackstrap molasses. It was used for all types of burns, cuts, tinctures, and teas, and to saturate homemade biscuits.

I was unable to use my hands, and for the first time in my life, I felt useless. I could barely lift a fork to my mouth or go to the bathroom without Grandma's help. Whatever I touched the sulfur and molasses would stick to like a magnet to metal. Having my independence taken away perturbed me. The only thing I hated more was the sight of Ant Bessie's evil face, which kept creeping into my mind.

After breakfast, Grandma tied fresh bandages on my hands, then sat down in the swing alongside me. I curled up with my knees to my chest, and she tried to calm my aching spirit with her humming. I can't describe how soothing the cool molasses felt on my hands. Before I knew it, I fell into a deep sleep. I didn't realize that Grandma had left, nor did I hear the noise from the black pickup truck that pulled in by the front gate. I was awakened by Grandma talking to what sounded like a young girl, a voice with a resounding southern twang that sent chills through me.

Shooting up, I ran to the screen door, hoping to catch a glimpse of what was going on in the front yard. I could see Grandma sitting in her chair, but the sun was so bright, I could only make out the silhouette of the person she was talking to. I had to press my face against the screen, then use my heavily bandaged hands to cuff my eyes so I could see the person.

It was Miss Daisy. What was she doing here? It had been a long time since she'd visited Grandma, more than four years. Her red hair was all curls that came down to her shoulders. Her clothes were almost as fine as Miss Sugar's and Miss Evelyn's. Her makeup accentuated her high cheekbones and deep-set eyes. She was so beautiful. She'd blossomed into a woman, but with a young girl's voice. I'd never heard her talk this much until today, as she sat with Grandma.

Miss Daisy was a grown woman, so Grandma expected me to show her the courtesies due to adults. I walked down the two steps to the front yard and said good afternoon. Miss Daisy smiled and nodded. I couldn't help but stare at how remarkable she looked.

Then, as expected, grown folks were talking, meaning I had to disappear. There was no way I could crawl under the house with ten pounds of molasses and bandages on my hand, so I went right back to my lookout post in the front porch swing. I lay down, thinking Miss Daisy's visit might be seren-dipitous. One of Grandma's favorite sayings was *God works in mysterious ways.* Another was how God put certain people in our life *for a reason and some for a season.* Maybe Miss Daisy coming here today, out of all days, was a sign. She had already been in my life a season. Maybe now there was a special reason for her to reappear.

From the swing, I heard Grandma and Miss Daisy laughing. Again, I ran to the screen door. Now I saw Miss Daisy unlatching the gate. Powerful emotions rose up inside of me. The next thing I knew, I'd run down the steps and grabbed her by the waist, hugging her wildly. This was the hug I should've given her the last time. I couldn't use my hands because of the thick wrappings, so I made do with my arms. When Miss Daisy hugged me back and kissed the top of my head, tears streamed down my face, and I began to apologize profusely. It was like something took ahold of me and words poured forth like a cloud bursting with rain.

"I'm sorry, Miss Daisy, for making fun at you. For all the times I usta laugh about your hair and your smelly clothes. And for sneaking and peeking in your house."

When I pulled away, her tears matched mine. I was touched, and even more impressed when she told me that my hands would heal whenever my heart gave them permission. Through my tears, I could see Grandma beaming. I guess she was proud of me. As she'd told me a few years back, I needed to learn how to step into someone else's shoes so I could feel their pain.

I'd never see Miss Daisy again, but like Miss Evelyn, she'd send Grandma postcards and letters. She'd moved to Lansing, Michigan, and started her life anew. Her letters described how she and another woman from down South had opened up their own beauty parlor in the basement of her house. Soon it was flourishing. My grandparents and I would crack up as I read them her stories about her customers. She'd send pictures, too—of the places she'd traveled and of herself. She wrote about how she spent every moment she could spare increasing her reading and writing skills. The thought of her being talkative, happy and free from traumatic thoughts brought me indescribable feelings of joy.

Later that day, Cuttin Jeff saw me with my hands looking a hot mess. He shook his head and exclaimed: "Chile, what you done got yoself into now?"

Before I could offer up an answer, Grandpa lifted me, rheumatism and all, and put me in the front seat of the truck, leaving
just enough room to take a seat beside me.

"Come on, Jeff," he said, "gots to get this chile over to Miss
Jubilee. We can gone to town whilst she works on this yere
chile's hands."

When Grandpa and Cuttin Jeff dropped me off at the path
that led to Miss Jubilee's house, I couldn't walk fast enough to
her front steps, barely paying any mind to all the weeds that
lined the path. I didn't see her standing on her porch, as she
usually did when she'd hear folks entering her property. I began
yelling her name, but with her kennel of hound dogs barking, I
wasn't surprised she couldn't hear me.

Miss Jubilee had about eight or so hounds of what seemed
like every breed imaginable. She used them back when she'd
hunt, before age caught up to her. By this time they all knew
me, and that day I had to slap them away. The smell of molasses attracted them, and they were going bat crazy, yelping and
barking, jumping on me and trying to lick my hands

Amidst that racket, I was glad to hear Miss Jubilee coming
up the dogtrot. She was what Grandpa called heavy-footed; each
time she took a step, you'd think she was walking with a ton of
clay wrapped around her ankles. Miss Jubilee didn't walk—she
stomped. Like Ant Bessie and Mama Nall, her shoes had a lot
of wear on them, so much so that the sole was completely gone
on one side. You could see her enormous baby toe protruding
through the torn leather.

I lifted myself up from the porch and yelled loud enough
for Cuttin Jeff to hear above his idling truck that I was all
right.

"Miss *Jubilee!*" My voice would've raised anything dead in
her fields out back. "Hey, Miss Jubilee, Grandpa and Cuttin Jeff
just dropped me off."

She appeared in her hallway. "Hey there, chile," she said.
"Come here and give Miss Jubilee some sugar."

When she saw my hands, she stared long and hard at them. I thought I saw tears forming in her eyes. She briefly looked away, then took both my hands and placed them on either side of her face. With her eyes closed, she began caressing them and mumbling something I couldn't make out. She didn't care that the residue from the molasses smeared her jaw. She just stood there, glaring through those beautiful deep-set eyes and telling me not to worry about a thing.

Turning, she led me to the small room where she kept all types of herbs, plants, and bottles of tonics and tinctures. The wooden shelves were lined with dried weeds, branches, and vines. It looked like a damn forest in there. There were no windows, so Miss Jubilee fired up two lanterns. It was scary as hell. But if she could heal my hands, I'd gladly put up with the dark dungeon. I was more than ready to rid myself of the sticky mess and the pain.

While I sat in the oversized rocking chair, which looked and felt like it was built for a giant, Miss Jubilee scurried from one side of the room to the other. She poured drops of liquid from various bottles into a large wooden bowl, then added crumbled-up dried leaves. Then she took a ladle and began stirring the concoction. My eyes darted back and forth and my heart started to pound. My mind went back to the superstitious talk I'd heard about Miss Jubilee. A lot of folks thought she wasn't a real person. Others spoke about her being a "root doctor." I tried to put it out of my mind, trusting that she wouldn't hurt me for anything in the world. I loved this old woman, and deep down inside, I knew she felt the same way about me.

Before I knew it, I was asking whether she wanted to know what had happened to my hands. But she never answered and I didn't repeat myself.

"Nigh I'm all finished mixin' the right concoction. We gone have you fixed up here in no time flat. Gone work on one hand atta time." Miss Jubilee removed the first sulfur-and-molasses-drenched bandage, then slowly and gently dipped my wrist into the wooden bowl. Leaves, grass, and buds of yellow flowers floated on top. As soon as my hands touched the water, it felt like shivers of ice shot through my entire body. Miss Jubilee continued holding my wrist, just in case I resisted. All I could do was close my eyes and think of anything hot or warm to keep my mind off the frigid wetness, which felt like a dozen bee stings.

Miss Jubilee never said a word. Her eyes were shut tight, and she rocked back and forth as though she was in a trance. After a few minutes, she lifted my hand from the elixir and placed it on a white piece of cloth. She wrapped my hand and wrist, overlapping the cloth several times. She did my other hand the same way. Then I sat there, both hands wrapped up like a mummy, staring at her. I felt absolutely no pain. Beneath the wrapping, my hands felt as normal as they had a day ago, before I'd put them into the scalding water.

I wanted so badly to remove the white coverings, but Miss Jubilee told me to let them be. She sat down in the rocking chair beside me and eyed me somberly, without saying a word. Even on the day I gave her the quilt of souls Grandma had made her, she hadn't exuded this type of melancholy. When she finally spoke, it was with such reverence, I knew I'd remember it forever.

"Let me tell you, chile: you carryin' so much on you rat now, and I wants you to let it go, else you ain't gone git all a them blessin's that's comin' yo' way. You carryin' all that spite in yo' heart and you gots no place to put it. I feels that hate in yo' heart. I knows it when I sees it 'cause Lawd knows I carry that kinda hate wit' me fo' so many years fo' massa, who sol' my family way from me. It takes me long times to gits over it. Don' thank the good Lawd let me finds my sista who sol' till I gets over it."

I didn't have to tell Miss Jubilee what had happened between me and Ant Bessie. She might not have known all the details, but somehow, she knew. Impulsively, I began to tell her about the strange incident last year, when I'd encountered Ant Bessie in the cotton field near her house in the Bottom. As I spoke, I began to choke on my own fear. My words seemed to get caught in the back of my throat.

"Gone, chile," Miss Jubilee said gently. "Talk to Miss Jubilee."

"Something in the woods grabbed me and I can't catch myself from falling in the stack of cotton Ant Bessie got piled up at the end of the row. When I look up, she gots the meanest look on her face, and she grabs my arm and snatch me up off that pile. I thought she was gone hit me, so I put my hands over my face. But she just pushed me and talk nasty to me."

I was crying so much I couldn't catch my breath. The whimpering became louder and louder, until Miss Jubilee said, "Hush, chile, come on over here and hug ol' Miss Jubilee's neck. She ain't gone let nothin' and nobody mess wit' you."

Miss Jubilee gently rocked her body back and forth, her eyes facing downward, while I described the rest of the awful details. This was the first time I'd talked about that day to anyone except Grandma, and I still didn't know which of my actions was worse: disobeying Grandma or receiving that horrible bashing from Ant Bessie.

"Ain't nothin' but the dev'l who tryin' stop you from usin' them hands to do good thangs. Miss Jubilee ain't gone let that evil Bessie put a chain 'round your spirit, chile. Long's Miss Lula and Miss Jubilee here 'live on Lawd's green earth, we gone fights the dev'l fo' you. And when me and Miss Lula gone to sleep with the angels, we gone always be 'round somewheres, watchin' over you. Miss Jubilee ain't got much longer for dis here world, but I wants you to know, you gots angels watchin' over you.

"But if you's carryin' hate, the good can't come through the door. So when Miss Jubilee takes deze yere rags from yo' hands, I wants you to let go all that meanness in yo' heart. Ya hear me, chile? Can't nobody do nothin' more to ya den you's already done to yoself. You won't 'mount to much if you carryin' 'round hate. Alls it can do is weigh you down. Can't lets nobody puts that much weight on you, chile."

I couldn't imagine, nor did I want to think about, Miss Jubilee going on to glory and not being able to see her anymore. When she finally removed the cloths, the palms of my hands had returned to their regular flesh-tone color, and the huge water blisters were gone. All that remained were circles of excess skin where the blisters used to be. Most of all, there wasn't a trace of pain.

I sat, looking at Miss Jubilee like it was the first time I'd ever seen her. Then I rose from the rocker and embraced her, so grateful to her for erasing the bitterness that had consumed me.

I spent the rest of the day sitting with Miss Jubilee, listening to her tales about the times during and after slavery. I was mesmerized by her ability to recall events that had occurred in her century-long life. She told bone-curdling and hair-raising ghost stories so vividly it sent chills down my spine. Even though her ghost tales scared the heebie-jeebies out of me, I couldn't resist them. Unlike Grandma, whose voice was soft and steady, when Miss Jubilee spoke, her voice cracked and trembled. But like Grandma, she could breathe life into her characters. Sometimes I'd hear eerie sounds as she talked and feel the sensation of someone lightly touching my skin with their fingertips. Occasionally, I'd pick at my face to try to pull off invisible cobwebs. Grandma described these webs as kind spirits passing by.

As Miss Jubilee rocked in her old beat-up chair with its straw bottom about ready to implode, she crossed her arms and began telling me the story of the Conkabayou Bridge and the mysteries that lay beneath it. She grasped the snake carcass and chicken feet that hung from her neck, clutching them with one hand as she spoke. She'd told me that these articles were for good luck and to ward off evil spirits.

"I knows why your Grandma don' ever wants you to go nowhere near where the waters come offa tha Conkuby. Ain't nothin' livin' down yonder but po' spirits. I hear dey still chasin' afta them evil dead white folks who kilt them. Them po' niggers spirit down thar tryin' to run 'em out. More niggers hang from them trees then pears. Them white folks killin' 'em every time you turnt 'round. Folks miles away say you hear cullud folk wailin' like cats fighting down in that Bottom.

"Miss Jessie, my friend, her lil grandbaby Good-Good kilt down thar. She no older than you is. She knows better than to go off down to that swamp, but Miss Jessie say she down thar lookin' fer her old Grandpa Sam. White folks kilt him fer nothin', say he stole, and Miss Jessie say he ain't bit mo' stol' nothin' then me sittin' yere. I reckon he already hangin' from a tree when Good-Good spot him. I guess she run into them white folks still celebratin' 'bout killin' her grandpa. When they spots her, that po' chile don' haves a chance in hell to get away.

"It pains me to no end what them evil white folks did to that lil gal. Folks say dey splits her insides wide open. Drag her through that swamp till she don' look lak a chile no mo'. Miss Jessie so tore up over losin' Good-Good and Ol' Sam, she los' her mind. Dey end up buryin' both of 'em near the part of the Bottom where yo' Ant Bessie live. Lots of folks kilt there, dey body there to this day. Dey's jus' lay out thar and rot. Niggers scared to go nowheres near the Bottom, and can't rightly blame 'em. Back when Miss Bessie catch you near the Bottom, Miss Jubilee know rat here, rat now you been casted, 'cause I can tell you it wa'n't nobody but lil Good-Good who toss you outta tha. She just ain't want you to be scared of them haints. Jus' not good fo' your young eyes to see."

As I reflected on what I'd encountered in that field, all I could think about was the little girl, Good-Good. I'd never met her, but I imagined her in my mind, and I wondered what her life was worth. What could she have done that would've made someone want to hurt her? I could've so easily been her.

Thinking about the brutality of her death brought back memories of an event that had occurred in my life a year earlier.

It was early September 1963, a very tumultuous period in American history and a time that further increased my understanding of how it felt to be a Black girl in the United States. I'd just turned ten. A few months before, my grandparents were given the gift of electricity, and my uncle bought them a large floor-model black-and-white television set. As he pushed it down the dogtrot and into our front room, I was thrilled to the point of speechlessness, jumping up and down like I was on a trampoline.

"Oooh-weeee! Lookit, Grandma, it got big silver knobs just like the one in the weekly reader magazine that Miss Clay hands out. Can I turn it on, Grandma, please? Please?"

My uncle barely had time to attach the rabbit ear antenna before I was fiddling with the knobs. It was sobering once I found out that, because our location was so rural, we could only get one channel. To add insult to injury, the television network didn't come on until eleven in the morning each day, went off at two in the afternoon, and didn't broadcast again until five-thirty, just in time for the local and world news. This television business was all new to Grandma. She really didn't care what time it came on or went off the air. Her rule was: the television was not to be touched until five-thirty, period. This was only if both her and my fieldwork and any other chores were completed. Otherwise, that television set might as well have been a piece of cute oak furniture. Work before play, case closed.

Our television set allowed the outside world to come into our little front room. And less than two weeks after my tenth birthday, me and Grandma sat in silence. We'd just seen the horrific pictures of four little girls killed by a bomb planted at the First Street Baptist Church in Birmingham. The girls were close to my age. All I saw as they showed their image on the screen was Black skin, innocence, and smoke oozing from the rubble.

When I looked into the eyes of those girls, or thought about what had happened to Good-Good and the many other Black children who suffered needlessly under the claws of a racist system, it seemed to me as though their lives had been deemed irrelevant, that society had acted as if there was no need for them to grow into adulthood. I thought about how Ella was treated too. She was as smart as she was brave, and I'm sure the young Mr. Young recognized that and tried to harness it. When he couldn't, he killed her. Over a half century has passed since little Good-Good and so many others died, yet Black youth are still trying to prove that their lives matter. That night in 1963, I stared at the television in disbelief; then, as always, turned to my grandma for solace. I saw real pain cross her face. It was a look that defied description, one that I hadn't seen before and never wanted to see again.

"Your eyes got no bizness watchin' all this evil in the worl'," she told me. "Them babies done gone on to where nothin' gone make them suffer like that no more. Go on, chile, find yo' grandpa and tell him we ain't gone be seein' nothin' else on this television tube no time soon. Gone now."

This was the first time Grandma didn't relate an experience to either a story from her past or from someone's else's life, as laid out in one of her quilts of souls. As I watched, she slowly walked to the other side of the room and placed one hand over her heart. With the other, she gently turned off the television. And true to her word, she didn't allow the set to be turned on again, not until months later, in November of that year, the same month in which President John F. Kennedy was assassinated.

All of these thoughts filled my mind as I sat quietly with Miss Jubilee. One particular memory came back to me. That day in Ant Bessie's field, as I flew through the air, an awesome silence had abounded. I'd never paid the quiet any mind. Too soon, it was interrupted by Ant Bessie's loud mouth. But one thing was for sure: someone was there with me. Again I saw myself flying, experiencing no fear, just absolute peace. It was only afterward, when I found myself staring up at Ant Bessie, that I began to feel afraid.

There are moments in my life that remind me of the dreams I had during my first few years in the country, dreams in which I was falling and couldn't help myself. Out of fear, I always woke before I landed. My experience that day in the Bottom was similar to those dreams, but it was my reality, and it had a very different outcome. Someone felt my fear, reached out, and guided me to safety. Now I could attach a name to my rescuer. It was Good-Good. Tears flooded my eyes as I looked at Miss Jubilee, who was still clinging to the stuff around her neck. She was smiling and nodding her head.

A strong wind blew the door to the room open, and a chill surrounded both of us. Then, as quickly as it had arrived, it left, and behind it came a breeze so fierce the door slammed shut. The resounding boom echoed through the house. Complete quiet followed, just as I'd experienced in the Bottom last year.

Me and Miss Jubilee sat and stared at each other, speechless. Then she winked at me through those deep-set eyes. As she was beginning to describe how she'd met Good-Good's grandparents, Miss Jessie and Mr. Sam, our conversation was interrupted by the sound of her dogs barking. She told me to go and find out what all the commotion was about. I ran down the dogtrot and heard the bushes swishing back and forth as someone made their way up the path. I knew it wasn't Grandpa, because I hadn't heard the sound of Cuttin Jeff's truck. I waited until I could make out who it was.

It was Mama Nall.

She had tied her mules and wagon next to Miss Jubilee's barn, then walked the two hundred or so feet to the house. When she saw me, she looked concerned and asked if Miss Jubilee had taken care of my hands. She'd caught wind of my injury through the country pipeline. I thanked her for asking and told her that Miss Jubilee was in the room.

"Hey there, Lizzie, how you doin' this mo'nin'?" Miss Jubilee greeted her. This was the first time I'd heard anyone call Mama Nall by her first name.

"I'm kickin,' but not high," Mama Nall responded.

"Come on in here and rest a spell. Been workin' on this chile's hands all mo'nin' long. She bees fine now. Had to heal that heart of hers, too, 'cause it was in worst shape den her hands. Show Lizzie yo' hands, chile."

When I opened my hands, showing my palms, Mama Nall grabbed my fingers and gently squeezed each one. I didn't have the slightest idea why, and I wasn't about to ask her.

"Well, Bay Sis, whatcha think? She gone live?"

"Yeah, I thank she gone be alright. I feels a mighty spirit in them hands."

Upon hearing Miss Jubilee call Mama Nall "Bay Sis," my mouth fell open. Grown folks' business be damned, I had to know what she meant. I'd deal with the consequences for getting out of a child's place later. I closed my eyes and blurted out in my most respectful tone: "Why you called Mama Nall Bay Sis?"

A part of me felt guilty, because I was raised to have deep respect for my elders, and Miss Jubilee and Mama Nall were both old enough to be my grandparents' parents. I was surprised when Miss Jubilee showed no hesitation at all in answering.

"Well, chile, 'cause she my sista. Didn't yo' grandma tells you 'bout it? 'Twas a lil while back Mollie Suggs come see yo' grandma 'cause she found them papers. If it wa'n't for her, I never know that Lizzie here my Bay Sis."

Not only was I completely caught off guard by this news, but the mention of Mollie Suggs sparked my interest. A long time ago, Grandma had told me the story of how Sheriff Suggs's widow, Mollie, used to visit her after the sheriff passed away. What papers had she brought? The horn from Cuttin Jeff's truck sounded then, and my heart sank. I wasn't ready to leave. I wanted to hear more about how these two women had found each other. My mind was bursting with questions. First Miss Sugar and Miss Evelyn; now Mama Nall and Miss Jubilee. Four women, two pairs of sisters separated at a young age, later brought together by fate and circumstance. Why did this all come to light at this time?

I looked at Miss Jubilee, and I knew she felt my longing to stay. She let go of my hand, then bent her oversized frame low enough to look at me, eye to eye. She told me that she loved me to death and not to worry 'bout a thang.

"Yes ma'am, Miss Jubilee."

The biggest shock came from Mama Nall, whose disposition was often chillier than an ice cube. To my surprise, she took her hand and gently rubbed the side of my face. I sensed warm, unconditional love from deep within her soul. Warmth traveled up my back and down my arms, and a pleasant serenity landed in my heart. It was him—the spirit of G. C. I thought about how Grandma had told me I possessed a sensitivity, an ability to feel those who lived in the spirit realm. At that moment, I knew G. C. was happy and free, and I'd been released from having to carry any more guilt about his passing.

As if reading my mind, Mama Nall reached into her apron pocket and pulled out a small, hand-carved rock. Its center was a picture of G. C. pasted on with glue. She smiled wide, showing her few remaining teeth, and winked at me with her uncrossed eye. Any residue of the aloofness I'd experienced in her after G. C. passed had vanished.

As I walked away, I couldn't help but turn around and glance at the two old sisters standing there, holding hands like little girls on a playground.

19

Transpired

WHEN WE MADE IT HOME, I couldn't climb out of Cuttin Jeff's truck fast enough. Instead of waiting for poor Grandpa to get out first, I leapfrogged over his lap, almost stumbling head-first onto the path. I was laser-focused on finding Grandma.

I searched for her, but she was nowhere to be found. I began screaming for her so loud, the chickens and ducks started flapping their wings and running under the house like they were being chased by a fox. I ran out the back gate, which led to the pasture and barn, searching. I was out of breath and panicking something fierce. It wasn't like Grandma to be unaware that I'd returned. She had to have heard Cuttin Jeff's truck, what with all the noise it made.

Winded, I stopped running and bent over with my hands on my knees, panting, trying to catch my breath. Some of the cows in the pasture stood there, hay hanging out of their mouths, eyeballing me. The rest of the herd was licking on large salt blocks that me and Grandpa had laid out for them yesterday. I sat in the grass to calm myself and watched the little calves slurp on the salt cubes. As I watched, my mouth started to water. I felt saliva flooding my mouth to the point that I just couldn't stand it any longer. The craving became stronger and stronger; the longer I watched, the greater the desire to do the impossible overwhelmed any logic I had to resist. I eyed one lonely salt block, sitting all by itself, no cows anywhere near it.

Before I knew what I was doing, I wandered over to it, fell to my knees, and started licking and lapping on that thing like crazy. I was so caught up, I didn't hear Grandma, but I felt her presence. There she was, standing only a few feet away, one hand on her hip. The other held a walking stick. I tried to look into her eyes, but they were partially blocked by the sun. The only thing I could do at that point was stay in the same position and shake my head.

"Chile, I know you ain't messin' 'round with that salt lick. Don' you know that salt dry you up like a piece of salt pork? Get on up to that house right now, and you best not let me get thar 'fore you. You know you knows better'n than that. You might as well gone get that switch off that fig tree when you get up to the house. Gal, I don' know whatcha thankin' 'bout. Lawd Jesus have mercy."

I cried like crazy. Grandma was so disappointed in my behavior that she hadn't even asked about Miss Jubilee healing my hands.

At the house, she gave me two heaping tablespoons of castor oil with two cups of warm water to drink behind it. I was gagging and throwing up as fast as it went down my throat. That didn't faze Grandma. She had another two tablespoons ready and waiting, which she pumped into me each time I barfed. I lost count of how many times I ran to the outhouse, suffering from an extreme case of the runs. But Grandma was determined to work every drop of that salt lick out of my body.

The next morning, I woke up, drained. I barely had enough energy to put on my overalls and wash my face. Even the dogtrot seemed much longer than it actually was. Before I got to where the hallway connected to the kitchen, Grandma was there, smiling and beckoning me for a hug. All I had to do was fall into those long arms of hers.

"I'm sorry, Grandma," I said. "For getting in that devilment with that salt lick."

"Don' you worry yourself none, chile, 'cause you gone be alright now."

I hugged her tight, and it filled me with joy, knowing that she'd forgiven me.

"Let Grandma take 'nother look at them hands. You's asleep when I seen them las' night. But they sho do look fine to me. Did you thank Miss Jubilee for the healin' she done? You knows she gots a healin' spirit. And she gots the Lord's favor too. Been knowin' Miss Jubilee for a long time now. She been 'round almos' fo'ever. Mos' folks don' know how old she is. Your grandpa tells me she crazy 'bout my lil grandbaby 'Stene. Grandma always loves your heart and your liver too. Jus' wants you to know that, chile."

I blushed as Grandma doted on me. It seemed like an opportune time to ask about the mystery of Mama Nall and Miss Jubilee, but before I could get a word out, Grandma sent me off to the smokehouse to get two sacks of clothes. One was a gray feed sack with a blue rope tie and a big "S" on the front label. The other was a dingy old yellowish pillowcase.

As I carried the sacks to the front yard, I thought about how nice it was to be finished gleaning the crops of peas, corn, and cotton. We had spent almost three days last week planting sweet potatoes, which wouldn't be ready for picking until late fall, and watering the roots of the pecan trees, which would be shook of their nuts in a few months. The persimmons and figs were ripe and ready for picking. It was nearing the end of summer, the time of year when Grandma would make jars and jars of preserves, and I'd sit, watching the process. I had a few weeks before school started, and I'd be turning twelve in

September. Apart from brief moments of childish indiscretion, like the salt lick, I thought I was mature.

By now, Grandma had made her way to the front yard, taking her regular position in her favorite chair. She removed a few pieces from one of the bags I'd brought and held them up, then picked out a few more. One of the bags contained leftovers from G. C.'s and his brothers' clothes. I was curious as to why Grandma had wanted this sack.

"I feel you wantin' to ask your Grandma somethin', chile, 'bout Mama Nall and Miss Jubilee. Edgar already told me he runs into Mama Nall at Miss Jubilee's place yestiddy. I see it all over your face. Jus' wants you to know that Grandma always know what you thinkin'. Don' matter what be happenin' in this worl', Grandma wants you to know that she always be right there, watchin' over you, come hell or high water. When Grandma gone on to glory, and you see a bird come near you or land on your windowsill, jus' want you to know that's your grandma checkin' on you. Don' ever wants you to forget that.

"I was gone get 'round to tellin' you what else I knows 'bout where Miss Jubilee come from, but like ol' Grandma tells you all the time, everything happen in due time. Everything got to be in God's timin' too. It ain't up to me, chile, 'cause I know God lets me know 'xactly when that time agonna come. Then a spirit comes to me las' night and sits right there at the foot of my bed, talkin' to me jus' like me and you talkin' here right now. And plain as the nose on my face, that spirit says it's time for the gal to know, 'cause she gone use it for good.

"I guess I gots a good mind to tell you everything that happen with Sheriff Gloster Suggs and how he come to know ol' Miss Jubilee."

I thought I'd misheard. Sheriff Suggs and Miss Jubilee! The news shocked the spit out of me. It seemed Miss Mollie, the sheriff's widow, had come to visit Grandma not long ago, on a day that I was in school. She'd found old papers buried in a shoe box in a chifforobe that hadn't been opened in so long, cobwebs and rot had overtaken some of the artifacts held within. They'd moved that chifforobe from the Suggs place long ago. Gloster, which was Sheriff Suggs's first name, never wanted to open it when he was alive, so after he died Miss Mollie just let it sit in its spot for some twenty-five years. Then one day she decided it was an eyesore. She wanted to get rid of it, but not before examining its contents.

To her shock, she found a bill of sale for slaves Thomas, Nellie, Lizzie, and a baby boy with no name, who were sold to Pax Jones, the first cousin of Gloster's grandpa, Joe Suggs. The bill was dated June 1864. Another, separate bill of sale recorded the original purchase of Thomas, Nellie, and infant Jubilee. It was right there in black and white: Joe Suggs bought them at an auction in Hattiesburg, Mississippi. The bill was dated March 1860. Four years later, Joe Suggs sold everyone in the family except for Miss Jubilee.

The very next day, Miss Mollie was sitting in our front yard, sharing this information with Grandma. The relationship between Mama Nall and Miss Jubilee was unexpected, yet it was satisfying to know how they'd finally found each other. There was another connection between Miss Jubilee and Sheriff Suggs, however. And that was an altogether different story.

At the thought of Miss Jubilee being subjected to the same type of humiliation my grandma had faced at Sheriff Suggs's hands, my youthful impulsivity kicked in, and my mind ran faster than my thoughts could keep up. Grandma was only at the beginning of the story, yet I'd already crossed the finish line, forming my own conclusions about what had happened. Grandma would warn me about this type of thinking, which she referred to as putting the cart before the horse. All I knew was, I didn't want to go through another 'twixt-Laurel-and-Livingston experience. It would be like tearing a scab off a sore that had taken a long time to heal. In my childishness, I'd learned to daydream the pain of my grandmother's suffering away. And afterward, Grandma didn't mention Sheriff Suggs or that road for almost four years.

She told many other stories in between, though, about folks' suffering. Each time, she laid out their losses and what they had to endure, and I grew to understand that I could no longer wish away someone's pain or lock it up in a box. I could not control the trajectory of another person's story. I wasn't eight years old any longer.

Tears began to roll down my cheeks. I had a visual in my mind of Sheriff Suggs mistreating Miss Jubilee, as clear as the nose on my face. Grandma had already been drawn into my despair, and she spoke to my feelings in the way she always had, telling me, "Chile, I wants you to let it all go, 'cause what you feeling now gone 'cause your heart to get hard. Can't let that happen to you. All that make you weak gone end up makin' you strong in the long run. I gots to prepare you before I leave on away from here. Don' wants you to let nobody set up they farm in your head.

"Now, I wants you to listen to what I'm a gettin' ready to tell you, 'cause Grandma ain't got long to stay here on this side. You gots to open your heart to receive what I'm gone tell you 'bout Sheriff and Miss Jubilee, lest I might as well be talkin' to your feet, if your heart closed.

"You don' know the whole story yet, chile. But once I tells you, you gone understand and it gone patch up your heart. Grandma and the Lord knows you ready to hear it now. Come tomorry, Grandma gone tell you. It's time."

Grandma's words saddened me. It was only yesterday that I'd listened to Miss Jubilee talk about goin' home to be with the Lord and how she'd be leaving this world for good. I couldn't bear a repeat of the going-home-to-glory speech from Grandma. Before today, when she'd told me and others I had an old folks' soul, I'd viewed it as one of her thousands of truisms. But sitting there in the front yard, I began to feel older than the oak tree that covered us. My transformation came in suddenly, like a gentle fall-like wind arising out of nowhere. It was like the quilts Grandma made: the placement of each piece of fabric provided support for the others.

My mind took me back to the days when I first came to Grandma, how fear had ravaged me. Sitting there under the tree, watching Grandma as she watched me, I thought of the women who'd been placed in my life, the ones that were here and those who'd passed on. Each of them gave my life purpose and filled me with a strength that defied anything I was about to hear about Sheriff Suggs. And though I knew I'd be sad whenever the day came for Grandma and Miss Jubilee to go on to meet the Lord, I had a feeling that it wouldn't take long for me to submerge myself in the river of acceptance.

Evening rolled in, and Grandma sat quietly, her face glowing. I knew she heard the thoughts inside my head, that I didn't have to say a word. In the silence, she began to sing one of her old spirituals, a song that further solidified my thoughts about how I'd weather at least a few storms in the years to come:

On a hill far away stood an old rugged cross,
A symbol of sufferin' and shame.
So I cling to the old rugged cross
Till at last I lay down;
I will cling to the old rugged cross
And exchange it some day for a crown.

On a visit to the site of my grandparents' farmhouse, which burned down many years ago, I discovered the frame of the old wooden gate that I spent many years swinging on.

20

Days of Reckoning

THE NEXT MORNING couldn't come fast enough; throughout
the night I tossed and turned, full of heated anticipation and
anxiety. Now I sat plastered to my chair, listening to Grandma.
The day was unusually hot for late August, but it fit well with
how I was feeling inside. Yesterday, the idea of Sheriff Suggs's
and Miss Jubilee's lives intersecting had created miles of curiosity inside me. Today, my level of eagerness could fit on an
island all by itself. What I was about to learn over the following weeks would answer many of my lingering questions about
Miss Jubilee. There was so much to unpack and unravel, like
a spool of yarn with tiny knots that had to be picked apart in
order to see how long the thread actually stretched.

The story began a few months after Sheriff Suggs passed
away. Miss Mollie had returned to see Grandma, just as she'd
promised. She longed to watch Grandma make a quilt of souls
out of the sheriff's old clothes, mixed in with pieces of clothing from their youngest child, who'd died at an early age. As
Grandma worked, Miss Mollie told her all about the sheriff's

unhappy childhood, as well as how he attached himself to Miss Jubilee.

Miss Mollie met Gloster Suggs when they were no older than me. Their fathers both had apple orchards. Miss Mollie's parents passed on when she was a young girl, and afterward her aunt moved into her folks' house and raised her. Mollie and Gloster would meet in the apple fields every day. They'd play amongst the trees and throw rotten fruit at each other, intentionally not trying to hit each other. Sometimes they were out there so long, Gloster's father, Granville Suggs, would come looking for him. Many times, Grandma told me, he'd take his whip from his back pocket and start beating Gloster right there in the field in front of Mollie. He'd accuse Gloster of being trifling, lazy, and no good. He blamed him for not doing his chores—slopping the hogs or feeding the cows. The apple grove was the only place where Gloster could go where he felt safe from this abuse. He and Mollie would sit for hours under the shade of the tall trees, plotting out their future. And this was where Mollie learned of the warm and loving relationship between Gloster and Miss Jubilee.

Gloster would tell Miss Mollie how Miss Jubilee was the only person who'd raised him. Since his birth, his mother never wanted to touch him and would say very little to him, no matter how hard he tried to talk to her. It was Miss Jubilee who tended to him when he was sick, sang to him, and told him stories. All the things a mother was supposed to do for her child, Miss Jubilee did for Gloster. She took care of him, because she knew how his papa felt about him. When Granville would go into one of his drinking fits, he'd come looking for Gloster. But Miss Jubilee always found a way to put his papa's mind elsewhere. To protect Gloster from the beatings, she stepped in and took the blame for his perceived shortcomings.

Miss Jubilee knew Granville Suggs well because they were around the same age. Both were born and raised right there on Joe Suggs's plantation. Even as a young boy, Granville was

as evil as they come. Miss Jubilee would witness him ridicul-
ing and mistreating his younger brother, who died early from
smallpox. Granville would beat and kick him mercilessly, right
there in the front yard. His parents never said a word. It was
in that same front yard that Miss Jubilee saw her folks carted
away, sold by Granville's father, Joe.

Years later, Granville married Gloster's mama on the steps
of the Suggs plantation, with its huge white columns. Gloster
was already born but not yet walking. His real father had been
killed on a hunting trip. A month later, his wife found out she
was pregnant with Gloster. No one ever found her husband's
killer, and Gloster's mother nearly lost her mind. Everyone
could see that she was half-crazy when she married Granville Suggs. People whispered about him marrying her for her
beauty. I assume that since he was also insane, their personalities canceled each other out.

And so Miss Jubilee came to raise Gloster. "She may as
well have been his blood mama," Grandma told me, "because he
loved her comin' and goin'."

As Granville grew, his stepfather's excessive drinking
further impaired their relationship. If Granville wasn't hunting,
drinking, or doing both, he was whaling on Gloster or mistreating Gloster's mama. Some nights, you could hear him out back,
shooting the sky until the sun came up. After his marriage to
Gloster's mother, Granville only lived in the main house for
a short time before moving to his hunting cabin, out past the
backyard. It was a showplace filled with his gun collection,
stuffed animals, and alcohol. He spent most of his waking hours
holed up there. He'd rail against Gloster day and night for not
keeping up with his chores, but Gloster was the one who kept
the farm functioning while his stepfather drank and hunted.

One night, Granville left on one of his extended hunting
trips. Before he left, he gave Gloster a list of things that needed
to be done, but not before telling him what he'd do to him if
the work wasn't carried out to his liking. When he was gone,

Gloster made a beeline to complain to his mama about Granville. It was like talking to a five-year-old. Even though Gloster knew that his mother wasn't in her right mind, he never failed to express how he felt about Granville.

That night was different, though. Lord knows what possessed his mother to go off, but she did, telling him Granville wasn't his real papa anyway, so he needed to stop all his whining. She showed Gloster a picture of his real father, which she had clutched in her hand. Gloster was almost eighteen years old, and this was the first time he'd ever heard that Granville wasn't his biological father. What went through his mind is anybody's guess. But it's easy to assume the shock and awe were unreal. Equally shocking: why did his mother wait until that moment to tell him this devastating news? Gloster was practically grown.

This was a question to which he'd never find an answer. And it set him on a temporary path of destruction. I can imagine him thinking about the daily verbal and physical abuse he took from Granville, a man with whom he had no blood connection. Granville may have taken out all of his frustration for not having biological children on Gloster.

As Mollie and Gloster lay in the apple orchard, he told her everything. She'd never heard him swearing and crying before. Clearly, he was planning something drastic, some revenge for all those years he'd endured his stepfather's wrath. Mollie heard it in his voice. The next thing she knew, he took off running through the orchard, disappearing into the woods as she called out to him, pleading for him to stay with her.

When he arrived back at the farm, he hid in the bushes near Granville's cabin, right next to the wood line. Over the years, he'd become well aware of Granville's comings and goings. Very seldom did his schedule change. Gloster was sure he'd spent hours getting liquored up with his friends over in Laurel, about a forty-five-minute drive from Meridian. Granville would come back to the cabin to get a couple hours of sleep before arising to go on his favorite deer-hunting jaunt the next morning.

Gloster saw the light come on in Granville's cabin right before midnight. He didn't hesitate, just ran down the small incline to the cabin and busted through the door like he was the police, armed only with the years of abuse he'd taken from his stepfather. The struggle began there. It must've sounded like World War II in that cabin. Granville had a huge weight and height advantage over the small-framed Gloster, and he easily got the best of him, even in his drunkenness. After beating Gloster nearly unconscious, Granville left with his rifle in hand.

When Gloster regained his composure and realized that once again he'd been beaten terribly by his stepfather, he headed to the woodpile and grabbed a bucket of kindling and matches. He doused the kindling in kerosene, placed the container inside the cabin, and torched it. He sat and watched it burn before absconding through the woods.

The fire awakened Miss Jubilee. If it wasn't for her and some of the folks who lived nearby, the entire cabin would've burned down. Fortunately, it had rained the day before and filled over a dozen ten-gallon washtubs with water. They were able to put it out, but Miss Jubilee had a horrible feeling that Gloster might have started the fire. She feared that Granville would suspect him, too, and probably half kill him as a result. So Miss Jubilee decided to do what she'd always done: fall on her sword to save Gloster's life.

Grandma told me that once she found out how Gloster had been mistreated, she felt sorry for him and what he had to go through, especially the beatings he had to endure. "Miss Jubilee says that Gloster beat more then any slave she know. When he suffer, she suffer jus' as bad. Through all that, chile, she gots a bond like you won't believe with Gloster. Miss Jubilee do anything' in this big ol' worl' for that boy. No difference then what mos' mamas gone sacrifice for they chil'ren."

Granville came home the next morning to find his place half-burned and in shambles. Miss Jubilee had a small house that sat below the main house, on the other side of Granville's cabin, about a half-mile through the woods. She knew he'd be coming to her as soon as he saw his place. He was aware of the close relationship between Miss Jubilee and Gloster, and when questions needed to be answered about Gloster, it was Miss Jubilee, not Gloster's mother, that replied. Granville would always blame her, his childhood playmate, for taking up for that "no-account boy," but it never deterred her from continuing to defend Gloster every step of the way.

That day, Grandma Lula told me, Miss Jubilee heard Granville screaming from a long way off. She wiped her sweaty hands on her apron and took a deep breath before opening the door. There he stood, a behemoth, hollering like a sinner who'd just ended up in hell and foaming at the mouth like a rabid hound dog. Miss Jubilee stood her ground, looked him right in the eye, and told him that she was the one who mistakenly set his cabin on fire. Before she had a chance to explain how, he took the butt of his shotgun and hit her so hard upside the head, the only thing she saw was red.

Miss Jubilee was almost seventy years old, but strong and resilient. She took off running and didn't look back. She knew Granville was still in somewhat of a drunken stupor, because he'd smelled of stale whiskey when he stepped in her door. He likely would not catch up to her, and if he started shooting, he wouldn't be able to aim straight. She didn't stop running until she arrived at the Reverend Cook's house, her forehead bleeding like a stuck pig. The Reverend Cook summoned some of the church folks to come and patch up the spot on her head.

In the meantime, poor Gloster was so afraid that he hid out in the woods until later that morning. Coincidentally, just a few hours earlier, Miss Jubilee had run through those woods, trying to escape Granville. After getting patched up, she snuck back to her house in the wee hours. She took the croker sack that contained her family's few pieces of clothing and other belongings. She knew that she'd never to return to that space or see her Gloster again.

It wasn't until later that morning that Mollie saw Gloster. He showed up at her front door disheveled. His face was streaked in blood, his bottom lip swollen to twice its original size, his shirt ripped. Mollie stood there, frozen and panicked at the sight of him. Slowly, she took a seat on the front porch and listened as Gloster paced back and forth before her, spilling out the story. A part of Mollie was proud of Gloster. For too many years, Granville had kept a tight yoke around his neck, never allowing him to speak or defend himself, right or wrong. For the first time in his life, Gloster had taken a stand, facing Granville like a man and taking up for himself.

Gloster told Miss Mollie how he'd burned down Granville's cabin, and said he felt no remorse. But Mollie tried to convince him to make amends with his stepfather. She told him she'd even give him some of the money left to her by her parents to pay for repairs. It was well known that the best way to get Granville's attention was money. At the same time, he was unpredictable, and so despicable that Gloster feared he might take the money and then beat Gloster to death. It took a great deal of coaxing for Gloster to agree. But he was willing to try—for Mollie's sake. He told her he'd find work to reimburse her.

Through puffy eyes and a busted lip, Gloster had another proposal, and that was asking Mollie to marry him, which she readily accepted. They decided to go find Miss Jubilee, tell her the news, and invite her to stay with them. On the same trip, Gloster decided, he would bring his mother to Miss Mollie's. Granville had absolutely abandoned her and there wasn't a stitch of love between them as husband and wife. Gloster knew that Granville wouldn't care if she disappeared, especially after hearing him repeat his dismay at marrying her in the first place.

When Gloster and Mollie arrived at Granville's half-burnt cabin, everything was dead quiet. They expected to see him somewhere nearby. When they didn't, they went up to the main house. There sat his mother in the bedroom, in her rocking chair as usual. She didn't look up; her head was down, and she was pulling on an old cotton wrap sitting in her lap. It was late afternoon, the time of day when Miss Jubilee would usually be tending to her or down in the kitchen, cooking. Today Gloster's mother's hair wasn't combed, and she was still in her night clothes. This had never happened before.

Gloster looked all over the house for Miss Jubilee. Miss Mollie told Grandma she could hear his voice shaking and trembling as he called. He even went out to the backyard, screaming her name. He knew that Miss Jubilee usually spent every other Sunday at church and with friends over in the Black settlement. But she returned in time to warm up dinner, feed his mother, and help her bathe. It was late Monday afternoon, and there was no sign of her.

It began to sink in that Granville might have had something to do with her disappearance, and Gloster took off out the back door, running like a bat out of hell to Miss Jubilee's little place. There was no sign of her. Gloster fought back tears. It was too painful imagining what could've happened to her. And how could she have disappeared without telling him or leaving word as to where she'd gone? He couldn't envision not having Miss Jubilee close by.

He decided to take Mollie's truck and check one last place—the Black settlement, easily accessible through the woods. There, he asked every Black person he came into contact with if they'd seen Miss Jubilee. No one knew anything—not until he asked two old Black women, who were sitting on their porch. They reluctantly told him they'd seen her and that she was safe. They refused to volunteer any additional information.

Most of the folks in the Black settlement knew exactly where Miss Jubilee was. They also knew that Gloster was closer than blood family to her. Unfortunately, Gloster was still a white man, and he represented the status quo in Alabama. It hurt Miss Jubilee deeply to hide herself from him, but she couldn't take the slightest risk of anyone finding out where she was. She really believed that Granville would shoot her on sight if he ever ran into her.

With a heavy heart, Gloster began to gather his mother's belongings so they could move her to Miss Mollie's place, which would become her new home. Before leaving, he said that he needed to feed the cows and slop the hogs; the cows had gathered at the front gate, near the barn, which meant they hadn't been fed. Mollie decided that she'd go with him to the barn. As they approached, they heard a moaning sound. The closer they got to what was left of Granville's cabin, the louder the sound grew. The moaning and groaning were so eerie Miss Mollie said that she wouldn't ever forget it, not in a million years.

Then, through the tall bushes, they made out the face of Granville. He was moving his hands and feet wildly, but his limbs were twisted and contorted. It looked as though he was trying to straighten them but couldn't. He scooted his body around on the ground, dragging dirt and grass with him. He'd try to talk, to mumble words, but each time, he'd gag. As they watched, he began foaming at the mouth, nearly choking.

Mollie and Gloster stood staring at him, incredulous. They were at a loss as to how to help, or even if they wanted to, after all the trouble he'd caused. But eventually Gloster squatted down and raised Granville's head to try to ease his suffering. The poor soul passed away right there in Gloster's arms, his eyes bulging from their sockets, his mouth stretched open wider than a dinner plate. No tears were shed. The only thing Gloster said before the undertaker took his stepfather's body away was this: he died the way he lived, a nasty old coot who wasn't worth the ground he was lying on.

Imagine the look on the undertaker's face when he viewed the twisted body of Granville Suggs! All his fingers and toes lay on top of one another. The undertaker had a mighty difficult time trying to straighten him out in the pine box for burial. Word of his condition spread like wildfire. Speculation was rampant among both Blacks and whites. Many knew that his death was something very unnatural. When word finally reached Miss Jubilee about Granville Suggs's passing, she felt enormous relief: now he could no longer make Gloster's life miserable. Since Miss Jubilee was a religious woman, more than likely a momentary tinge of grief crossed her mind, although she still felt it was all for the best in what she had to do to bring peace to Gloster's life, and closure to her own.

Granville's father, Joe Suggs, had sold her family away. He and Granville were cut from the same cloth: mean, evil, and hateful. Both of those Suggs men would kill you without blinking an eye and carry no regrets. For years, Miss Jubilee had carried the memory of her parents crying and screaming as they were dragged away from her on that fateful day in 1864. She never forgot her mama's pleas for mercy, the way her eyes burned deep into Miss Jubilee's soul, the sand kicking up around her feet. She could still see her father's unconscious body being thrown in the back of the wagon after he'd tried to put up a fight. Her parents didn't want to leave their oldest child behind.

She remembered, too, the tobacco juice running down the lips of Old Joe Suggs as he spat in the sand under her feet. He'd reared back with his open hand, ready to slap her silly, before Mr. Hitch grabbed her up and carted her back to the front steps of their shanty. Miss Jubilee said that to that day, she could hear the chains of the wagon wheels and see the sweat and grief on her mama's face. Mama Nall, who was also sold, was about two. The girls' baby brother was still nursing.

Even though Joe Suggs was responsible for selling Miss Jubilee's family, she couldn't punish him, because he died not long after. So she waited to seek her vengeance. It wasn't by design that she ended up punishing his son. She believed that Granville had carried on his father's tradition of hatred and scorn. If given the chance, he would try everything in his power to destroy her and Gloster, just like his father had destroyed her family.

To me, Miss Jubilee described the roots or hex she put on the man she only referred to as Old Man Suggs. Many enslaved Black folks believed in casting roots on their slave-owners. It was a gift from Africa or the Caribbean, passed down through the chain of generations. Miss Jubilee told me that she was the one who cleaned Granville's room. She said she took out his piss pot every day, so she was able to gather some of his pee in a bottle. She'd plotted this way before the fire, but to conjure up the hex, she also needed two pairs of chicken feet.

Now, Miss Jubilee said, Granville hated chickens worse than the plague. Nor did he like geese or ducks; in fact, he despised anything in the bird family. The only animals he would keep around the house were his six or so hunting dogs, and of course his horses, cows, and pigs. He'd buy chickens and ducks from a cousin who lived in Laurel and bring Miss Jubilee the bird to cook feather-free and already sliced up. His papa Joe had been the same way. In the end, Miss Jubilee had to get the chicken feet from a Black woman who lived on old man Scatt's plantation.

Miss Jubilee believed it had to be the right time of the month to put the roots on somebody. When we talked, she'd go on and on about not ever wanting to mess up a potion. The roots had to work the first time. If they didn't and the slave-owner got wind of it, the roots caster would be whipped to death. That's why some slave-owners wouldn't allow chicken feet to be preserved or kept by the slaves for any length of time. One of the things that scared white plantation owners the most was a fear of the roots.

To be safe, Miss Jubilee hid the chicken feet and the small jar of piss deep in the woods, where she knew they wouldn't be found. Late on the night when she came back to the Suggs plantation to get the croker sack that contained her family's few remaining clothes, she stopped momentarily to unearth them. The roots worked best, Miss Jubilee told me, when you cast them under a dark sky, illuminated by stars. That next night, after moving to Coatopa, Alabama, a small town just outside of Livingston, she found the perfect spot under a cluster of tall pine trees, sat down, and pulled out the pair of chicken feet and the bottle of Granville's urine. She took each foot one at a time and twisted it, until the claws ended up on top of one another. When she placed them in the jar, they looked like one big glob of gristle and toenails.

Before pouring the piss in with the feet, Miss Jubilee said a few words, prayed, then turned the small vial upside down until every drop of piss landed in the jar. She screwed the metal lid on until it was so tight that her hands felt weak. Then she shook that jar so hard, the pee inside it started to bubble. On both knees, she scratched and clawed into the earth as far as she could go without passing out, laid the jar in the hole she'd dug, and covered it with dirt. She could feel that her mission was complete: all the fear she had of Granville dissipated, and she felt a release, like she was draped in a cloak of freedom. It was a feeling she'd never had, not even when old Black Sam had run around the plantation years ago, at the end of the Civil War, announcing, "We be free, we be free."

There, under the pines, Miss Jubilee knew that she'd rendered the person who'd treated her with such disdain helpless. He would never harm anyone else in his miserable, hopefully very short life. A smile crossed her face in the darkness. Later, she found out through the rural grapevine that old Granville Suggs had passed away. Word came that his body was more twisted than a crooked rattlesnake carcass. Most Black folks who were familiar with casting roots never let on, but they knew the signs. For many years, Miss Jubilee never spoke a word to anyone about putting the roots on Granville Suggs. Grandma and I may have been the only people she ever told.

Even though Miss Jubilee believed that she was responsible for Granville Suggs's demise, no one could factually attest to this being the case. But according to folklore, the roots and spells were as real as the sun, moon, and universe. This was something that many southerners believed in so deeply they could write a book about it.

It took years for me to understand why Miss Jubilee chose to keep this story, and Gloster's name, so close to her chest. It was, after all, the Deep South in the early 1900s. Even the hint of a Black woman killing a white man, planned and executed by means of spiritualism, mysticism, knifing, shooting, or any other act of foul play, could mean an automatic death sentence. Miss Jubilee knew the risks. As a result, she kept quiet about what she'd done for many years. I can only imagine how she must've struggled mentally and emotionally, because she desperately wanted to seek out Gloster, to tell him that she was alive.

Miss Jubilee ended up moving permanently to Coatopa. A few years later, Grandma met her at a church service. Since Miss Jubilee never had children of her own, I imagine Grandma was the closest thing to a daughter for her. The more she came to know and trust Grandma, the more Miss Jubilee began to talk about incidents and people from her past, including her family, who had been sold away. Finally, one Sunday after church, Miss Jubilee named the plantation of Tom and Granville Suggs in Meridian, Mississippi.

Grandma was able to conclude that this was most likely the family of the Sheriff Suggs she'd encountered week after week 'twixt Livingston and Laurel. When she told Miss Jubilee about her encounters with him, about how bitter he had come to be, Miss Jubilee somehow understood the depth of his anger. He was unable to forgive her, as he thought that she'd abandoned him. She told Grandma that she'd long ago concluded she'd never see that boy again in her lifetime. She wanted desperately to reach out. But there was so much fear of the unknown, of what might happen to her if white folks knew that she'd put the roots on Granville. She had no choice but to remain silent and stay as far away from Meridian as possible.

In time, however, Grandma told Doc Murphy the story of Miss Jubilee and Sheriff Suggs—excepting the roots that

Miss Jubilee had put on Granville. Doc Murphy in turn made arrangements to personally speak to the sheriff, and two weeks later he assigned Grandma that new driver.

When Doc Murphy's father was alive, he knew practically all of the large plantation owners up and down the state of Mississippi. That's how his father, who was also a big-time hunter, first met Granville Suggs. Close to fifty miles separated Laurel from Meridian; another forty miles stretched from Meridian to Livingston. Not much happened within this radius that folks didn't eventually find out about, especially when it came to the larger white families. Doc Murphy and his father before him knew the Suggs family, because it was good politics for upper-crust whites to know officials from nearby cities.

With that said, it was a hundred percent certain that the Murphy family knew what had happened to Granville Suggs. Many whites, including Doc Murphy, also knew how he'd treated his stepson. Those in and around Meridian had seen him beat Gloster in public, in plain view of town folks, when the Suggs men would bring their apples to town to sell and the corn and cotton to the mill.

It was a shame, I thought, that Grandma never told Doc Murphy about how she'd been mistreated by the sheriff. It would've eased her burden significantly. But Grandma was so appreciative of the kindness that Doc Murphy extended her, she considered it disrespectful to complain. And when she found out that the sheriff was the Suggs boy that Miss Jubilee had raised, Grandma only searched for the good. That's why, when she told Doc Murphy about his and Miss Jubilee's relationship, she never, not once, indicated how he had mistreated her. Of course, it just so happened that Miss Evelyn *did* tell Doc Murphy. The splendid way this all came together felt to me almost like a mystical coincidence.

Before Stump left for college, Doc Murphy arranged for him to go to Livingston to retrieve Miss Jubilee and take her to Meridian to reunite with Sheriff Suggs. Stump and Miss

Jubilee were the only ones that witnessed Gloster's reaction. Miss Mollie wasn't around that day. But when Gloster told her about it, he had the biggest smile on his face. Miss Mollie said it was as though a huge burden had lifted from him. It was the first time she'd seen a glimpse of his return to that young lad that she'd romp with across the apple orchards, all those years ago.

Miss Jubilee was an old Black woman who became Sheriff Suggs's surrogate mother from almost the first moment he entered this world. Even though she didn't carry him in her womb, they were connected by an umbilical cord of love. Her devotion and nurturing toward him had nothing to do with race; however, it was race that kept Miss Jubilee from reaching out for Gloster after she left Meridian. And each time Sheriff Suggs looked at Grandma, I realized, he saw Miss Jubilee. That's why he'd sit under the tree and watch her and Stump for hours.

I'll forever remember Grandma's words that day: "You see, chile, Gloster was mournin' that his Miss Jubilee left him. He wa'n't mad at Grandma and Stump, either; he mad at the world for givin' him a mama who never treat him like her chile and a papa, no tellin' jus' how much he hate that boy. Wa'n't that much love in this here worl' for poor old Gloster, 'cept for Miss Mollie and Miss Jubilee. Miss Mollie try so hard to soften his heart over how his step-pa treated him. But when you got only one somebody who care for you, like Gloster since he was a baby, and now they gone, all he gots to turn to is a whole bunch a hate. Now, that's somethin' his papa teach him. Folks don' come outta they mommas hatin'; they learnt it from this sinful worl', baby. Sheriff don' find hate—hate find him."

As Grandma spoke, I realized that, in some ways, Sheriff Suggs was like the young me. I'd came to Grandma so afraid, full of misplaced anger and confusion over why I'd been taken from my family. I could somehow cast myself in the same lot as Gloster, who'd never received his mother's love. He had difficulty finding forgiveness for Miss Jubilee after she left without explanation. I couldn't help but compare his situation to my mother, who'd sent me away.

I was blessed to have Grandma as a mother replacement, to teach me how to walk in someone else's shoes. In turn, I had found ways to forgive. But I'd missed my family something terrible when I first left Detroit. If it wasn't for Grandma, I probably would've found something inside me or someone to take my frustration out on. In the same way, Miss Jubilee was the voice and face of all that was good from Gloster's childhood to nearly adulthood. All that anger at not seeing her, at missing her and grieving her loss, was taken out on Grandma.

Grandma didn't allow this to happen to me. She'd always tell me that I couldn't bottle my pain up like the preserves and jellies we'd make in the fall. She said everyone needed a salve to put on their hurt. Mine was her and the love she gave me. Finally, I understood. Every time Grandma spoke about Gloster, she drew out our similarities. As time passed, more and more I had to admit to myself that Gloster and I had suffered a childhood trauma that was more alike than different. Questions stared me right in the face, questions I could no longer ignore. Miss Daisy, Miss Sugar, and I were all abandoned by our mothers. Yet, unknowingly, did I choose to give these mothers a pass because of the color of their skin? Were they less guilty than Gloster's mother, who neglected him utterly? In one way or another, all four women discarded their children, and Gloster, Miss Sugar, Miss Daisy, and I each suffered as a result. Their choices were the cause of our discontent, not the color of it. I had to ask myself if I viewed Gloster's turbulent childhood as a condition of his race, rather than it being predicated on circumstances beyond his control—a condition that had nothing to do with his skin color.

I believe Grandma's ultimate goal was to make me understand that color and gender don't necessarily impact one's feelings about loss, desertion, and its impending hurt, especially when perpetrated by a parent or someone close to us. That's why she'd constantly say to me, "It don' make no difference who you is and what your color; when you hurt, everybody cry wet." I remember the times when she'd stop in the middle of her sewing and ask me, had I ever seen dry tears fall from someone's eyes? I could only answer with an emphatic "no."

I tried never to get ahead of Grandma or the ways in which she told her stories. All this time, she knew the complete story of Sheriff Suggs; Miss Jubilee; and, just recently, Mama Nall. But she couldn't reveal it to me until she felt I was ready. It was a gradual process, which I tried to relate to my quilt of souls. Over time, Grandma told me, it would all become a part of me, just like the quilt itself would become whole.

Sitting there, listening to Grandma's story, I took a deep breath. Then I lifted the unfinished quilt from her lap and placed it around my shoulders. It began to come alive in my small hands. Gently, I folded it and placed it in an empty croker sack. Soon, we would complete it. As I returned the bags of rags to the smokehouse, I looked forward to that day, but a small part of me was sad, because this beautiful story would soon come to an end.

As always, the way in which Grandma told her stories, and her ability to look at the good that came from them, was a balm to my spirit. It led to my own forgiveness of Sheriff Suggs. Grandma told me that he lived for only a few more years after reuniting with Miss Jubilee. He became very weak one day after plowing his fields. Before he died, he asked Miss Mollie to take him back to the apple orchard, where he took his last breath. I thought how fitting it was that his last wish was to return to the place he loved, stretched out on green pastures.

The ending of this story was one I never expected. But as my grandma spoke, I realized: the shape of our lives can never be predicated on one piece of information. They are layered and immense, threaded into an area the size of Livingston, with all its many fragments somehow connected, just like Grandma's quilts of souls.

The headstone and final resting place
of my grandma, Lula Horn

21

A Season of Loss and Remembrance

MY GRANDPARENTS' PASTURE was filled with a mesmerizing array of green, gold, and red fall leaves, which had gathered under and between the trees. The farm was like a painting, especially this time of year, with its towering backdrop of blue skies and naked pines, its kaleidoscope of colorful foliage. There was so much space for me to run, jump, dance, and play. I had just turned twelve, stood over five feet tall, and was all legs.

It was Saturday morning, the day Grandpa made his biweekly trips to town with Cuttin Jeff. Since we'd gone to town last Saturday, I paid no mind to Cuttin Jeff's arrival. He'd probably just come by to chitchat with Grandpa.

It was 1965 and the school year was starting, which meant that Grandma and I had less time for quilting. In a few short weeks, the fall crop would be reaped, picked, pickled, canned, and stored away in the smokehouse. Grandma had turned eighty-two that August, and Grandpa was three years older. They were ageless wonders, especially Grandma, who was still plowing the fields, chasing cows that had gotten out into the pasture, and doing endless rounds of baking. Not to mention the hours she put in canning jar upon jar of jellies, preserves, and pickles. As I lay there, wrapped in stillness under the endless blue skies, I found myself craving those delicacies, imagining filling one of Grandma's homemade biscuits with her fresh fig preserves.

Suddenly, I heard Grandma yelling my name, and I took off running. By the time I got to the front yard, Grandma had four sacks of clothing sitting near her rocking chair, or what I called her sewing chair. I recognized three of them. One was a beige croker sack with the leftover scraps of Sheriff Suggs's clothing and other stray pieces. Then there was the off-white pillowcase with pieces of overalls and shirts from G. C. and his brothers, Mr. Nall's trousers, and other unidentified scraps. The last one had the partially finished quilt that we'd worked on last month, made with pieces of fabric from G. C., his brothers, and Sheriff Suggs. The fourth bag, sitting closest to Grandma's chair, was one I'd never seen before.

"You ready to help Grandma with her sewin', chile, 'cause we don' wants to be still workin' on this here quilt come this time nex' year?"

This was Grandma's way of saying we needed to make haste. Someone was probably waiting on the quilt to be completed. But her demeanor took me aback. Grandma looked a little sullen. Usually, she would be enthusiastic about making a quilt. And her voice let me know that something lay heavy on her mind. I'd been around her long enough to recognize and understand her mood, which was usually unchanging. She avoided eye contact, then grabbed me by my forearm and brought me closer. I searched her eyes, looking for the reason her spirit was low.

"Miss Jubilee and Mama Nall gone home to be with the Lord, chile. Don' want you to worry yo'self none, 'cause they gone be alright. They left here together. The Lord got them in his lovin' arms, and they ain't struggling no more."

No words could fill the wound Miss Jubilee's passing made in my soul. I think all my tears must've reversed course. Instead of water gathering in my eyes, waiting to flow down my face, it felt as though they'd backed up—like I was drowning from the inside out. I couldn't breathe. I felt myself gasping, and the only thing I heard was Grandma telling me, "Let it out, baby, let it out."

I closed my eyes and tried to visualize the times I'd spent with Miss Jubilee, the stories she'd told me of her family, of slavery and casting roots. It was as though I was looking at her life on a projection reel. In every frame, she was in a different pose, from the time she was young to the way she'd looked the last time I'd seen her. I felt her holding my hands, telling me how much strength there was in them. She had told me never to forget it.

"Chile, you gone be okay; Grandma got you, baby. Poor thing, I think you passed out. You know Miss Jubilee was crazy 'bout you. Chile, Mama Nall crazy 'bout you, too. I hear them two sistas leave out this worl' holdin' hands; they ready to go. Lord keep them on this earth till they find each other and Miss Mollie sho nuff prove they sistas alright. They souls at peace now, chile; they so at peace—that's all you need to know. They your angels, now. You best believes Miss Jubilee gone be here, watchin' over you. Jus' likes when Grandma fly 'way to glory, she gone be watchin' over you, too, God willin'. Your cuttin Jeff dropped off this here bag with Mama Nall's and Miss Jubilee's clothes a lil while ago. Pearlie gathers they belongin's after they pass. She wants to make sure I make a quilt so she always has her grandma and antee nearby."

Grandma reached into the bag and began pulling out two long grayish-blue dresses, the ones Miss Jubilee had worn almost every time I'd visited her. As Grandma picked up the scissors, I cried out, "No, Grandma, I want to cut Miss Jubilee's dress. Please let me do it, please, Grandma. I want to do it myself."

I couldn't stand the idea of anyone, not even Grandma, piercing the fabric of someone I cherished so deeply. I wanted to have the opportunity to hold Miss Jubilee's dress in my hands before it was torn apart. Grandma handed it to me and I held it to my nose, inhaled its smell, then took the scissors and carefully cut the sleeves and part of the midsection before giving the shears back to Grandma. Not a word was uttered; the only sound was the whistling of the fall wind.

I tried to avoid thinking about Miss Jubilee. The pain and sadness were too pronounced, too new. I wondered how I would feel on my next trip to town, passing by the grassy road that led to her house. I thought about her being buried under a mound of dirt, and how she didn't deserve that. She should be covered in a bevy of flowers and green grass, surrounded by her herbs and tinctures.

Grandma sewed the pieces of Miss Jubilee's and Mama Nall's clothes into the quilt, forming a beautiful zigzag pattern that dominated the middle. There was Miss Jubilee's dress, with alternating rows of Sheriff Suggs's shirt squares and Mama Nall's green plaid gingham dress crisscrossing around the middle and sides. A large swatch of cloth from G. C.'s bib overalls and clothing from his brothers were included in two separate squares, surrounded by cloth from their great-grandma Mama Nall's dark brown dress.

I'll always remember one part of that quilt in particular: a huge square made with strips of cloth from Miss Jubilee's scarf, which I'd seen her wear many times. Inside the square were small pieces of Sheriff Suggs's khaki britches. This symbolized that Miss Jubilee was still watching over him, even in the afterlife.

For the rest of the day Grandma sat there, sewing the unfinished quilt of souls in silence. How had she known to leave this particular quilt incomplete? I guess it suffices to say that she somehow knew Mama Nall and Miss Jubilee weren't going to be on this earth much longer. The layout and timing of this quilt was foretold.

It was early Sunday morning when I again heard the familiar sound of Cuttin Jeff's truck in the distance. Grandpa was all dressed up in what Grandma called his Sunday-goin'-to-meetin' clothes: dark blue gabardine dress slacks; a white shirt; a red, blue, black, and gray necktie; a wide-brimmed felt hat; and, of course, his signature suspenders, adjusted so high the waistband of his pants nearly reached his armpits. Yes, Grandpa was sharper than a tack. He had the quilt we'd completed yesterday neatly folded under his arm. He'd be taking it with him to Mama Nall and Miss Jubilee's home-going service, or funeral. After the service he'd hand it over to Pearlie, from whom it would undoubtedly pass down to her only living son, little Backus. I could only hope that he'd cherish and maintain a second quilt of souls for the rest of his life.

I couldn't see myself staring at either of the two old women's remains. I chose to remember them the way they'd looked as they stood on the front porch of Miss Jubilee's house, holding hands. Grandma knew how I felt, and not once did she try to discourage me. She was staying home, too. In all my many years living with my grandparents, I can never recall my grandmother leaving the confines of our farming community— not by vehicle, by wagon, or any other mode of transportation. I never understood why, and I never asked.

Since it was still early, I figured I'd retreat to the spring. I wanted to think about Miss Jubilee and Mama Nall. Cuttin Jeff would be sitting around with my grandparents in the front yard, talking, before he and Grandpa headed up the road. At the spring, I stretched out along the banks, my back against the green grass, my overalls cuffed to my kneecaps, and allowed my feet to hang over the dirt bank, into the warm water. Lingering thoughts of G. C., his brothers, and Miss Jubilee consumed me—I envisioned them at absolute peace. Was Miss Jubilee thinking about me, wherever she was? How happy she must be that she'd found her sister and discovered a larger family that she never knew existed. Even though she'd never had any children, she found her lost sister, nieces, and nephews, too.

I was incredibly sad over Miss Jubilee's passing, but knowing that Mama Nall was with her in the end and that they'd entered paradise together made my heart smile. And I felt content knowing that their loved ones would find peace within each strip of clothing, beautifully woven into a quilt by the hands of my grandma Lula. Lying next to my watering hole, I realized that this was the place where my life had begun to take shape almost nine years ago. Each time trouble came to me, after Grandma set me on the right path, this is where I'd end up. In the quiet, for a quick second, I thought I felt Miss Jubilee's presence. An overwhelming sense of gratitude fell over me, like a warm country day in May.

Many times, Grandma had shown me that each piece of clothing in her quilts was married to misery, pain, and sometimes joy. Mama Nall and Miss Jubilee, Ella, Cooter, Sheriff Suggs—they were real people who lived and put up with many a struggle. I just hoped they had all found happiness in their afterlife. My own quilt was filled with their clothing. I remember so well the way I wanted to cry when Grandma told me that Sheriff Suggs's shirt was meant to be a part of my quilt. I couldn't wrap my head around it. The clothes of a white man, with whom I thought I had very little in common, intermingled with the clothes of women I admired and honored so highly?

When I asked Grandma about it, she told me in her own way that his fabric represented forgiveness, which had been difficult for me to grasp. She wanted me to know that each time I looked at my quilt, it would remind me how important it was to be compassionate toward others and identify with their struggles. I remember her exact words, the same ones she repeated so many times:

"Chile, Grandma never wants you to look at the bad in folks and go backward. I wants you to look at the good in them and go forward. If you jus' look at the bad, you gone find 'xactly what you lookin' for. Even the worst folks got a speck of good; you jus' got to find it."

Cuttin Jeff's truck wailed as he started pulling away from our house with Grandpa in tow. I got up the hill just in time to wave good-bye. As I crossed the road, I saw Grandma sitting in her usual seat under the oak tree. When I got closer, I could see that she had my quilt draped over her lap. By now it was nearly complete. But except for a few pieces of Ella's dress, the middle portion was empty.

I took a seat next to Grandma as she began pulling out pieces of Mama Nall's and Miss Jubilee's clothing from the bag that sat before her. Tears began to well up as I realized their clothes would finish my quilt, that Miss Jubilee's fabric would join with Ella's in its center. Along with Ella, her fabric would hold all the other pieces together. How fitting: the grand finale and the closing frame for my quilt of souls.

Grandma had waited all these years so that I could familiarize myself with the lives led by the owners of each piece of cloth, from Ella to Cooter, from G. C. and Sheriff Suggs to Mama Nall and Miss Jubilee. Now, the storybook of my quilt of souls had been exhausted, and it was Miss Jubilee who gave it closure. She'd told me that my hands were a tool I'd use to do great and wonderful things. Little did I know that one day, her words would fall right out of the palms of my hands and land on the pages I'd write to tell the stories I needed to live.

When Grandma stood and opened wide my quilt, the setting sun fell on top of it, and every inch of fabric glowed. She handed it to me. The tattered piece of cloth I'd wrapped myself up in as a scared four-year-old had become a masterpiece, a living testament to all the men and women who'd worn these pieces of clothing. The tattered pieces were whole.

I sat quietly under the familiar old oak with Grandma, caressing my quilt. My thoughts were like grains of sand, and as the wind approached, it blew each granule across the universe, turning the sky a lovely ashen gray. My reflections scattered about, encircling the globe, returning in unison to the outpost of my memory. Once there, they reformed, skipping, dancing, gathering, then sprouting forth like the branches on a tree.

Then, right in the middle of my daydream about Miss Jubilee, out of nowhere a strong gust of wind appeared, kicking up a circle of dust. Even Grandma was surprised by the suddenness of it. A few seconds later, the air calmed.

"Chile," Grandma said, "that was jus' ole Miss Jubilee's spirit lettin' you know that all is well."

Epilogue

ALL GOOD THINGS must come to an end.

My years with Grandma ended in the summer of 1966, as I approached my thirteenth birthday. It had been a little over nine years since I'd first laid eyes on my grandma, and there I was, tall, scrawny, and packed with more knowledge and wisdom than a child my age could imagine. I possessed an abundance of self-confidence, because I'd received so much guidance and direction from the strong women who had surrounded me over the course of my years in the country.

When my mother and my uncle Guicy arrived that day to bring me back to Detroit, I was stunned. As I realized that I was being taken away from my home of nine years, I screamed and cried. Grandma was crying as hard as I was. That let me know this was for real, and not a dream or a silly joke. She wiped her eyes with her apron, sat up straight, and said to me, "Wipe your face, chile." Then she hugged me so hard I thought I might break. "Don' you cry, chile, trouble don' las' always."

I was ripped away from the only love I'd ever known. I flashed back to when I'd first arrived, in a big car full of big people. How fitting that it all ended the way it began. My life was over.

Seven years would pass before I saw my grandparents again. Those years were hard years and have their own story—a story of my own journey through a troubled adolescence and my relationship with my mother and how it went through so many different phases. But throughout, my time with my grandma was lying beneath my challenges and giving me the strength to go on. As I came into my own and left my mistakes behind and developed my own adult sense of assurance, I often thought about how proud Grandma would be if she knew how I had made something of myself.

In 1973, after I had completed high school, joined the air force, and completed basic training, I finally got the opportunity to reconnect with my grandma for the first time since leaving Alabama. It was beautiful. A homecoming of sorts. We pulled up in the long driveway of Ant Phyllis's house, and there was Grandma, standing at the front door. I can't remember whether I ran or jumped into her wide-open arms, but I know she wrapped me in a tearful embrace, saying, "Chile, chile, chile, you a sight fo' sore eyes. I sure do love yo' heart and yo' liver, too."

Everything was right again. She hugged me so long and hard, at one point I could barely breathe. That energy, her warmth and love, provided me with enough oxygen to last a lifetime.

Unbelievably, Grandma lived for another thirteen years, to the amazing age of 104. By then I was living in Atlanta and able to visit her regularly, including her last night in this world, when she called my name, patted the sheet for me to sit down beside her, and said, "Grandma loves your heart and your liver, too. Don' wants you to forget when you comes to where I'm a-goin', Grandma be waitin' for you on the other side of the Jordan."

Over the years, thoughts of my grandmother's quilting acumen, her kindness, thoughtfulness, love of humanity, and, most of all, her willingness to forgive have inundated me. I'll forever be grateful for her attributes and how she instilled them in me. I consistently strive to emulate those same behaviors and remember the guidance she provided to me over the years. As I ran into life's obstacles, I only had to remind myself of my grandmother's teachings to overcome the stumbling blocks.

I'll never forget the most troubling period of my life. It was about three years before my grandmother passed away. I struggled mightily with college. I'd completed my sophomore year by a thread while working full-time and raising two boys. With all that going on, I only had the late evenings and early mornings to catch up on my reading assignments and prepare for the next day's exams.

During my junior year, in the middle of night, it all came to a head, and I broke down and cried. I couldn't do it any longer. The rigors of trying to maintain a home and be a mother, wife, student, and employee all caved in on me at once. Not only was I fatigued beyond belief, I felt broken and defeated. I got up before daybreak the next morning. Feeling like I hadn't slept since I'd first enrolled in college, I lumbered to the coffeepot: I needed a heavy dose of caffeine.

It was late fall. The sun had just begun to come up, and the wind was howling outside. I'd watched the weather the day before so I could dress my kids appropriately for school. I was surprised to see the wind raging, as there'd been no talk of rain or high wind for that day. As I sat at the kitchen table, my face in my hands, deep in thought, I started thinking about how I was going to compose a letter to the university to tell them that I had to drop out. My thoughts were interrupted by a loud crashing sound from the backyard. I ran to the back door and saw that our medium-sized oak tree had split from the cold and wind and fallen on top of our large metal barbecue pit. Staring at it, exhausted body and soul, I thought, "Another mess to clean up."

I took a closer look. The tree was stripped of all its leaves except for one lonely limb. Just one leaf still hung from it. Tears began to flood my face as I remembered how Grandma would always use the tree-and-leaf analogy to encourage me. There it was—the leaf that represented me during this juncture in my life. I was still standing. The storm and wind had raged, then subsided, and here I was, looking at this little leaf that had resisted all the elements. Even though Grandma was still alive and over a thousand miles away, without a doubt this was a message from her, reminding me that I was the leaf that refused to fall—that I must never give up, turn back, or digress from what I was meant to do.

I remember thinking about my quilt of souls and how I'd have loved to have wrapped myself in its comfort. I imagined it draped around my shoulders as I sat there for the next hour. All was quiet except for the sound of snoring coming from my kids' room. I thought about Ella and her yearning to learn even under difficult circumstances; Miss Cooter, who worked, raised children, and hauled clothes all over Livingston; Miss Jubilee and Mama Nall, forcefully torn apart from each other as mere babies. I felt their presence.

Miss Evelyn and Miss Sugar came to me that morning, too. Though their clothing wasn't included in my quilt, I was able to physically embrace them in real time. Their self-assured, dynamic personalities helped form and mold me, and in this way I wove their words and lives into my heart, just as Grandma sewed the lives of her loved ones into my quilt of souls.

I stood in solidarity with all these women, and after that fall day I never again suffered any misgivings about what I could accomplish. This included years working as a counselor with incarcerated youth, abused women, and the homeless, and serving as a retired member of the US military. In time, I received a master's in creative writing. Grandma was the catalyst for all these accomplishments and what I'd go on to achieve as a professional counselor, writer, and storyteller. I would pass down the stories she told me to my own granddaughters, repeating them with the same energy, vigor, honor, and respect. To see the twinkle in their eyes and the smiles on their faces when I talk to them about their grandma Lula is priceless.

Quilt of Souls is a tribute to everything I learned about slavery, the resulting African American servitude in this country, and the bravery it took for many women of that era to eke out a semblance of dignity from a culture of white supremacy that tried to deny them their basic humanity. Books, articles, documentaries, and movies have detailed the plight of African Americans before slavery and during and after Reconstruction. But it is past time to tell the story of how this same group, particularly Black women, uplifted themselves and overcame injustices while shielding their families from a host of retributions.

My grandmother and so many other women of her era are largely unknown. They did not have the name recognition necessary for inclusion in the few histories of great African American women. Yet their boldness and bravery, their refusal to succumb to the injustices that stared them in the face, is a story that can benefit so many. It is what I am most proud of. The women who stood in the shadows or worked behind the scenes in the lives of the well-known Harriet Tubmans, Sojourner Truths, and Mary McLeod Bethunes beg the question: Who lifted these patriots up? Who was their backbone? Who paved the way for them?

The answer is: so many unidentified women like my grandma, my aunt Ella, Miss Daisy, and all the others I've attempted to bring to life. Now you've heard my story, and theirs.

It is time to write yours.

Acknowledgments

I FACED MANY OBSTACLES while writing this book, and I would never have had the energy or strength to overcome them without God's intervention and the anchor of my deep faith. I am also grateful to a group of special individuals who kept me upright when those obstacles seemed insurmountable:

My husband, Reginald Elmore: You are my life force, always standing beside me and never allowing me to falter. There aren't enough words in the dictionary to define our love and friendship, which has grown over almost forty years. You're my rock and the yin to my yang. I love you to the moon, stars, and universe and back again.

My friend of fifty years and closest confidante, Janet Stone: We were giggly teenagers when we first met, but even then you were constantly trying to convince me to write my story. I love you and will forever cherish our special friendship, sisterhood, and unbreakable bond.

My sons, Lafayette and Yaftahe Williams: You are the impetus behind my powerful desire to complete this book.

You're also the catalyst for passing down these stories to my beautiful granddaughters and the generations that follow them.

Marie Wall and Cass Scopino: I lost count of how many times you've read the draft manuscript and its many revisions over the past five years. Your comments and critiques were always timely, enlightening, and helpful. I love your hearts and your liver too. Bella, Gianna, and Phoebe: My inspiration throughout. Love you to the moon and back. Robin Age: You were mother, soldier, sister, and one of my greatest allies. Your loyalty and energy are infectious and your compassion is off the radar. The encouragement you offered always provided me with hope. Cecilia Mariaca: What more can I ask for in a friendship? You're my caterer, photographer, "battle buddy," and much more. You're also a bundle of walking, talking, comedic relief. You provided belly-aching laughter when I needed it most.

Tanyia McLaughlin: Thank you for the creativity, friendship, and energy that you displayed over the years. Leslie Caplan: Your vision and originality always put me in the perfect space. You've been a wonderful writing coach, friend, and talented poet who mesmerizes with every line. Your poems helped me to look deep inside myself as I put my own words to paper. Fran Lebowitz: Your tutelage was invaluable. Thank you for bringing *Quilt of Souls* out of the shadows. I'll be forever grateful to you for placing my book in the hands of those who went on to elevate it to the next level. Genevieve Gagne-Hawes: You're an editing phenomenon who can turn two sentences into a twelve-part symphony. I believe God put you on this earth to fall in love with my grandmother and her stories. I'll never forget you.

My agent Susan Ginsburg: How can I ever begin to thank you? You've been an absolute joy to work with. Always accessible and possessing incredible ingenuity and calm. I haven't witnessed this type of peace and serenity in an individual since my grandmother. I'm beholden to you and my editor, Kevin Stevens at Imagine Books, for giving me this opportunity to

tell my story and share it with the world. Our author/agent/
publisher relationship wasn't happenstance. I firmly believe
Quilt of Souls was destined to fall into your world at the appointed
time. Kevin: You've been a delight to work with. You're an
awesome taskmaster who always gave clear and concise directions each step of the way. I breathed life into the characters
in my book, but your editing acumen gave them permission to
speak for themselves. Catherine Bradshaw: Thank you for the
sunshine that seeped through every email you sent. Your effervescent personality was always a pleasure to hear and feel.

Thank you to the Biffle-Horn and Elmore-Loyd families
for their undying support. And finally, thank you to all the
people I met during my speaking engagements and via social
media. You've been persistent and devoted followers. Reading
your daily comments has brought smiles and sometimes tears.
You took Lula Horn and made her part of your family. I can't
express how honored I was to be uplifted by the thousands of
you who gave me a platform. You opened doors for me to tell
this story. I will never forget the dedication you've shown me
over the years.

About the Author

BORN IN DETROIT, MICHIGAN, Phyllis Biffle Elmore was sent at the age of four to the tiny town of Livingston, Alabama, to be raised by her grandmother, Lula Horn. In 1973, she joined the United States Air Force, and her military career included service during the Vietnam War, Desert Storm, and Operation Enduring Freedom. She served as an aviation operations specialist and equal opportunity adviser until she retired from the US Army in 2013. Her civilian career has included working as a counselor for incarcerated youth and women victims of domestic violence, and ten years as a counseling supervisor for youth and adults suffering from alcohol and substance abuse.

She has traveled extensively, telling the stories of her grandmother's quilts of souls in the media and as a guest speaker at libraries, genealogical conventions, quilting clubs, book clubs, colleges, and schools throughout the United States. She has a bachelor's degree in sociology and women's studies from the University of Maryland Baltimore County and a master's certificate in creative writing from the University of Denver. She lives in Florida with her husband, Reginald Elmore, and has seven granddaughters who are the love of her life.